D0938945

WALL STREET

AND THE

SECURITY MARKETS

WALL STREET

AND THE

SECURITY MARKETS

Advisory Editor
Vincent P. Carosso

Associate Editor
Robert Sobel

*See last pages of this volume
for a complete list of titles*

The
NEW WALL STREET

RUDOLPH L. WEISSMAN

ARNO PRESS
A New York Times Company
New York – 1975

Reprint Edition 1975 by Arno Press Inc.

Copyright © 1939, by Harper & Brothers
Reprinted by arrangement with
   Harper & Row, Publishers, Inc.
   All rights reserved.

WALL STREET AND THE SECURITY MARKETS
ISBN for complete set: 0-405-06944-8
See last pages of this volume for titles.

Manufactured in the United States of America

—◦◦◦—

Library of Congress Cataloging in Publication Data

Weissman, Rudolph Leo, 1900-
   The new Wall Street.

   (Wall Street and the security markets)
   Reprint of the 1939 ed. published by Harper, New
York.
   Bibliography: p.
   1. Wall Street. 2. United States Securities
and Exchange Commission. 3. Securities--United
States. 4. Stock-exchange--United States. I. Ti-
tle. II. Series.
HG4572.W4 1975   332.6'42'0973   75-2684
ISBN 0-405-07245-7

The
NEW WALL STREET

by

RUDOLPH L. WEISSMAN

Author of
"The New Federal Reserve System"
Formerly Financial Editor of the "American Mercury"

HARPER & BROTHERS PUBLISHERS
NEW YORK AND LONDON
1939

THE NEW WALL STREET

To
B.W.
E.M.W.
G.W.

CONTENTS

PREFACE

THE Old Wall Street is dead. The new is now emerging. No institution has undergone more drastic change. I have tried to portray something of the spirit of Wall Street and its people, and to describe the New Wall Street's workings in terms of the significant changes that have taken place. This book has been written for those in Wall Street who may wish to find in proper perspective a convenient recital of things familiar, and for the larger number who are interested in the financial world, but who are bewildered by the glimpses that they catch of the differences between the Wall Street that they knew, or have heard about, and present realities.

Since the book is not intended to be a survey of Wall Street, or a financial history, the conditions out of which the new controls grew have been sketched with brevity. There is another purpose in emphasizing the present. It would be well for both Wall Street and Main Street if, instead of rehearsing the mistakes of the past or defending abandoned positions, the possibilities of the New Wall Street were recognized. Nor is the book a compendium of the mechanics of Wall Street or a complete description of the Securities Act of 1933 and the Securities Exchange Act of 1934. I have confined its scope to what I believe are the most important developments and tendencies.

I have been frank in making observations, regardless of whom they may please, without, I trust, falling into the habit of seeing nothing but black or white.

Anyone writing on Wall Street today must acknowledge the value of the tremendous accessions to the available material in the publications of the Securities and Exchange Commission. Readers will observe that liberal use has been made of this material. I have to thank the friends and associates with whom all the main parts of the book have been discussed and whose suggestions and criticisms have been of the utmost help. For the opinions expressed I alone am responsible. The proposals set forth are the result of many years of experience in Wall Street.

If this book measured up to the standard of Justice Louis D. Brandeis, Mr. William O. Douglas, Chairman of the Securities and Exchange Commission, Mr. William McC. Martin, President of the New York Stock Exchange, and others like Justice Felix Frankfurter and Mr. A. A. Berle, Jr., who are either responsible in great measure for the creation of the New Wall Street or whose energies have been devoted to the promotion of the well being of both the New Wall Street and the nation, I should express my indebtedness to them at greater length.

I plead guilty to a point of view—it is that the investor, as never before, is now receiving a square deal so far as it is possible for this to be accomplished by the authorities and the Stock Exchange. Wall Street is on the way to becoming a potent instrumentality in the promotion of economic democracy. To describe this achievement is the main purpose of this book, in the course of which several suggestions are made to help reach the goal.

Brooklyn, New York   RUDOLPH L. WEISSMAN
January 15, 1939

P.S.—Since the manuscript went to press, the Chairman of the Securities and Exchange Commission, William O. Douglas, has been appointed a Justice of the United States Supreme Court. In the death of Mr. J. D. Ross, formerly a member of the Commission, and later head of the Bonneville Dam project, the nation lost a faithful and able public servant.

The Commission has modified its rules concerning short sales. The new rule permits a short sale at the price of the last sale; previously, a round lot short had to be made a price above that of the previous short sale. This notable step indicates that the Commission is open minded, and is in line with the hope expressed on page 145 of this book.

March 30, 1939   R. L. W.

The New Wall Street

CHAPTER I

PEOPLE OF THE STREET

EXCEPT for a few sketches of spectacular careers, Wall Street's people have been entirely overlooked. The financial world is still the subject of detailed, close study. The mechanism, nevertheless, is not self-operating. No one thinks of farm tenancy in terms only of crops, lease provisions, or even statistics of income. The farm tenant and his family are the center of the examination of the farm tenancy problem. Likewise, Wall Street should be reexamined in terms of the people of Wall Street—their environment, background, intellectual interests, social views, prejudices and opinions; that is, in terms of their activities and lives as human beings. Unfortunately, no Lynds have entered the "Street" to make such a study as they did of Middletown. A study of this kind would require the aid of a staff of trained investigators for many months. The result would be a notable contribution to a better understanding of Main Street, Wall Street, and Washington, and their relations.

Human beings are more than brokers, dealers, or investment brokers. Investment trust managers, salesmen, security analysts, traders, etc., are not fully known unless we know something about them as citizens and husbands, their ideals and desires, social relations and mode of living. Conceding the vast significance of the economic interpretation, other interests activate individuals. The interrelation of these and economic interests make up the whole life of an individual, no one part of which can be severed from all other parts. In the absence of such a study, the writer will approach the problem, aware of the limitations of a discussion by one who is not a sociologist and who may not possess the objectivity of the most satisfactory observer. In the end, our respect may be heightened or our low opinion confirmed. Whatever the conclusion, it will rest on more than superficial impressions.

1

THIS IS WALL STREET

For purposes of ready classification the financial district as it relates to investment banking, brokerage firms and dealers, may be reduced to the following groups:

Members of the New York Stock Exchange
Partners or officers
Salesmen (and customers' men)
Research
Traders
Office workers

At the beginning of 1938 there were 47,300 employees of members and member firms of the New York Stock Exchange. The Exchange had 1,375 members: there were 652 firms, and 936 partner members, of whom 916 were general partners; these firms had 2,768 nonmember partners.

The Commission has published the most comprehensive data ever assembled on the number, personnel and branch offices of brokers and dealers. This information is as of May 27, 1936. At that time there were within the continental United States 5,761 firms with 16,973 partners or officers. Employees totaled 76,062, or an average of about 13 for each firm. The total number engaged in the securities business was 93,035. Almost half the total, 46,220, were in firms with principal offices outside New York City. The employees were divided as follows:

Salesmen	13,852
Traders	3,286
Customers' men	5,732
Others	53,192

In attempting this description of Wall Street types, the writer must discuss composite figures. The result will probably represent no single individual with photographic accuracy. There is no average except in the mind of the compiler of the average. To describe individuals would furnish an even less accurate picture. Accordingly, it is hoped that none will take offense if the portrait is not entirely flattering. The sole purpose is to approximate the truth as the author sees it and to convey to the outsider something in addition to impersonal facts and statistics, all of which are the effect of human activities, experience, aspirations, mental attitudes, prejudices, and habits.

The New York Stock Exchange in its latest yearbook devoted some attention to the age and birthplace of its members. On January 1, 1938, the average age of the members of the New York Stock Exchange was forty-five years, 822 were in two brackets, 30 to 39, and 431 were between 40 and 49. Thirty-seven states and seventeen foreign countries are represented in the list of birthplaces of the members. Out of 1,295 members born in the United States, 805 were New Yorkers and 123 were born in Connecticut. Of the 54 foreign-born members, 14 were natives of Germany, the largest number from one country. The active members are divided as follows:

Members of commission and investment firms	550
Bond brokers	67
Specialists	360
Odd-lot dealers and brokers	123
Floor brokers	165
Floor traders	34
Private bankers	9
Total	1308

MEMBERS OF THE EXCHANGE

The Stock Exchange member is more often than not a college graduate, the son of parents either of the upper middle class or of some wealth. His early education probably was at private schools. As a rule, the members are fond of athletics and of outdoor activities. The floor members are generally nervous and energetic. The severe strain of the excitement of active markets requires good health. Politically, the Exchange member has been traditionally a steadfast Republican. Before the New Deal the Democratic party was disliked; since the New Deal it has been anathema. For reading, outside the daily newspapers and financial news, the popular magazines and mystery stories probably get the greatest part of the member's reading time. Historical novels and accounts of contemporary journalists have had a good market among members. Serious economic studies of a factual nature as well as the more solid historical and political treatises are not popular, probably because they are not easy reading and the Stock Exchange member likes opinions rather than the tortuous processes through which opinions are reached. As a rule, the opinions must not be qualified, but bold and vigorous. The member is more likely to attend a musical show than a Shakespearean revival, a football game than a lecture. Since a member of the Stock Exchange in the halcyon days before the war drew an intimate vignette of his colleagues no other writer has been as generous in his praise. W. C. Van Antwerp, in *The Stock Exchange from Within* (1913), wrote: "It would be difficult to find anywhere a more intelligent and interesting group of men than the members of the New York Stock Exchange. Some of them are men of peculiar personal charm, others are distinguished for especial ability in various ways, others are men with hobbies, nearly every one knows something that is worth knowing, and what is better, talks of what he knows in the manner of culture. Naturally, in the cosmopolitan atmosphere of the Stock Exchange tastes are catholic and run to wide extremes. One of the members is a student of Russian literature in all its phases; he can tell you of its folklore, its peasantism, its liberal thought and its ethical ideals of society; Dostoyevski is his hobby and Melshin the poet. Beside him stands a man who has mastered the culinary art; the joy of his life is to prepare with his own hands, for the palates of his fastidious guests, dainty dishes and wonderful sauces that make an invitation to his table something worth having." The writer goes on to say that one of the members is an animated concordance of Shelley and another is a disciple of Heine. It appears that many of the members were collectors of paintings, old silver, Elizabethan early editions, ceramics, postage stamps, and tapestries. The civic and other public activities were described with warm admiration. Undoubtedly, although the members are an interesting group, Mr. Van Antwerp's description might leave the reader with a somewhat exaggerated idea of the intellectual attainments of the average member. Unfortunately, the work was not revised and no member has written a comparable up to date survey.

The member is not tolerant of political differences, especially now that the leading political questions relate so directly to the Street. The tolerance that is prevalent in the City in London does not find its counterpart in Wall Street. While there are members who read liberal publications like the *Nation* and the *New Republic*, what a sensational news item it would be to read of a member who is a leader in an organization like the League for Industrial Democracy? Few, if any, Stock Exchange members are also members of the American Labor party, to say nothing of the Socialist party. One wonders if a sponsor could be obtained for an applicant for a seat with such political affiliations. The average member could not understand how one with radical or socialistic opinions reconciled his views with membership on the Stock Exchange. It is doubtful if one entertaining such views openly would be successful in obtaining business from other brokers; he might suffer social ostracism or at least be made to feel that he was not welcome. Yet, one of the charter members, and the secretary for many years of the Fabian Society, a socialistic educational organization in England, was the late Edward R. Pease, a member of the London Stock Exchange. Mr. Pease was the author of a history of the Fabian Society and one of its active members. None thought these activities incompatible with his membership on the Exchange.

In all fairness it should be added that Maurice Wertheim of Wertheim & Co., a prominent investment firm, was for a time the publisher of the liberal *Nation* and is a trustee of the New School for Social Research. One of the most energetic members of the reform group of the New York Stock Exchange, now its president, William McC. Martin, Jr., is a trustee of this institution. He is also interested in an important periodical, the *Economic Forum*, and has been identified with it since it was founded. Edmund C. Stedman, author of a History of the New York Stock Exchange and a member for many years, was a poet and literary critic of distinction. James Truslow Adams, one of the foremost American historians of the present day, was at one time a member of a stock exchange firm.

Members and executives alike, aside from a thorough technical knowledge of the machinery of finance, including rules imposed by the Exchange and by law, seem to have little interest in the things in which they deal. It is rare to find in the financial district partners or other executives who catch a glimpse of the intricate economic machine or who are interested in the evolution of modern industry and finance except as instruments of gain. To this extent Wall Street leaders have not attained the professional instinct.

Few are so attracted by the forces of applied economics that they would not leave the financial district if better money-making opportunities presented themselves elsewhere. There is nothing reprehensible or uncommon about this. In the tobacco, furniture, glass, or shoe business it is rare to find the executive who has a feeling for the industry expressed in his love of lore concerning it, or his library. Building a business is itself an art. Finance, trading in securities, and even underwriting are less permanent or concrete in affording chances for constructive work or artistic impulses. Hence, all the more reason why the Wall Street leader should find a great fascination in his work. As everyone in the financial district knows, markets are the most sensitive barometers. To catalogue the myriad influences bearing on prices is beyond my purpose. The selection of a few will illustrate amply the diverse nature of the events and forces making prices. Court decisions, crop reports, foreign exchange fluctuations, international events, congressional legislation and reports of committees, reports of fact-finding agencies like the Brookings Institution, the conversations of statesmen on international policies, the habits of Indians and Chinese in buying or selling gold and silver, the developments in chemical laboratories, changes in social customs (smoking by the female sex), changes in population trends, diet, besides the direct influences like earnings of corporations, accounting policies, etc. The wonder is that more have not been attracted by the sheer thrill of the nerve center of the world as a post from which to observe the ever-changing, fascinating scene.

The majority have relied on contacts and business adroitness for success. Contacts, as the result of family connections or school associations, supply business. The execution of orders is conducted with reasonable skill, care, and probity by one broker as well as another. Contacts are equally valuable in the search for new financing. Keen market sense and ability in negotiation are other attributes of success in the financial world. In the small number of instances where individuals have been recognized for knowledge of certain aspects of security values or corporate finance, there seems to be the beginning of a more professional type. The author of many studies on foreign bonds is a well-known partner of a bond firm. He not only knows the current prices and markets, but has a vast fund of information concerning the debt record of leading borrowers like Brazil or Germany and the political and social histories of these countries. His knowledge is supplemented by a study of the chief economic and political documents and periodicals of foreign nations, by conversations and discussion with leaders in business and government. Another expert in railroad finance has traveled widely and knows the physical factors concerning properties securing the Buffalo, Rochester & Pittsburgh Railway Company Consolidated mortgage 4½s due 1957, or the St. Louis Southwestern Railway Company 1st mortgage 4% certificates due 1981, and of railroad bonds generally. Contacts with shippers keep him informed of their opinion of railroad managements; he is constantly studying the tremendous body of material published by the Interstate Commerce Commission. Railroad finance has taken him back into economic history and the influence of the general east-west character of railroad building on American history before the Civil War; it has taken him into the future in the study of the entire transportation problem.

Several partners of investment banking firms have become experts in reorganization and in the setting up of plans of recapitalization that reconcile the differences of various groups of creditors and owners. One has reached a philosophical attitude of rights founded in legal principles for the give-and-take spirit that is necessary in overcoming financial difficulties. Not everyone is intellectually inclined or fundamentally a student, but the commodities of Wall Street—securities—whether one is engaged in their "manufacture" through new financing, or in their purchase and sale, or in the giving of counsel, offer to him who knows decided advantages. In the graduate business schools a broader outlook is developing, which in time may affect the Street.

Friendly relations with bank officials were at one time sufficient to establish oneself in business or gain a partnership, but this is no longer true. Capital, accompanied by average talents, still goes far, as it does in any other business. The restrictions of the Securities and Exchange Commission, the changes wrought by law and by the Exchange itself, as well as the diminution in activity, have stiffened competition. Ten years ago a member of a firm of accountants who did a large business in the financial district expressed doubts as to the possibility of many partners remaining in other businesses for a year. He went so far as to describe the typical broker and investment banker as ignorant and arrogant. In these ten years a perceptible change toward a more informed, more serious individual has been observed.

Affability and good breeding are not substitute for a high degree of integrity and an awareness of the responsibilities of a business affected with a public interest, involving often a relationship of virtual if not legal trust. It would be unkind and unfair to leave the subject with a recitation of breaches of trust and sheer moral turpitude which shocked none so violently as those in the financial community. The Street itself must ever beware an attitude that might be misconstrued as an excuse or indulgence. One is reminded of the biting remarks of Macaulay in his famous essay on Milton. Discussing the defense of Charles I, he asked: "And what, after all, are the virtues ascribed to Charles? A religious zeal, not more sincere than that of his son, and fully as weak and narrowminded, and a few of the ordinary household decencies which half the tombstones in England claim for those who lie beneath them. A good father! A good husband! Ample apologies indeed for fifteen years of persecution, tyranny and falsehood! We charge him with having broken his coronation oath; and we are told that he kept his marriage vow! We accuse him of having given up his people to the merciless inflictions of the most hot-headed and hard-hearted of prelates; and the defence is that he took his little son on his knee, and kissed him! We censure him for having violated the articles of the Petition of

Right, after having, for good and valuable consideration, promised to observe them; and we are informed that he was accustomed to hear prayers at six o'clock in the morning!" The financial community, whose prosperity and very existence rest on confidence, must excoriate and denounce every evidence of breach of faith or practice that throws suspicion on its character. Internal reform is worth infinitely more, and discovery of crime loses half its sting if the initiative is taken by the financial world without waiting for the public authorities. The lead taken by the Stock Exchange in the establishment of sound and informative accounting practices is an example of what can be accomplished.

SALESMEN

Today's salesmen are tomorrow's partners and officers. The few exceptions prove the rule. The well-known story of "from college graduate to bond salesman" in order to make money quickly and easily was true of the twenties. The majority of salesmen are college graduates recruited mainly from the same families and social group as the Wall Street executives.

Those who have become salesmen in the past five years have been more serious and on the whole definitely more competent than their prototypes of the preceding decade. The security salesman generally is first put through a preliminary stage of training as runner or messenger and often works in the bookkeeping department. He may spend six months in the research department. The youthful salesman soon decides on one course or another. He either makes a determined effort to keep abreast of financial and economic developments and to learn the elements of security values or he gives up this sphere and concentrates on selling. Often the most successful salesman is one who makes no pretense of advising the client or of appraising securities. Important clients are glad to know that the salesman, instead of relying on his superficial knowledge or shouldering a responsibility not justified by his experience, has made it a practice to consult a partner or the firm's research department. Other salesmen, especially those who deal with the smaller investor, are required to act on their own judgment, since an expression of doubt or a frank admission that the salesman does not know enough about a security to express a worthwhile opinion, may result in the loss of the account.

The salesman must trade on his friends and acquaintances. A social standing that brings him into friendly contact with persons of wealth is an invaluable aid. "Cold" selling is a most difficult task. A week end at the home of the parents of a friend may lead to results that months of business calling could not hope to achieve. Commissions range from one-third to 40 per cent of the gross profit if the salesman has a drawing account, to 50 per cent if the salesman is purely on a commission basis. High-pressure salesmanship is not so common as it was in the twenties.

The social and economic opinions of the salesman vary little from the conventional Wall Street type. Nevertheless, it is true that the younger men, many of whom have been exposed to the "liberal" or "red" (depending on the individual who makes the judgment) opinions of instructors in the social sciences, are more tolerant of the recent tendencies of legislation and national policies. Since they have only heard of the "good old days" and have been trained during the period when present restrictions have been effective, the constant comparison of what might have been done before the Securities and Exchange Commission is not before them. Accordingly, the restraints do not appear to be so irksome. In fact, salesmen find that the watchfulness of the Securities and Exchange Commission is of assistance, as prospective buyers are more inclined to place credence in statements supported by the prospectus. A few probably use the fact of registration illegally, despite the boldface type used on the first page of every prospectus declaring "It is a criminal offense to represent that the Commission has approved these securities or has made any finding that the statements in this prospectus or in the registration statement are correct."

The difficulties of the securities business have reduced the number of young men eager to become salesmen and many of those with experience have had to seek other business activities. The shafts of criticism leveled against securities salesmen for the losses of the twenties were largely misdirected. The "merchandise"—whether South American bonds, public utility holding company issues, or investment trust stocks, to mention three classes of new financing in which losses were heaviest— was not created by salesmen but by their superiors. In the uncritical atmosphere prevailing in a boom, the approval and example of those to whom they naturally looked for guidance, and the material gains to be derived, were more potent factors than mere indifference to the investors' interests or downright callousness as to the welfare of customers. Salesmen's courses in corporation finance and investment analysis help the salesman to guide his customers intelligently. Large firms often provide an intensive course of study in their offices during the training period.

One of the problems of security selling, whether for a dealer or an investment banking firm, is the margin of profit. In the late twenties "long profit" bonds, in which the gross commission for the salesman was anywhere from three to five points, almost invariably were securities of third grade. They had no place in the portfolio of either banks or individual investors. Competition and the emphasis on a "good market," that is, one in which the spread between the bid and ask price is not great, and in which purchases and sales may be effected in reasonable amounts, have narrowed the commission on sound securities. Two evils have followed and have persisted in the securities business. The salesman is tempted to interest the prospect in inferior securities, and following a sale the salesman again is under the urge of "trading" his customer whenever an excuse presents itself, so that he may consummate another sale. If the commission on sound securities were larger in the first instance both evils would tend to disappear. The fault is not with the salesman's employer so much as it is with the structure of the business. The public undoubtedly stands to benefit from arrangements that permit the salesman to make a reasonable profit. This development must await a public that is more income-minded and does not scan the financial pages of the newspaper nightly. It may never take place. With the exception of tax-exempt securities and the demand for bonds by financial institutions and estates, the ordinary investor's interest has centered increasingly on equities.

The customers' man, in a sense, is a salesman for a brokerage house. A broker-dealer firm may employ both customers' men and salesmen. The customers' man in such cases may also sell securities in transactions in which his firm is acting as a principal. Primarily, and generally exclusively, a customers' man accepts orders for the execution of purchases and sales of securities so that his firm acts as a broker. As noted above, the number of customers' men is only about 40 per cent of the number of salesmen. Partners act as both so that their inclusion would not change the ratio to a material extent.

The disrepute in which the customers' man fell during the twenties was justified. Many had no training and were ignorant of the most elementary principles of corporation finance and investment. Ignorance might have been overcome, for the inexperienced could rely on the better informed individuals of the firm. Unfortunately, the customers' welfare was not the concern of the customers' man, whose principal aim was to obtain commissions. Investigation revealed shocking relations with pools. Customers' men recommended the purchase of stocks and received options on stocks, or a fee based on the number of shares purchased. At dinners they were reported to have found bank notes for large sums under their plates. Liberal expense accounts enabled them to entertain their victims. To some extent, the laxity or indifference of firm managers and partners contributed to the ease with which such practices were carried on. Low margin requirements also helped. More than any single cause, the casino aspect of the board room, the supercharged atmosphere, and the general atmosphere of finance in the twenties made it possible for the worst types of customers' men to flourish. The race track tout might easily have passed for this type of customers' man. The most absurd rumors were communicated to customers. "I hear" prefaced prophecies of earnings, dividend declarations, mergers, buying by the "house on the corner" (J. P. Morgan & Company), and activities of large speculators whom the rank and file followed eagerly. Every device was resorted to in order that customers might be induced to sell what had only recently been highly recommended for a new "sure bet." The mortality rate among customers was high in the boom period. After the collapse in 1929 and in response to growing complaints, the Stock Exchange moved to eradicate the mischief created by unprincipled customers' men. In May, 1930, rules were issued requiring a customers' man to sign the following agreement:

I agree as follows:

1. That I will not represent to any customer that I will personally guarantee the account of such customer.

2. That I will not either directly or indirectly lead any customer to believe that he will not suffer loss as the result of opening an account with my employer, or as the result of any dealings in connection therewith.

3. That I will not, directly or indirectly, take or receive a share in the profits of any customer's account.

4. That I will not maintain a speculative account, nor be directly or indirectly interested in such account.

5. That at any time upon the request of the Committee on Quotations and Commissions or any other Committee of the New York Stock Exchange, I will appear before such Committee and give evidence upon any subject under investigation by any such Committee, and that I will upon the request of any such Committee produce all of my records or documents relative to any inquiry being made by any such Committee.

6. I am familiar with the rules and the regulations of the New York Stock Exchange pertaining to the employment of so-called customers' men and others engaged in the solicitation of business or the handling of customers' accounts, and I agree to abide by the existing rules and all amendments thereto.

In November, 1933, a standing committee on customers' men was created. At present they are required to have at least six months' previous experience and they must be successful in passing an examination by the New York Stock Exchange Institute. The Institute offers a customers' man course in stock exchange practice, brokerage office practice, and security analysis. According to the annual report of the Stock Exchange for the year ended May 31, 1937, about 1,100 applicants had been examined since the inauguration of the course in February 1, 1936. Without question, the heavy mortality rate of customers' men in recent years has removed most of the undesirables. At best, the relations of an employee whose compensation is based on commissions and who acts in a semifiduciary capacity are full of difficulties. The customer who has opened an account expects more of the customers' man than merely the transmission of orders. He generally reports the news, and must avoid coloring it in accordance with his views or desire to obtain orders for the purchase or sale of securities. In many instances he acts as investment counsel. Recognizing the conflicting interests, a spokesman for the Exchange has said: "The goal as I see it is the creation of public confidence in the advice of an unselfish nature that will attempt to answer the problems of the particular customer asking the advice, so that it will be advice uncolored by a desire to turn the customer purely into a producer of commissions."

Former abuses are disappearing. The reforms of the Exchange have contributed to a higher standard of conduct; also the entrance of a better qualified, more responsible individual into the ranks of customers' men. Higher margin requirements, restrictions imposed on floor traders and on short selling, and the higher cost of trading have reduced the volume of in-and-out trading upon which rapid turnover depends. The gradual change to a greater reliance on investment business is a potent force in rendering impossible the return to the abuses of the twenties. The author has no desire to offer a defense of practices so palpably vicious. Yet one must recognize that many customers' men are competent and conscientious, and that the greed and unreasonable expectations of businessmen—not widows and orphans—invite overtrading.

One of the few who appraised the markets accurately from the summer of 1937 to the spring of 1938 was a customers' man in a New York Stock Exchange firm. In his advice to customers he advocated and followed a do-nothing policy for those who did not care to sell short. He was responsible for the conservation of the capital both of his clients and of his firm. To his chagrin he found that businessmen chafed under the inactivity and that a fairly large number of accounts late in 1937 and early in 1938 were transferred to other firms. From the standpoint of the national income or welfare it matters little if the honest efforts of customers' men are not rewarded by business success, as in the case above cited, but we are not now concerned with this broader phase of the significance or value of speculation. Unless intense speculation develops in the securities markets or there is a complete reversal of recent tendencies by the authorities, the customers' man will have to accept a permanently reduced income or repair the reduction through the handling of a greater number of accounts. The latter possibility does not hold great promise, since the very diminution in activity intensifies competition in the securing of new business.

Unless segregation of dealer and broker follows, it may be that the sale of securities, especially open end investment funds, will be permitted and will furnish an added source of income. So long as the customers' man is recognized as a part of the market machinery reasonable supervision should be observed, for under the stress of earning a livelihood the abuses sought to be removed may crop up. With the reduction in the overhead of offices, possibly the customers' man will receive as salary a larger part of the commissions produced. The capital invested in the business may have to accept a reduction in earnings. Although customers' men are not paid directly in relation to the commissions earned, salaries over a period of time do bear an undeniable relation to the firm's commissions on business for which they are responsible.

SECURITY ANALYSTS

Among the "others" in the classification of Wall Street personnel are the statisticians, but they are of sufficient interest to justify a brief discussion of their duties. Except as applied to a small number, the term "statistician" is misleading. "Security analyst" is a more accurate description, since few of the statisticians pretend to be expert in the mathematics of statistics. Depending on their activities and size, firms will have in their statistical or research departments from one to twenty or more. Duties include the study and interrelation of financial and economic developments, supervision of accounts, review of investment portfolios, recommendations to partners, salesmen and others, the preparation of special studies, the search for special situations of unusual interest, the preparation of circulars, selling material and market letters. In the twenties the market letter was more important than in recent years. Greater care is now exercised as to the statements made in such letters, which must be examined by a partner and filed with the Stock Exchange. The research department also works with the buying department in underwriting firms in the study of new deals, comparison of similar securities as to price, and economic characteristics of the industry in which the corporation to be financed operates. Since the Securities Act of 1933, the research department has less to do with the preparation of the prospectus than formerly. The research department keeps files on individual corporations, special subjects, listing statements, etc., and receives the various investment advisory services and manuals to which the firm subscribes.

In the financial district it is usually taken for granted that the inveterate pipe smoker with the mass of papers on and around his desk is the statistician. Ordinarily the young man who is a student rather than a salesman by temperament interests himself in this work. At present many of the research departments are composed largely of men who have received part of their education at one of the recognized collegiate schools of business administration. Some of the younger men look upon a short period in research work as rounding out their training. Others find in it a permanent appeal. In point of hours of work, the members of the research department probably stand highest in the Wall Street hierarchy.

In the small firm the statistician will be called upon to do or be expected to know the most varied assortment of things. He may be called upon to write an analysis or report of the Standard Oil Company of New Jersey or the American Telegraph & Telephone Company. A harried customers' man may want to know in the next fifteen minutes if National Steel or Bethlehem Steel is the better purchase. A salesman wishes to know if Toledo Edison Corporation is likely to refund its 5 per cent bonds in the near future. A partner discussed the desterilization of gold the night before and now wants to send a memorandum to one of the disputants on the significance of the policy and the process of reserve credit. Can United States Steel "break even" at 45 per cent of capacity of operations? Will the Reconstruction Finance Corporation lend a railroad enough money this year to prevent its going into receivership? How are the Erie Railroad Consolidated prior lien bonds likely to come out in reorganization? Has he any opinion on the acquisition of X Company by Chrysler? The most exasperating inquiries are not those manifestly impossible to answer; they are the demands to prepare a letter or memorandum on why a prospect or customer should sell a sound security to buy one that is being offered by the firm with which the statistician is associated. Bits of gossip are passed on to the statistician to investigate; offerings of other firms are submitted to determine whether or not the firm should participate. Executives and salesmen and often customers look to the statistician, who, being free from the necessity of selling or producing commissions and at least a step removed from news ticker and ticker tape, is moved more by facts and less by the interests of the moment or the vagaries of the market than are those engaged in other work. A capable, experienced statistician, with the assistance of the investment services generally available and the contacts gained over the years, may do a good job for his firm. If it is true—and the veteran of the markets can hardly doubt it—that securities now move in greater unison with values and that more information than ever before is obtainable for the formulation of an intelligent opinion, the statistician's worth is likely to increase. A more intelligent investing public seeking factual information will place greater weight on opinion founded on painstaking analysis, without expecting the statistician to be an infallible prophet.

The large firms have research departments similar to those of investment trusts. Under the direction of the department head, who may be a member of the firm, the work is planned on specialized lines. One or more may be assigned to the various important fields of study: railroad, public utility, merchandising, steel, and other single industries. Less reliance is placed on data generally made public and more attention is given to field work, including conferences with corporate officials. If investment counsel service is rendered, account managers, to whom the research department submits material and recommendations, handle a limited number of accounts. Investment banking firms follow particularly the affairs of the corporations with which they have been identified in new financing. Monthly reports are studied. Members of the research department in this way become familiar with the details of corporations, and are more objective observers than officials and the directors; they suggest valuable ideas and direct attention to undesirable tendencies. Sometimes they become directors, or eventually become associated with these corporations as officers.

Although a part of the research department's work is of passing value, and not thorough when judged by severe standards, it often represents in concise form the honest opinion of serious students whose accumulated experience is of value. The conclusions may be the same whether expressed in a brief paragraph or in a comprehensive, many-page report. Few investors care to read a voluminous study; the conclusion is the essence of a report. The data on which the conclusion rests usually is of as little interest to the investor as the lawyer's brief is to a litigant. The more formal studies of many firms are of recognized excellence. *The Earning Power of Railroads,* prepared under the direction of Mr. Floyd W. Mundy, and in its thirty-second year, is a standard reference work of railroad analysts. Monthly analyses of specific industries and special studies of certain firms compare favorably with the best work of university economists.

Because the statistician is not able to trace the value of his work directly in sales or commissions, his position has sometimes been inferior to the sales department or customers' man. If the research department is competent, and not placed in a subsidiary position, it may be a valuable adjunct. The natural tendency toward enthusiasm or unbridled pessimism should receive its check in this department. Diversity of opinion and clash of temperaments are needed for clarity of vision and contribute toward a necessary brake on hasty action.

Their associates and outsiders often look upon statisticians or security analysts with a little disdain. If the members of the research department really know security values, why is it that they are not the most successful group in their speculative ventures or as investors? This is a fair question, but there are sound answers. Speculation is an art, not a science. It requires the ability to make quick decisions, to shift positions rapidly, and to cut losses. In other words, while a knowledge of values may prompt a course of action that will prove profitable in the long run, important swings of great importance to the speculator are completely lost. The analyst is not likely to be so successful in correct timing as the nimble trader with a poorer equipment in the way of knowledge but a keener sense of markets and market movements. Moreover, specialization often creates a false perspective. Railroad bond experts with an intimate knowledge of railroad finance and traffic movements have been notoriously wrong in their opinions of the future course of prices. Prices are often the result of waves of emotion or prejudice which the expert rightly feels are beyond prediction or logical interpretation. Nevertheless, the purchaser of a bond at 60 who sees it carried down to 40 cannot be wholly undisturbed even if the purchase eventually turns out profitable. The analyst, who in addition to being a student of values and of the forces that ultimately make prices, also develops a trading sense, combines the qualities most essential for satisfactory advice.

CLERICAL WORKERS

The large number of Wall Street employees in clerical positions are at the foot of the ladder. They have no influence, and in general mirror the opinions of their superiors. Through the educational facilities of the New York Stock Exchange Institute and the evening schools, opportunities for broadening their knowledge are now afforded. In the smaller organizations officials may come in contact with the office force. In the larger firms, however, partners may not be aware of individuals with many years' service. From the standpoint of personal advancement, this phase of the work of Wall Street is least attractive, and the positions are occupied mainly by those with less education and of a lower social rank than those engaged in other branches of the business. Wall Street firms have been generous in the past in the distribution of bonuses and in reference to hours of work, vacations, and absences. In all but a few firms working conditions are pleasant. More recently the machinery of the financial district has been excessive in relation to the volume of business, working great hardships on the clerks and those least able to bear loss of income. Adjustments, partly because of the volatile nature of the business, have to be made rapidly. The life of the average firm is relatively short. Changes in partners, liquidation of firms, the addition or dropping of departments is frequent, involving an unusually large turnover. Absence of steady policies aggravates an already serious condition. A more deliberate attempt to stabilize conditions might be helpful to all, employers and employees alike, in modifying the prince-and-pauper aspects of this business. As a result of the large lay-offs in the spring and summer of 1938, and the clear evidence that much of the unemployment was permanent, a special committee of replacement was formed by representative stock exchange firms. This committee registered over two thousand former employees and endeavored to find suitable employment for them in other industries.

Wall Street, to a large degree, is Main Street in Wall Street. John Combs, an expert in margins, resides in Montclair, New Jersey, and has gained his position as head margin clerk only after many years. William Sinsheimer, cashier of a stock exchange firm, lives with his family in a Westchester suburb. He was graduated from the evening division of a university after seven years of study. Wall Street is not composed entirely of Whitneys. The usual order may pass through the hands of four or five skilled persons who happen to be making a livelihood in the financial district; otherwise, they are indistinguishable from thousands of other office workers.

INCOME

The nearest approach to a complete survey of income of the brokerage business was submitted to the United States Senate Subcommittee on Banking and Currency for the five years and eight months from January 1, 1928, to August 31, 1933, and is summarized on page 21 from the tabulation in *Security Speculation* by John T. Flynn.

These figures are interesting chiefly because of the extreme fluctuations in gross income and profits, which make planning almost impossible. Since they do not include underwriters who were not members of the Exchange, dealers in over-the-counter securities, or firms which were members of the New York Curb Exchange only, they are of little aid in obtaining any

NEW YORK STOCK EXCHANGE MEMBER FIRMS

	Total Income[1]	Expenses	Net Income[2]	Number Firms In-cluded	Number Firms Regis-tered
1928	$547,295,754	$209,367,140	$332,821,808	611	437
1929	653,921,232	298,106,040	321,113,197	665	480
1930	341,458,118	256,879,880	61,778,406	649	495
1931	223,784,667	213,373,929 (Def.)	6,923,304	621	534
1932	176,451,346	168,559,665 (Def.)	8,722,061	610	571
1933	210,307,754	115,721,014	88,304,717	618	598

[1] Includes commissions, interest, profits on trading, dividends, underwriting, etc.
[2] Exclusive of odd-lot firms, and after accounts receivable written off, net of recoveries.

estimate of the size of the gross income or profit in the securities business, or of the capital employed. Comparisons are likely to be more striking than significant. It is common knowledge that aside from the underwriting of high-grade issues, principally for refunding, profits have been small or entirely absent over the past five years.

The value of the services of the financial world can never be appraised accurately. An exaggerated notion of the value probably existed in the past. The two genuine services rendered are the furnishing of capital to industry and the creation and maintenance of a market for securities. Other services, such as aid in the investment of funds or speculative activities, may be helpful to individuals or particular institutions, but they do not add to the aggregate well-being of the nation. It has been true in all likelihood that the financial world's returns in relation to the services rendered have been high. Individuals found finance an easy living without the industry or specialized training generally necessary for success in other businesses and the professions. For some years it was not even necessary to sell; one merely accepted orders. Partners and others withdrew amazing sums. This has not been true in the past five years. Already polls taken in the senior year of colleges show that finance has lost much of its attraction. The difficulties of earning a livelihood in finance have been no secret. Those affected most by the change cannot be expected to bear it without a sense of bitterness or hope for a return of the "good old days." From the national standpoint concern must be felt rather over the possibility that in the cutting down of the financial world's income industry may be hurt.

Critics of the functions performed by finance, especially of the stock exchanges, point out that the greatest part of the trading and fluctuations in securities does not affect the issuing corporations. They argue that after the original financing, a corporation often finances its further development entirely through the reinvestment of earnings and without seeking new funds in the capital markets. Hence, all the trading thereafter renders little if any service to it. Except as the price of a stock may indicate approaching failure or a spectacular rise advertise unusual success, the changes in the market affect only the security holders as distinguished from the corporation. The point, in part, is well taken. Through the legislation against manipulations and the vigilance of the stock exchange authorities, manipulation has been virtually stamped out. However, the importance of the market is not to be measured entirely by the frequency with which a corporation seeks to obtain new capital. Without the expectation of a continuous ready market, a great part of the new financing could not be undertaken. Investors refuse to invest funds in enterprises where they are certain to be "locked in." Experience of investors in corporations with few stockholders, and in which they are minority shareholders without an active participation, has been none too satisfactory. In the event that the investor must sell, the difficulty in obtaining a bid and the greater difficulty of obtaining a fair price are well known. Market price with all its aberrations is more likely to be a fair measure of value than the price obtainable when one of ten or twenty stockholders must obtain a bid from fellow stockholders who are made aware that his stock is being offered. In addition, the ability to borrow on securities is of no little importance. Security loans, with good reason, have been restricted and discouraged. Nevertheless, after years of effort in this direction and the deflation of security prices, such loans at this writing still amount to about $2,600,000,000. Omitting loans against government securities, this remains an imposing sum. Security loans, properly safeguarded, have a permanent place in our banking system. These loans would not be made by the banks if the securities had no market or were not considered liquid.

The Securities Exchange Act of 1934 itself recognizes the great importance of market prices. It states the need of doing away with manipulation and avoiding sudden and unreasonable fluctuations, which "hinder the proper appraisal of the value of securities and thus prevent a fair calculation of taxes owing to the United States and to the several states by owners, buyers and sellers of securities, and prevent the fair valuation of collateral for bank loans and/or obstruct the effective operation of the national banking system and Federal Reserve System." The service of the markets is not accurately gauged by fixing attention solely on the number of times that a corporation has obtained additional capital. Accordingly, while the financial community is not in every activity a contributor to the national efficiency or welfare, its members perform services of value at other times than in the sale of securities representing new financing. Unless we are prepared to embrace a philosophy of unlimited state intervention, a policy advocated by no responsible authority, the alternative is to permit errors of judgment, especially since no one is omniscient. Liberalism implies the right to choose and to make errors. Within a framework of the greatest possible equality of the parties, preservation of the right to be wrong is more precious than the elimination of error. The attempt to guide, and later to govern, every element in the vast interplay of forces and activity, the total of which is our economic life, inevitably leads to the totalitarian state.

FINANCIAL JOURNALISM

FINANCIAL journalism is an integral part of Wall Street, exercising an influence far beyond that suggested by the small number engaged in writing for the financial press. The term includes the financial columns of the daily newspapers, and the periodicals devoted wholly to finance and investment. My remarks will be confined largely to New York City newspapers and magazines.

The most striking fact in examining the leading newspapers is the great number of pages given over to financial news and comments. Twenty years ago the daily financial report of the New York *Times* was compressed into two pages, including the list of trading and quotations of the New York Stock Exchange, which amounted to less than a column. Ten years later six or seven pages were required, and now ten or more pages. The New York *Times* traces the development to the awakening interest in securities following the sale of Liberty bonds, which made it necessary to expand the space given to matters relating to finance and securities and to change the character of the reporting so that it would be intelligible to more than a few outside Wall Street. A similar transformation has taken place in England, where at the turn of the century the financial columns of *The Times* consisted mainly of an article under the general title, "The Money Market."[1] The quality of the news reporting and comment has improved markedly in the last decade. For speed and accuracy the financial departments of the newspapers and the news ticker organizations are probably unsurpassed. The possible effect of careless reporting or

[1] "The Financial Press," by A. R. Hobson, Lloyds Bank Limited, January, 1934; the New York *Times* has printed a helpful pamphlet on "Financial News: How to Read and Interpret It," and the New York *Herald Tribune* has published a similar booklet, entitled "The Financial Section of a Newspaper."

"inspired" articles in a sensitive market, which often revolves on the news, requires both a high degree of accuracy and absolute integrity. The New York *Times* has developed a corps of more than forty experts whose daily work is to record and call attention to points that will bear watching.

Every important newspaper's financial department centers around the daily column of comment on the market and the other financial events and news of the day. The column is, first, a factual summary and, second, a running commentary on the day's developments. This second function gives it great importance, since the editor's opinions are bound to influence his comment, however objective he may try to remain.

Comment in the leading papers seems to suffer little from the delicate problem of the relationship of advertising to freedom of criticism. It is probably unreasonable to expect that writers will altogether ignore the need of their papers to maintain friendly relations with important advertisers. On the whole, investment banking firms, whose new issue advertising is an important source of income, and the issuing corporations seem to take an enlightened attitude. Critical remarks on financial policies are frequent. In American, as in British journalism, according to Mr. Hobson, "there is nothing in the remotest degree resembling the system of subsidy and blackmail that prevails in a portion of the French Press." The ideal situation, a newspaper such as we are accustomed to on a completely self-supporting basis and independent of income from advertising, is out of the question. In England important corporations pay for the printing of the chairman's report at annual meetings, but in this country such addresses are only now becoming common, and the reports of stockholders' meetings are simply considered news items. Comment on individual securities may degenerate into tipping. The leading New York newspapers, aware of the danger, avoided the practice, but it was not until the Securities Exchange Act of 1934 became a law that the practice was almost entirely stamped out. Instances of "tips" that were bought and paid for were introduced before the investigations of the United States Senate committee and earlier had been condemned in his usual vigorous manner by Fiorello H. La Guardia when he was a member of the House of Representatives.

The periodicals devoted to finance and investments leave something to be desired. The *Commercial & Financial Chronicle,* for many years indispensable to everyone in the securities business, is composed primarily of source material. Its conservative editorial policy is steeped in the Wall Street tradition. During the period leading up to the 1929 crash its editorials represented the minority viewpoint and were sharply critical of what they repeatedly referred to as a speculative debauch. In contrast to many economists of academic standing, the gigantic increase in brokers' loans did not appear to the editors to be, as it did to President Coolidge, a "natural expansion of business."

Barron's, the foremost weekly read by individual investors, is an outgrowth of Dow, Jones & Co., the publishers of the *Wall Street Journal,* and has grown in excellence over the past five years. Editorially it, too, embodies largely the Wall Street point of view.

The *Magazine of Wall Street* and the *Financial World* are two other financial magazines read by individual investors.

The *Annalist,* published by the New York *Times* has valuable statistical features and its index of business activity is widely noted. The comments on the general business situation are independent and provocative. Remarks on individual securities, however, are limited, apparently as a matter of policy.

Unfortunately, there is no American financial publication of the excellence of the London *Economist,* probably the world's greatest financial periodical. It contains not only comment on company reports, observations on specific securities for the guidance of investors and the usual summaries of prices, dividends, etc., but also editorials of the highest standard on international finance, economics, and politics. Its special review of the New Deal before the 1936 national election was regarded as one of the best studies published here or abroad. Editorially its policy is enlightened and marked by a liberal attitude that is rare in American financial comment. The special correspondence from foreign countries, a reflection of the international character of the London market, is notable.

Possibly the excellence of the financial departments of the great New York dailies, with their Sunday financial sections, supplants the need of a weekly like the *Economist*, but it is the writer's hope that a similar publication will make its appearance in this country. The growing interest in economics and finance lends weight to the belief that it would be commercially profitable. A liberal financial magazine might serve as an equivalent of the minority security holders' national organization broached from time to time, but which is faced with formidable obstacles. At the same time, criticism of financial policies of a liberal national administration from such a source would be respected; at least, it could not be lightly dismissed. When the London *Economist* disagrees with a Conservative government we witness the interesting circumstance of a financial publication that is often more liberal than the prevailing government. In the past it has not spared the Liberal party or the Labor government. Its established position makes it more than a financial magazine. The *Economist's* observations cannot be dismissed by suggesting that it speaks only for the City or the financial world.

The dean of American financial journalism, Alexander D. Noyes, of the New York *Times*, writes with a fine sense of historical perspective. Besides being the author of two standard books on the financial history of the United States he has written his reminiscences of a half century in *The Market Place*, a fascinating book. The author has taken full advantage of his listening post. His daily column is rich in historical allusion. Mr. Noyes kept his balance in the years preceding 1929 and in the storm and strife period ending in 1932-1933. Around him he has gathered an able staff which is responsible for careful and thorough special articles. Mr. Noyes leans toward the political and economic faith of Senator Carter Glass, to whom he dedicated his latest volume. Never has the task of a financial writer been more aptly described than by Mr. Noyes: "Naturally, a conscientious writer for the press had to be on his guard. In a Stock Exchange community, dissemination of tips concocted for speculative purposes, and for which professional speculators wish to get newspaper publicity, is always present. The recourse taught by experience to newspaper writers of character was simple: to abstain altogether from personal speculation, which is the only way for preserving an unbiased mind; to see to it that the Stock Exchange fraternity should understand this attitude; to refuse all favors except being put in touch with legitimate news as a matter of professional duty; never to venture into the corridors of the Stock Exchange itself (where the very atmosphere unsettles sober judgment); to be scrupulously careful regarding habitual affiliations; to judge every rumor by the source from which it comes, but until the rumor, from whatever source, had been investigated, to receive it with cool skepticism. Such rules were perhaps in those days honored more often in breach than in observance; but the financial column of a newspaper was sure to indicate unmistakably whether the writer of it did or did not shape his own course according to them." Mr. Noyes has been a frequent contributor to the editorial page, where his discussions of financial topics bore the unmistakable stamp of large perspective, accuracy and, almost always, significant historical analogies or contrasts.

C. Norman Stabler and Edward H. Collins, of the New York *Herald Tribune*, write with a greater degree of partisanship than their contemporaries of the *Times*, but also maintain a high standard for completeness and accuracy. The financial editor of the New York *Sun*, Carlton A. Shively, is always interesting. His barbs against the New Deal and the Roosevelt administration are caustic. What his comments lack in even temper they make up for in liveliness. At times his criticism of high finance and the New York Stock Exchange have been equally blunt and unsparing, and he makes no attempt to appear unprejudiced. He has never descended to the ill manners of one of the few professional economists engaged in New York financial journalism, who in a diatribe against the present administration used the marital problems of a member of the Roosevelt family to sneer at the futility of the New Deal's program. Ralph Hendershot, of the *World-Telegram*, is somewhat more to the center than the financial editors of the leading morning papers. The articles of John T. Flynn appear in the financial pages of the *World-Telegram* and cover a broader field than the usual financial column. They are characterized by independence and an individual viewpoint. It is difficult to classify Mr. Flynn. Critical of speculation, he has been equally critical of many of the New Deal's economic measures.

The *Wall Street Journal* is the most important daily financial newspaper. The late Clarence Barron, owner of Dow, Jones & Co., publishers of the "broad tape" news ticker and news sheets, was for many years also the publisher of the *Wall Street Journal*. A large part of the paper consists of dispatches and reports that have appeared on the news ticker the previous day. In the past decade the paper has made important strides. Valuable articles contain firsthand information of corporate activities. The attention devoted to foreign news has increased. Excellent articles appear from time to time concerning financial developments in the principal European countries. In Thomas F. Woodlock, former member of the Interstate Commerce Commission, the *Wall Street Journal* has one of the best exponents of the conservative point of view. His articles show evidence of broad reading and experience. The editorials, often given over to discussions of special interest to the brokerage and investment banking interest, have a more limited interest than the special news items or the reports of its Washington correspondents. Commodity news is now given more space than formerly. The Dow, Jones & Co. averages of stock prices are still the most generally used. The interpretations of the late William P. Hamilton, for many years the paper's editor, have become classics in this field. Able successors continue the interpretation.

The New York *Journal of Commerce*, the leading contemporary of the *Wall Street Journal*, is one of the city's oldest newspapers. It is less exclusively devoted to finance and investment than the *Wall Street Journal* and devotes greater attention to commodity news and trade developments. The editorials, while the paper was edited by the late H. Parker Willis, were noted for their sharp, unsparing observations on monetary and banking policies, especially when the authorities departed from the views of commercial banking and Federal Reserve policies closely associated with Dr. Willis. The present editor, Dr. Jules I. Bogen, an associate of Dr. Willis, carries on the conservative tradition, but in a more moderate way.

Gradually a tradition is being developed around financial journalism. Recently an organization consisting of approximately a hundred financial writers of the daily New York press was organized and at its meetings the members are addressed by important figures in the world of finance and industry. This should be instrumental in promoting and maintaining a high sense of responsibility on the part of its members.

London has been fortunate in its outstanding representatives of financial journalism. The editor of the *Economist* since 1922 has been Sir William Layton who was a member of the Balfour Mission to the United States in 1917; financial adviser to the Indian Statutory Commission, 1929-1930; a British delegate to the World Economic Conference in 1927; British member of the Organization Committee of the Bank for International Settlements, 1929; and of the Advisory Committee under the Young Plan, 1931. His studies of prices and related problems are standard works. Walter Bagehot, early editor of the *Economist*, wrote the classic *Lombard Street* in addition to a noteworthy study in political science. He also attained fame as a literary critic. Hartley Withers has written a sheaf of books on finance, the most popular of which is *The Meaning of Money*. Francis W. Hirst, who became editor of the *Economist* at the age of thirty-four, has written *The Stock Exchange, Local Government in England,* and biographies of Thomas Jefferson and John Morley. Recently he wrote an important essay on "Economic Freedom." These English financial writers have a breadth of view that is uncommon in this country; it probably shows a greater maturity, which we may reasonably hope to achieve.

The Wall Street Mind

Through such books as *How the Other Half Lives,* by Jacob Riis, and a long list of realistic novels and dramas the physical aspects of poverty and want were well understood even before the beginning of tremendous unemployment. I wish that Wall Street equally understood how the other half lives mentally, that is, the great American tradition of dissent and liberalism.

Formal schooling, it appears, has left no mark of the Americanism of Thomas Paine, Wendell Phillips, or Theodore Parker. Henry Thoreau wrote vigorous essays on "Civil Disobedience," as well as *Walden* and *The Maine Woods*. The cry for social justice is quite as American as the stock ticker. Henry Demarest Lloyd's *Wealth Against Commonwealth* and the persuasive eloquence of Henry George's *Progress and Poverty* are as much a part of the American scene as the monopolies which they denounced, or New York's Richard Croker and Pennsylvania's Boies Penrose. Edward Bellamy's utopian romance, *Looking Backward*, was one of the most popular books of the day, and Henry Adams meditated profoundly and skeptically on a society of political democracy and economic plutocracy. The vision of the good society moved the Populist leaders and nourished the Grangers. Before the New Deal there was the New Freedom; and before that, Jacksonian democracy. American monetary heresies run back to the early colonial period. Benjamin Franklin, for all his homilies on the virtues of industry and patience, impatiently worked out and contrived a paper money scheme as a short cut to the operation of "natural" economic forces in an attempt to invigorate languishing trade and reverse the downward tendency of commodity prices.

One wishes that a treatise like the late Vernon Parrington's *Main Currents of American Thought* were as familiar in Wall Street as the writings of some of the popular columnists. Many of the most significant writers in American literature hardly represented the conservative idea. The encompassing love of the great masses characteristic of Walt Whitman; the critical portraits of the American middle class, ranging from William Dean Howells to Sinclair Lewis; the great contribution to the study of American society and history of Charles Beard and his school—all point to the dissenter's large place in American life. In economics the so-called Wisconsin group, led by Richard T. Ely and John R. Commons, has not escaped criticism for its searching examination of our institutions. Abroad, the most widely read American authors are Mark Twain, Jack London, and Upton Sinclair.

The financial world is in imperative need of understanding

this position, strange as it may appear to those who have been sheltered intellectually to the point that all dissenters are classed as un-American. Only by understanding its roots can the conservative meet intelligently and, therefore, effectively the opposite idea. Tinkering with machinery is an old American habit. It is not to be wondered at that periods of economic and social distress set in motion a desire to tinker with the economic and financial machinery. To some observers the deeply rooted desire to create greater national well-being represents tinkering that shows vigor and freshness. So long as it prevails there is less danger of capitulation to the extremes of fascism or communism or any closed system of life, for at the bottom of this spirit is a restless, inquiring mind unwilling to accept as inevitable the surrender of political freedom, and convinced of the ability to remove the curse of unemployment amidst plenty.

Side Lights on Wall Street

In one's business or professional career some incidents or episodes stand out from among the numberless day-to-day happenings. Sometimes they are in themselves of minor importance. Their peculiar quality, however much they may vary in other respects, is to catch with singular sharpness the character of the participants or the spirit motivating them. The "side lights" that follow, I trust, will help to create a better understanding of the virtues, defects, and problems of Wall Street as they appear to one observer.

Sentiment in Wall Street

To re-create the mood of a period is a task for a literary historian. Let us, nevertheless, sit in as invisible chroniclers on a meeting held in February, 1932, in the conference room of one of the most important investment banking firms in New York City. All the partners are present. The room is richly furnished but without ostentatious display of wealth. The firm members, with one exception, are graduates of a famous eastern university and have added to inherited wealth.

One of the partners suggests that the firm transfer a large sum to one of their foreign offices. The possibilities of loss are slight. The domestic situation is desperate. Prices of common stocks, after their calamitous decline from 1929, are still sinking almost daily. Bonds, both high and low grade, are tumbling under constant liquidation. The banking situation is ominous and the three supports of American economy in the lush decade are prostrate—farm income, automobile sales, building activity. Commodity prices seem to find no bottom. Now that England has taken the long step of abandoning the gold standard, without disastrous results, gold is moving out of the United States in great amounts, and is being hoarded internally—is it not inevitable that the dollar will be devalued? Prudence dictates the transfer of funds out of dollars, either in deposits abroad or in the large-scale purchase of foreign securities. Here is irrefutable logic, and if it carries weight, where could a better hearing be obtained? In Wall Street circles, in the heart of the world of finance, certainly the appeal to reason, coupled with safety as the minimum gain and substantial profits as a reasonable probability, must be irresistible.

As a matter of fact, no sound financial or economic reason was presented for not adopting the policy recommended. However, two of the senior partners having the largest capital investment in the firm demurred. One, who had served overseas in the war, somewhat embarrassed to have to reveal his real motive, fumbled with his fraternity key. He said something about feeling that the worst was over and that recovery would shortly take place in security and commodity prices. Yet, for months he had counseled against undertaking new commitments. The other partner was more frank. Turning first to the partner responsible for the meeting, he said: "Bill, nothing I say is meant to be critical of you. I appreciate your efforts to conserve the firm's capital. We have taken a real beating in the past two years. You know I shared in your idea about buying good gold-mining shares partly as a hedge against further deflation or ultimate currency devaluation." He continued: "Gentlemen, this is a hell of a situation, but my family, starting with nothing several generations ago, built up a fortune in this country. If the dollar is about to go, I am willing to go with it. This may sound foolish, but I can't take a major step that is a wager on America's weakness and will in itself contribute to the growing fear and panic. I'd hate to make money that way."

After some further discussion, nothing was done. Within a year the dollar was devalued by approximately 40 per cent. The firm had lost a chance to profit to the extent of many thousands of dollars in a period when profits were rare. The sentiment that governed the policy was muddleheaded. Logically, every sale of securities contributed to the general undermining of confidence. The purpose of reciting this incident is not to uphold the position of the partner who held to his faith in the dollar with fervor. The fact is that monetary gains were sacrificed knowingly, that sentiment overpowered self-interest and intelligent action. Somehow one's admiration is stirred by this sentiment. A little madness is a relief in a debit and credit world, especially when we find it where only profit and loss are supposed to govern men's actions. The economic interpretation of history is inadequate.

A Psychological Interpretation

To the jobholder whose office work has become more or less routine, to the retailer and small businessman, identification in any form with something big and powerful provides a feeling of vicarious importance. After John Smith has bought an odd lot of General Motors, Standard Oil of New Jersey, or Du Pont de Nemours, he reads the newspaper with renewed interest. Mr. Sloan, Mr. Teagle, the du Pont family and he are faced with great decisions in business matters, or in politics; the international situation is now something to worry about. Taxes deprive him of so many cents per share. The advertising of his company is set mentally alongside other advertising. Quarterly reports are read carefully. Decisions at dividend meetings take on additional meaning.

Mr. John Smith, moving out of the narrow range of daily humdrum affairs becomes a part of a far-flung business empire. If he had sold his stock when he wanted to he could have bought it back 15 per cent cheaper—if only Mary hadn't interfered. Many men derive out of financial sheets a satisfaction that is similar to that obtained by their wives and daughters out of the motion pictures. Wall Street is the western frontier of many a quiet, uninteresting straphanger or occupant of the 8:15.

CLEAN HANDS?

Mr. Jackson had been president of the —— Gadget Company since the death of the "old man," four years ago. He had an interesting matter to discuss—would Brickley, Wendell & Company, an investment banking firm, care to listen to the story? Mr. —— of the new-business department made an appointment with Mr. Jackson. The story, briefly, follows: "As you can see from these statements, we haven't made much progress in the last two years. Our position is quite strong and it isn't in connection with any new financing that I wanted to see you. When the old man died, control passed to two sisters who are getting along in years and to a nephew who is a Latin instructor in a western university. We have in all about fifty other stockholders, none of whom owns a substantial interest in the company. The stock is rarely dealt in and is quoted nominally around 40. There are outstanding 10,000 shares. I own about a thousand. We could have made a better showing. Our inventory is undervalued by more than 25 per cent, and we have been making some plant expenditures that we could have charged to capital instead of as an operating expense. Really, we could have shown closer to $100,000 net than the $60,000 that we reported."

Mr. Jackson chuckled. "Furthermore, the Steel Company has made us an informal offer for several acres adjoining their plant and we can undoubtedly get a handsome price. Our plant is sufficient and we can expand on the south side if necessary. Now, I want to obtain control myself or jointly with a friendly group. My idea is to make a bid for the stock of the old man's relatives, and I should like your aid. We haven't paid much in dividends and they would probably sell around the present price. I could offer a little stock down to around 35 to establish a low price. If we held the stock for a while, split it four or five to one and then showed our real earnings, there would be a handsome profit in it."

In other words, Mr. Jackson, who probably denounced the

Wall Street bankers in his conversation, had come to Wall Street to obtain its aid in consummating a reprehensible scheme. When business ethics are higher, Wall Street's morals will be less open to attack.

In Praise of Municipal Ownership

Wall Street has exhausted the English language, rich as it is, in the denunciation of public ownership and operation of electric light and power properties. Public ownership and operation are inefficient; they cannot compete successfully with private companies unless subsidized or exempted from equal taxation; public ownership, it is said, stifles initiative and is un-American. The debater's handbooks of twenty years ago contained every basic argument that has been advanced on either side of the question. The issue will be warmly debated for many years to come. Facts and logic may have less to do with the ultimate decision than clever propaganda and spread-eagle oratory. The subject is introduced here to show the financial district as an enthusiastic endorser of a municipal power and light system.

Partly because of the constant opposition of the world of finance to such projects, sales resistance to bonds secured on the properties of publicly owned power systems is powerful. The opportunity to finance the plant of the city of Seattle, Washington, brought forth several interesting studies by bond houses setting forth in detail the merits of the city's power and light system and its bonds. The reader, in effect, was told: "Forget whatever you have read about municipal ownership in general or what we have said about it in the past. Listen to this story of a successfully operated property, ably managed and worthy of consideration by you as an investment. Frankly, we were as astonished as you will be when you have read this study. This may seem to be an inconsistent position, but we haven't changed our general opinion. Anyway, aren't we all a little inconsistent?" From these studies the following has been extracted or paraphrased.

Seattle has been furnishing service since January, 1905. Generating capacity has been increased from time to time and has grown to approximately 245,000 kw. from 10,400 in 1904.

In 1937 the plants of the city generated 331,173,583 kw.-hr. The domestic rate was only 2.52 cents per kw.-hr., as compared with the national average of 4.69 cents. The city is considered to be the best lighted in the United States, with an average residential consumption of twice the nation's average. The system operated in competition with Puget Sound Power and Light Company, but under the superintendence of J. D. Ross, has gained the respect of its competitor for fair dealing and efficiency. Depreciation charges have been liberal. In the opinion of a prominent firm of engineers who examined the properties, the "department operates with smaller overhead costs than many, if not most, privately owned utilities of the same character and corresponding magnitude." In discussing the revenues and expenses, it was remarked: "Unlike the private utilities, City Light's capitalization consists of bonds alone— no preferred or common stock." The underlying purpose of a municipal utility is to furnish service at cost, the same circular points out. One of the underwriters commented sensibly on the situation. The firm stated that it had no desire to take sides in the controversial question of municipal versus private ownership, but believed that the next few years might witness a rapid growth of municipal power and light bonds. At one time municipal water revenue bonds were also regarded skeptically, so that precedent was not the sole proper guide.

At the same time that public activities have been categorically condemned, bonds of public corporations such as the Port of New York Authority and the New York City Parkway Authority have become recognized media for conservative investment. Broad statements supported principally by prejudice may serve as a boomerang and interfere seriously with the ability of underwriters to merchandise the sound issues of public corporations, besides leaving the financial district open to the charge of patent inconsistency.

CHAPTER III

THE SECURITIES AND EXCHANGE COMMISSION

ORGANIZATION

THE Securities and Exchange Commission was created pursuant to Section 4 of the Securities Exchange Act of 1934, which was approved by President Roosevelt on June 6, 1934. The Securities Act of 1933 was administered from May 23, 1933, the date of enactment, until September 1, 1934, by the Federal Trade Commission. On the latter date, under the provisions of the Securities Exchange Act, the administration and enforcement of the Securities Act was transferred to the Commission.

The act provides that the Commission* shall be composed of five members, to be appointed by the President, by and with the advice and consent of the Senate. Not more than three commissioners shall be members of the same political party. The salary is $10,000 a year and appointment is made for a period of five years, after the expiration of the terms of the first appointees who were to hold office for periods of from one to five years. One of the five commissioners is annually elected chairman. The commissioners act as a board and hold daily meetings at the Commission's offices in Washington, D. C. They pass upon policy of all matters within the jurisdiction of the Commission. The Commission has set up ten administrative zones in the United States and maintains a regional office for each zone. For the sake of efficiency, several divisions were established in Washington, D. C. The regional offices and the areas covered by each zone are shown on the following page.

Compared with the Federal Reserve Board of Governors, the Commission is smaller in number. Members of the Board of Governors, seven, are now appointed for fourteen years at

* "Commission," when used hereafter, refers to the Securities and Exchange Commission.

Regional Office	Zone
New York	New York, New Jersey, and Pennsylvania
Boston	Massachusetts, Connecticut, Rhode Island, Vermont, New Hampshire, and Maine
Atlanta	Tennessee, North Carolina, South Carolina, Georgia, Alabama, Mississippi, Florida, and the portion of Louisiana east of the Atchafalaya River
Chicago	Minnesota, Wisconsin, Iowa, Indiana, Missouri; and Kansas City, Kansas
Cleveland	Ohio, Illinois, Michigan, and Kentucky
Fort Worth	Oklahoma, Arkansas, Texas, Kansas (with the exception of Kansas City), and the portion of Louisiana west of the Atchafalaya River
Denver	Wyoming, Colorado, New Mexico, Nebraska, North Dakota, and Utah
San Francisco	California, Nevada, Arizona, and Hawaii
Seattle	Washington, Oregon, Idaho, Montana, and Alaska
Washington, D. C.	Virginia, West Virginia, Maryland, Delaware, and District of Columbia

an annual salary of $15,000. There is no restriction on the number of members of the same political party. The structure of the system with its regional banks is embodied in the Federal Reserve Act. The arrangement of regional offices of the Securities and Exchange Commission is its own creation. In the light of the importance of the Commission's functions and the need of obtaining officials of the highest ability, no valid reason seems to exist for the difference in salary. The term of office might well be extended to from eight to ten years, and the salary of commissioners raised to $15,000 annually.

Divisions and Their Functions

The functions and activities of the several divisions and offices which have been established to promote efficient administration are as follows:[1]

The Legal Division is responsible for (1) the rendering of opinions and advice to the Commission on general questions of law arising in connection with the administration and enforcement of the three acts over which the Securities and Exchange Commission has jurisdiction; (2) the rendering of opinions and the drafting of interpretive letters in response to

[1] Based on a description of the divisions published by the Securities and Exchange Commission.

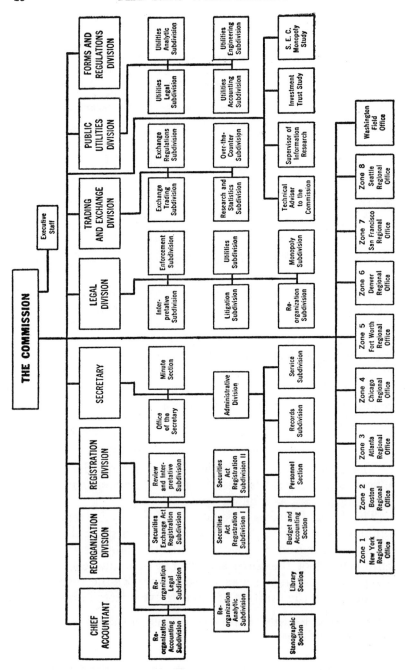

inquiries regarding the interpretation of the statutes administered and enforced by the Commission: (3) conducting hearings before the Commission, in all cases except those involving refusal or stop order proceedings under Sections 8 (b) and (d) of the Securities Act of 1933, which are conducted by the Registration Division, and hearings relative to the continuance, extension, termination, or suspension of unlisted trading privileges on national securities exchanges, which are conducted by the Trading and Exchange Division; (4) supervising the conduct of investigations of alleged violations of the acts; (5) representing the Commission in all judicial proceedings, including proceedings to enjoin violations of law and proceedings for the review of orders of the Commission (under existing legislation all civil court actions, including actions for injunctions, proceedings for the review of Commission orders and a variety of proceedings in which the Commission or the members of the Commission are defendants, are handled directly by the Commission's legal staff, whereas criminal proceedings are referred to the Department of Justice); (6) preparing criminal cases for transmission to the Department of Justice and to the Post Office Department for prosecution and the cooperation in the trial of such cases; and (7) collaboration with other divisions of the Commission in the preparation of reports to Congress as required under the Securities Exchange Act of 1934 and the Public Utility Holding Company Act of 1935.

The Registration Division is responsible for the examination of all registration statements covering the proposed public offering of securities in interstate commerce or through the mails, filed pursuant to the Securities Act of 1933; prospectuses and offering sheets filed pursuant to the Commission's regulations providing a conditional exemption from registration under the foregoing act; applications for registration of securities on national securities exchanges pursuant to Section 12 of the Securities Exchange Act of 1934; reports of security ownership and transactions as required of directors, officers, and principal stockholders under Section 16 of the Securities Exchange Act of 1934 and of directors and officers under Section 17 of the Public Utility Holding Company Act of 1935;

and applications for the confidential treatment of material contained in any application, report, or document filed under the Securities Exchange Act of 1934. This includes the examination not only of statements, applications, and reports proper, but also of accompanying financial statements, certificates of incorporation appraisals, prospectuses, and other documents, as well as periodical annual reports and amendments to the foregoing; the preparation of reports and letters of deficiency; the making of field investigations by engineers and accountants; the conduct of hearings for the development of facts and the verification of data submitted in registration statements and applications; and the conduct of hearings in refusal-order and stop-order proceedings under Section 8 (b) and (d) and in examination proceedings under Section 8 (e) of the Securities Act of 1933; the preparation of recommendations to the Commission on the above matters and, after the Commission has acted, the preparation of the Commission orders.

The Trading and Exchange Division is responsible for (1) the examination of registration statements filed by exchanges for registration as national securities exchanges and the exemption of exchanges from registration; (2) the formulation of rules for the regulation of floor trading by members off the floor of exchanges, and for the limitation of dealings by specialists and odd-lot dealers; (3) the detection of excessive trading and unlawful practices on exchanges, including wash sales, matched orders, pool operations, the tipping of pool operations, the dissemination of false and misleading information concerning securities, and other manipulative or deceptive devices; (4) the review of field investigations into trading activities; (5) the formulation of rules for the regulation of pegging, fixing, and stabilizing operations on exchanges and in over-the-counter markets; (6) the formulation of rules for the regulation of puts, calls, straddles, and other options both on exchanges and over-the-counter; (7) the formulation of rules for the regulation of short selling and stop-loss orders; (8) the study of the effect of Federal Reserve margin regulations on trading in securities; (9) the formulation of rules relating to the borrowings of exchange members, brokers, and dealers, and relating to the hypothecation of customers' securities by exchange members, brokers, and dealers; (10) the study of exchange rules and the formulation of rules governing miscellaneous exchange practices; (11) the formulation of rules with respect to "when and if issued" trading; (12) the formulation of rules for the regulation of over-the-counter markets, including rules providing for the registration of brokers and dealers in over-the-counter markets and for the elimination of the unfit, rules regulating trading practices and dealings in over-the-counter markets, rules to ensure to over-the-counter investors protection comparable to that provided in the case of national securities exchanges, rules for the regulation of securities salesmen employed by over-the-counter houses and rules for the regulation of investment counsel; (13) the formulation of rules and regulations governing the continuance or extension of unlisted trading privileges on national securities exchanges of rules governing the withdrawal and removal of securities from unlisted trading privileges and the examination of applications for the delisting of securities listed and registered on national securities exchanges; and (15) the conduct of hearings before the Commission or an officer of the Commission held on such applications.

The Secretary is the chief administrative officer of the Commission and as such is responsible for action on, signing, and service of all Commission orders, actions, and certifications; preparation and defense of the budget estimates before the Bureau of the Budget and the Appropriation Committees of Congress; preparation of the Commission's Annual Report to Congress; action on all allotments and expenditures of appropriations; and assistance in the coordination of the many activities of the Commission. The Secretary also has general supervision over (a) the Recording Secretary, who is responsible for the preparation, maintenance, and indexing of official minutes of the Commission and the drafting of memoranda to division heads and regional administrators indicating actions taken on matters presented to the Commission, and (b) the Administrative Division, the functions of which include: (1) all service activities such as the establishment of field offices, the preparation of leases, the preparation of contracts for miscellaneous services, all duplicating activities, the purchase, storage, and issuance of supplies and equipment, the maintenance and distribution of forms, rules, regulations, instructions, opinions, press releases, etc., the compilation of statistical information by means of card punching, sorting, and tabulating machines, and the editorial and printing work; (2) the preparation and maintenance of the dockets and records on all registration statements, applications, declarations, etc., filed with the Commission; (3) the maintenance of the central files of the Commission; (4) the maintenance of the Public Reference Room and the dissemination of information with respect to all public documents filed with the Commission; (5) the maintenance of the Library, the central mail room and the stenographic pool for servicing all divisions of the Commission; (6) the maintenance of the Commission's appropriation accounting records and the auditing of vouchers and pay rolls covering expenditures; (7) the conduct of general correspondence not relating to technical subjects or matters; and (8) examination of and action on all applications for admission to practice before the Commission as attorney or agent.

The Public Utilities Division, in general, is charged with the administration of the Public Utility Holding Company Act of 1935. Its financial, accounting, and engineering staffs make studies of the operations and financial structure of the registered holding company systems and pass upon the declarations or applications filed by the holding companies or their subsidiaries with respect to matters requiring approval of the Commission, such as the issuance of securities, the acquisitions of securities or utility assets, reorganizations, organization of service companies, and similar matters. The division is also responsible for making studies of holding company systems with a view to determining the best methods of achieving the integration of systems and the simplification of rules and regulations with respect to various aspects of holding company activities, such as intercorporate loans, redemption of securities, declaration of dividends, sales of assets, solicitation of proxies, transactions with affiliates, the keeping of accounts, the filing of reports with the Commission, etc.

The Chief Accountant of the Commission is responsible for

the rendering of advisory service to the Commission in connection with accounting matters; for the conduct of studies, investigations and researches involving accounting theory, policy, and procedure; for the conduct of conferences with accounting authorities and members of the staff regarding matters involved in the drafting and interpretation of accounting rules and regulations; for the supervision of the accounting work of the Commission whenever unusual matters, new procedure, or new policies are concerned; for supervision over the promulgation and administration of rules regarding uniform classification of accounts; for drafting and establishing procedure to be followed in the conduct of audits and accounting investigations; for rendering advisory opinions and instructions to the accountants assigned to the various divisions and regional offices of the Commission in connection with the disposition of highly technical auditing and accounting questions; for the preparation of accounting briefs, reports, and memoranda regarding accounting matters under the jurisdiction of the Commission in connection with the administration and enforcement of the Securities Act of 1933, the Securities Exchange Act of 1934, and the Public Utility Holding Company Act of 1935.

The Research Division is responsible for the collection of information bearing upon current development in the securities market, and the observation of the financial policies of corporations under the jurisdiction of the Commission; the maintenance of statistical and analytical information on security markets, corporate earnings, and other subjects of interest to the Commission; the maintenance of statistical records on the activities of the Commission; and the organization and presentation either for internal use by the Commission, for other governmental agencies, or for publication of the statistical material collected by the Commission in the exercise of its administrative functions. It is further charged with advising the Commission on current developments and problems in the above fields and with drafting special reports on technical and economic aspects of the issuance of and the trading in securities. The division also engages in research on basic economic and financial problems connected with the administration of the Public Utility Holding Company Act of 1935 and advises the Commission thereon. A section of the division conducted the study of investment trusts and investment companies authorized by Section 30 of the Public Utility Holding Company Act of 1935 and by resolution of the Commission under Section 18 of the same act.

The Supervisor of Information Research is responsible for disseminating public information regarding the activities of the Commission by means of correspondence and press releases. The legislation under which the Commission operates specifically directs that publicity be given to its rulings, regulations, opinions, and findings, as well as to the filing of registration statements, the effective registrations, hearings held, and reports and statements filed with the Commission by security issuers, officers, directors, and principal stockholders. This information is made available to the public by the Supervisor of Information Research through releases issued to the press and through mailing lists established for the convenience of those who wish to receive releases currently.

The Forms and Regulations Division is responsible for (1) the preparation for submission to the Commission of rules, regulations, and forms in collaboration, where appropriate, with other divisions of the Commission; (2) the conduct of accounting, legal, and economic researches for the purpose of developing facts, policies, and customers regarding specific industries to be affected by the promulgation of such rules and regulations and forms; (3) the conduct of conferences and interviews with representatives of accounting and legal societies and associations, stock exchange officials, and others for the purpose of securing suggestions concerning proposed forms and regulations and in order to ascertain the reaction of these representatives to the proposed forms and regulations, particularly with respect to burdens that may be imposed upon industries as the result of their promulgation; (4) the conduct of studies in connection with forms and rules and regulations now in existence to determine whether they should be amended, revised, or modified; and (5) the preparation of legal opinions and interpretations concerning those rules and regulations. This work involves the preparation of rules and regulations and forms for use in connection with the regulation of stock exchanges of the country, the flotation of new securities and the registration of securities listed on exchanges by a great variety of security issuers. The Employment Research Division is charged with the responsibility of handling all personnel matters for the Commission. It includes the conduct of correspondence, the maintenance of personnel records, the interviewing of applicants, and all administrative work regarding appointments, pay rolls, transfers, reinstatements, service records, promotions, demotions, separations, and classification work.

The Protective Committee Study Division was charged with the responsibility of conducting investigations and hearings for the purpose of assembling data and facts for use in the preparation of the Report to Congress as required under Section 211 of the Securities Exchange Act of 1934. The division was also charged with the actual drafting of the report. The investigation related to the work, activities, personnel, and functions of protective and reorganization committees in connection with the reorganization, readjustment, rehabilitation, liquidation, or consolidation of corporate persons and properties. Investigations terminated early in January, 1936. Since that time the division prepared and published reports to Congress on the subject.

The Securities and Exchange Commission is represented in the Temporary National Economic Committee which is charged with the duty of making a full study of monopoly and financial concentration. The studies assigned to the Commission include insurance companies, investment banking, and corporate practices.

The regional offices are charged with the responsibility of conducting trading, accounting, and legal investigations and hearings with a view to the efficient enforcement of the Securities Act of 1933, the Securities Exchange Act of 1934, and the Public Utility Holding Company Act of 1935. Each regional office serves the general and investing public within the zone over which it has jurisdiction, and aids registrants and accounting, legal, and investment firms in complying with the statutes and the rules and regulations administered and enforced by the Commission.

The work of the Accounting Division in establishing uniform and sound practice is of great importance. The McKesson and Robbins case emphasizes the importance and opportunities of this division. The schedules required in connection with registration statements and the establishment of rules for the forms of annual reports give the Commission opportunities to use its influence and power for the promotion of helpful standards.

From time to time general statements are made as the result of the questions that have arisen in a particular case, if the principle in question has wider application. The Commission was asked whether it is proper for a corporation to treat as income dividends applicable to shares of its own stock held in a sinking fund. Many preferred stocks of industrial corporations now contain provisions for the establishment of a sinking fund. Such stock is generally canceled, but a corporation that must require 5,000 shares of stock annually may take advantage of market conditions to purchase 15,000 shares, or three years' requirements. Shall it show in the income account the dividends on this stock? A simpler case is illustrated by the repurchase of stock which is held as treasury stock. Through its Chief Accountant, the Commission made reply and published the reply in its Accounting Series.[2] The answer was that dividends on a corporation's own stock held in its treasury or in sinking or other special funds should not be included in income. The treatment of such dividends as income results in an inflated showing of earnings inasmuch as the earnings from which dividends are paid have already been included in income or surplus during the current or prior accounting periods. When a corporation's own stock, the opinion observed, is held in a sinking or other special fund, the requirements in respect of which are such that earnings accruing to the securities held therein must be added to the fund, dividends applicable to the corporation's own stock held should not be treated as income.

The authority vested in the Commission is nowhere catalogued; it is scattered throughout the statutes and the rules adopted by the Commission. Its powers are broad, but are properly conditioned as to the giving of notice, the holding of hearings and the right of appeal. The variety of matters within the Commission's jurisdiction is described in the discussion of the Commission's work and the divisions established by it. Without enumerating its powers with respect to exchanges and securities, their wide range may be illustrated. For instance, the Commission, under certain conditions, may suspend for twelve months the registration of a national securities exchange, or any member of such an exchange. The Commission may suspend trading in any registered security for a period of not more than ten days; or, with the President's approval, summarily suspend all trading on any national securities exchange for a period of not exceeding ninety days. It has authority to fix reasonable rates of commission, and over the solicitation of proxies by the use of the mails or any means or instrumentality of interstate commerce.

The efforts of the Securities and Exchange Commission in behalf of minority interests, the classification of accounting methods where honest differences of opinion may arise, the constant efforts to win adherence to the standards of full and fair disclosure will have an incalculable influence on corporation finance. Already annual reports are beginning to reflect the new standards. Leaflets with nothing more than a balance sheet and profit and loss statement expand into pamphlets containing comment on the changes in important items and a fairly comprehensive narrative account of the period's developments, accomplishments, and problems. The specific examples of activities in behalf of fairer plans of recapitalization, of more accurate accounting practices, of fuller disclosure of relevant facts, of the exorcising of misrepresentation are, after all, of limited application even if they affect corporations having assets of hundreds of millions. The deep, pervasive influence exerted by these examples, in preventing unfair plans from being presented to security holders, in honest descriptions of purpose in proxies and letters, in the more frank disclosure of value-making or -destroying developments, in the stillbirth of schemes representing anything from artful, deceptive plans to outright fraud simply because of fear—these are the measure of the gains to the security holder and the nation.

[2] Securities and Exchange Commission Release, Accounting Series 6, May 10, 1938.

CHAPTER IV

THE WORK OF THE COMMISSION

ADMINISTRATION OF THE PUBLIC UTILITY ACT OF 1935

ADMINISTRATION of the Public Utility Holding Company Act alone is a formidable task. The summary report of the Federal Trade Commission to the United States Senate[1] shows that the eighteen top holding companies on which hearings were held had total assets in 1932 of $4,119,769,627, and their subsidiaries produced 35,577,517,490 kilowatt hours.

As of June 30, 1938, public utility holding companies with consolidated assets on December 31, 1937, of $13,869,830,000 had registered with the Commission under the terms of the Act.

Far-reaching developments may be anticipated from the administration of Section 11 providing for the simplification of holding company systems, the so-called "death sentence." Former Commissioner J. D. Ross, now administrator of the federal government's Bonneville dam project and an expert in the field of electric power and light management, described the duties and powers of the Commission in the following words:

"Section 11 goes much further than the previous Securities and Exchange bills in that it allows the S.E.C. to determine the value of a security by studying the financial condition of the concern. To determine the value of a concern requires more or less a valuation of its properties. It seems very probable, therefore, that the investor will expect more from the S.E.C. in the case of utility company offerings and will take it for granted that there is the proper value back of each security. In other words, it will put a considerably greater load on the Commission than it now has in requiring an

[1] *Utility Corporations,* 70th Congress, 1st Session, Document 92, Part 72-A (1935).

honest disclosure of all facts as specified by the previous laws."[2]

Under this section the American Water Works and Electric Company, Inc., one of the principal public utility holding companies, submitted a voluntary plan to the Commission for corporate simplification of its system. This was the first application of its kind. The company contended that its electric properties extending over parts of five contiguous states— Pennsylvania, Ohio, West Virginia, Maryland, and Virginia— are either physically interconnected or capable of physical interconnection, and that its other businesses, including water, transportation, and miscellaneous activities, are reasonably incidental or economically necessary or appropriate in its operations. The plan involved the dissolution of the West Penn Electric Company, its largest intermediary holding company. Upon the completion of the realignment, the four principal subsidiary companies—West Penn Power Company, Monongahela West Penn Public Service Company, the Potomac Edison Company and West Penn Railways Company— will be its direct subsidiaries. There will then be in the system no subsidiary companies which in turn will have subsidiaries that are holding companies. The plan would be carried out by the purchase of subsidiary company securities and assets, and by approximately $44,000,000 of new financing. In connection with the fair and equitable distribution of voting power among its security holders (a necessary condition for obtaining the approval of the Commission), the company pointed out that the stock capitalization of each of its subsidiaries will consist of a single class of capital stock, or of common stock, or of common stock and a single class of preferred stock, and a single issue of first mortgage bonds.[3] This large company with consolidated assets of $384,000,000 and annual gross revenues of $52,053,052 did not find it difficult to obtain the cooperation of the Commission because its plan was fair and it desired to take advantage of the Public Utility Holding Company Act to simplify its financial structure.

[2] Address before the "New Wall Street" symposium at the New School for Social Research, New York, March 31, 1937

[3] Securities and Exchange Commission, Holding Company Act Release No. 793, August 25, 1937.

That the "death sentence" would be administered cautiously was indicated by the opinion of the Commission in the reorganization of the Peoples' Light and Power Co. Although the plan contained a number of features that were open to criticism, the Commission recognized that "preservation of the system for the time being may facilitate eventual integration on terms which may at least protect security holders from the sacrifice which anything resembling forced selling at this stage might involve." The tactics adopted by some holding companies while the bill was debated and the irresponsible statements made after it had become a law might have had serious consequences if, in the administration of the law, the Commission adopted a vindictive attitude or held to the letter of the law, regardless of the consequences. In the exercise of such broad powers, the difference between reasonable administration and a dogmatic spirit may be as important as the statute itself. The long and expensive litigation over registration by some utility interests delayed refunding operations and was costly to security holders in many ways. It might have engendered bitterness that would have been even more costly. The statesmanlike attitude of the Commission in the Peoples' Light and Power case foreshadowed judicious and considerate treatment. The broad principles set forth were that "the problem of consummating integrated public utility systems under the Act is of necessity in many cases an evolutionary rather than a revolutionary process. As a practical measure it will often be necessary to accomplish the ultimate objectives of the Act by a series of steps rather than by one direct and final step."[4]

Every registered holding company must file a declaration regarding the issue or sale of a security and the Commission, before permitting a declaration to become effective, must find that:

(1) the security is reasonably adapted to the security structure of the declarant and other companies in the same holding company system;

[4] Securities and Exchange Commission, Holding Company Release No. 885, November 16, 1937.

(2) the security is reasonably adapted to the earning power of the declarant;

(3) financing by the issue and sale of the particular security is necessary or appropriate to the economical and efficient operation of a business in which the applicant lawfully is engaged or has an interest;

(4) the fees, commissions, or other remuneration, to whomsoever paid, directly or indirectly, in connection with the issue, sale, or distribution are reasonable;

(5) in the case of a security that is a guaranty of, or assumption of liability of, a security of another company, the circumstances are such as to constitute the making of such guaranty or the assumption of such liability to a proper risk for the declarant; or

(6) the terms and conditions of the issue or sale of the security are not detrimental to the public interest or the interest of investors or consumers.

Section 7 of the Holding Company Act also prohibits the Commission from permitting a declaration concerning the issue or sale of a security to become effective unless it makes findings relating to the security of the issue or the purposes of financing. Without an effective declaration, except for obligations maturing in nine months or less, it is unlawful either to use the mails or any means or instrumentality of interstate commerce for the sale of securities.[5] These safeguards do not mean that the securities issued will not fluctuate or depreciate in price. The Commission does not possess omniscience, nor does it pass on the price at which a security is sold unless it be grossly inadequate or excessive.

The soundly financed company usually has no difficulties. Let us take an example and see how the Commission proceeds. San Antonio Public Service Company, a subsidiary of American Light & Traction Company, which is a registered holding company, filed a declaration pursuant to Section 7 of the Public Utility Holding Company Act with respect to the issue and sale for refunding purposes of $16,500,000 first mortgage bonds 4 per cent series due 1963, $2,500,000 aggregate

[5] Section 7, Public Utility Holding Company Act: Declarations by Registered Holding and Subsidiary Companies in respect of Security Transactions.

principal amount of 4 per cent serial notes (maturing 1939-1948), and 28,000 shares of no-par value common stock. The new bonds were to be secured by a direct first lien on all property and franchises with certain exceptions; the serial notes were to be unsecured obligations.

After appropriate notice a hearing was held. The declaration was open to examination by anyone interested. On May 25, 1938, the Commission made an order that the declaration become immediately effective. The findings and opinion of the Commission showed what matters were considered in its deliberations.

After the refunding operation it was found that the capital structure would be as follows:

	Amount	Per Cent of Total
Total Funded Debt........	$19,000,000	64.0
Preferred Stock...........	4,500,000	15.2
Common Stock and Surplus.	6,189,646	20.8
Total Capitalization.....	29,689,646	100.0

The Commission found that the average interest rate on the funded debt will be 4 per cent and the interest requirements for the first year will be $760,000, a gross saving of $221,400. Amortization of expenses incident to the new financing will reduce the gross figure to $121,015. After the notes are paid off, a sinking fund is to become operative for the retirement of the new bonds making for a progressive decrease in funded debt. The common stock will be sold to the parent company for cash at the stated value, $70 a share, and will provide $1,960,000 equity money. The bonds are to be sold for 96¾ per cent of their principal amount to the underwriters who will sell them to the public at 99. The Commission observed the close connection of the principal underwriters with interests associated with the parent company and that there had been no public bidding. However, testimony given at the hearing with respect to the fairness of the spread satisfied the Commission as to its reasonableness. The earnings were reviewed with respect to the coverage of interest. The total proposed debt would represent 63 per cent of the net property account, which is not excessive. The basis of the book value of the property account was set forth and the Commission discussed the provisions for depreciation. There was some question as to whether retirement provisions had been adequate. The Commission passed no opinion on this subject, but pointed out that the new bonds were protected by provisions in the supplemental indenture requiring a "maintenance and replacement fund and prohibiting payment of dividends except after compliance with a certain minimum standard with respect to maintenance and depreciation.[6] Here, too, the Commission did not insist on perfection or the ideal.

In this everyday work the Commission will stand as a vigilant guard of the investors' interests. As the holding companies and investment bankers recognize the value of the Commission's findings, financing should be made easier. Declarations, of course, do not relieve the companies of registration and the issuing of a prospectus; but, whereas it is illegal to represent that the Commission has approved a security or has made any finding that the statements in the prospectus or registration statement are correct, it is not unlawful to present the prospective investor with a copy of the findings and opinion in making a declaration effective. The opinion of the Commission, ordinarily more conservative even than the investment advisory service, may be used by alert underwriters to supplement the opinions of these organizations.

Not all the problems arising out of reorganization or recapitalization of holding companies concern the larger systems; size is not the criterion of either the standards under the misnamed "death sentence" provisions or Section 7 which gives the Commission power to permit or refuse to permit the issuance of new securities. One of the most significant cases in which the Commission has acted has been that concerning the reorganization plan of the Genesee Valley Gas Company, Inc.[7]

The Genesee Valley Gas Company, Inc., was organized under the laws of New York State in 1926 for the purpose of

[6] Securities and Exchange Commission, Holding Company Act Release No. 1120, June 9, 1938.

[7] In the matter of Genesee Valley Gas Company, Inc., Holding Company Release No. 981, January 24, 1938, and Address of A. Fortas, Assistant Director of the Public Utilities Division, Securities and Exchange Commission, July 14, 1938.

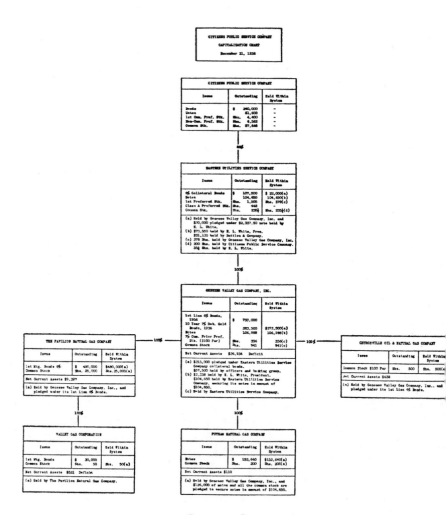

CORPORATE STRUCTURE

Genesee Valley Gas Co., Inc., System

acquiring the common stocks of certain gas utility subsidiaries. These subsidiaries serve natural and manufactured gas to twenty-one communities in New York State. Total population served is about 28,000. Capitalization at the end of 1936 was as follows:

Funded Debt
First Lien 6s, due 1956......................	$733,000.
10-year 7% Debentures, due 1936............	283,500.
Secured Notes.............................	106,987.

Capital Stock
7% Cum. Prior Preferred Stock ($100 par).....	33,600.
Common Stock (no par).....................	55,111.
	(941 shares)

The capital structure of a small company was merely the focal point of a complex holding company superstructure. The principal subsidiary, Pavilion Natural Gas Company, from which the parent company derived practically all its income, had gross revenues of only $181,430 in 1936. As the accompanying diagram shows, the Genesee Valley Gas Company is an intermediate holding company with two tiers of holding companies above it, Eastern Utilities Service Company and Citizens Public Service Company, and a group of operating companies below it, consisting of Pavilion Gas Company, Valley Gas Corporation, Churchville Oil & Natural Gas Company, and Putnam Natural Gas Company. The major assets of Genesee Valley were the common stocks and certain obligations of its subsidiary companies.

The origin of this structure is of some interest. Genesee Valley's common and preferred stocks were issued to the bankers in consideration of promotional services; the acquisition of the stocks of the subsidiaries was financed through the sale to the public of the mortgage bonds and debentures. In 1928 Citizens Public Service was formed to acquire the common stock of Genesee Valley; it issued its debentures and preferred stock for part of the common stock, but the banking group retained the bulk of the issue, enabling it to keep control. After avoiding financial difficulties which arose as early as 1931, Genesee Valley effected a reorganization in 1933 through the formation of a new company, Eastern Utilities Service Company, which was interposed between Genesee Valley and the top holding company, Citizens Public Service Company. The plan cut the debenture interest in half, as the holders of Genesee Valley debentures received $500 in new collateral trust bonds of the new company for each $1,000 debenture. I have asked the reader to follow this maze because the essence of holding company evils is unnecessary complexity stemming from artificially created entities enabling someone to disguise the exact facts.

Proceedings for the company's reorganization were commenced in December, 1936, and a plan was filed with the Securities and Exchange Commission in May, 1937; subsequently a public hearing was held. The immediate cause of receivership was the company's inability to redeem or refinance its 7 per cent debentures which had matured in September, 1937.

The plan provided that the first lien bonds remain undisturbed. The debenture holders and general creditors were placed in the same class. The former were to receive a total of 24,097.5 shares of common stock, or approximately 85 shares for each $1,000 debenture with interest. Other general creditors were allocated a total of 328 shares, or approximately 58 shares for each $1,000 claim with interest. The secured notes were placed in separate classes because of differences in security. A secured note on which $2,600 was due was allocated 1,600 shares of common stock, an arbitrary figure (see by whom this note was owned for a possible explanation), and another note on which $121,000 was due was allocated 10,465 shares of common stock. The old common and preferred stock was given a total of 739 shares of new common stock.

In sum, the proposed plan, upon consummation, would result in 48.8 per cent of the voting control passing to the public and 51.2 per cent remaining in the hands of the present management, since the secured notes were held by the president of the company and its bankers.

The plan was disapproved by the Commission. The Pavilion Natural Gas Company, as already noted, provided the parent company with approximately 92 per cent of the total income received by it in the form of dividends or interest from the time of organization to the close of 1936. This operating company, with a gross income in 1936 of some $57,000, had attempted to support a superstructure of three tiers of holding companies having outstanding securities of approximately $2,200,000, with annual dividend and interest requirements of about $139,000. The Pavilion Company, without the approval of the Public Service Corporation, had transferred $196,000 from its depreciation reserve to the earned surplus account. Except for this transaction, all dividends subsequently declared would have been paid at a time when the earned surplus account in reality showed a deficit. The Public Service Commission had under examination the propriety of this transfer, made in 1927, at the time the plan was submitted for approval.

More significant from the general standpoint of the reorganization plan was the doubtful propriety of the allocation of the new stock representing an equity over and above the first lien bonds, as follows:

Security	Total Claim Principal and Interest	Number Shares New Common Stock to be Distributed	Basis of Exchange per $1,000 Due
Debentures	$392,647	24,097.5	61 shares
Secured note	121,000	10,465.	86 shares

The Commission pointed out a glaring discrepancy in the relative treatment of the debentures and secured notes. Using the treatment accorded the secured note as a yardstick, it would be necessary to issue to the debentures 34,430 shares. The value of the security was only about $8,000, for which the noteholders were being allotted, in fact, 3,572 shares, or about 446 shares per $1,000 of secured claim. Estimating the value of the new shares on the basis of the allotment to the $8,000 secured portion of the other secured notes, it would be necessary to issue to the debentures 175,525 shares. Plainly the treatment of the debentures made it impossible to justify the issuance of new shares to the old stock.

The fixed assets had an aggregate book value of only $991,060, including a substantial amount of abandoned property, against a total capitalization to be outstanding of

$1,339,008 and a gross income of only $83,000 annually. This might be reduced because of the inadequacy of the accruals to the depreciation reserve and annual maintenance requirements. Neither the value of the properties nor likely earnings justified the participation of the old shareholders in the plan. It would aid materially in perpetuating the control of the management. The sacrifice of the creditors of their prior rights was unaccompanied by any consideration by way of assessment of the old stock or otherwise.

The Commission in this case went so far as to suggest a plan that in its opinion would meet the standard of fairness under the statute. It commented on the total absence of any provision for eliminating the intricate holding company system. It said: "Admittedly, the effort toward simplification of Applicant's capital structure is a step in the right direction. Nevertheless, the crucial factors underlying the system (and which have made necessary the present reorganization) urge something more than a mere palliative—removal of three uneconomic structures from the back of an income-producing unit might well be considered as the first requirement of any effective therapeutic." The Commission suggested a plan which would include the distribution to the company's first mortgage bondholders of the pledged collateral—the first mortgage bonds of Pavilion—constituting 65 per cent of the face value of the security; this, together with the allocation of par value common stock for the balance would place the bondholders in possession of an obligation reasonably adopted to the security structure and earning power of the Genesee Company. A sinking fund was also proposed so that eventually the bonds might be retired, in which event the capital structure would consist of only common stock.

This case illustrates the audacity of some corporate interests and the need of a police agency like the Commission. It also shows that the vices to be corrected are by no means confined to the large holding companies. Smallness and comparative obscurity in themselves are not virtues or a guaranty of soundness.

By a ruling made August 5, 1938, the Commission declared the Genesee Gas Company, Inc., exempt from the provisions of the Public Utility Holding Company Act, since the company was not a subsidiary of any holding company. The assets of Eastern Utilities Service Corporation had been distributed on its dissolution in April, 1938.

WORK OF THE SEC

One of the many ways in which the Commission exerts influence on the financial policies of corporations is illustrated by an early important opinion under Section 7 of the Public Utility Holding Company Act of 1935.

Northern States Power Company in February, 1937, conducted a refunding operation. It sold $75,000,000 principal amount of first and refunding mortgage bonds 3½ per cent series due 1967 and 275,000 shares of $5 series cumulative preferred stock. Northern States Power Company of Delaware owned all the common stock and in its turn is a subsidiary of Standard Gas & Electric Company. The preferred stock was sold to the underwriters at 100¼ and this issue was offered to the public at 103. On October 14, 1937, the underwriters still owned 69,500 shares although the public offering price had been reduced to 98½. The bonds had been successfully offered.

About the time the preferred stock was offered, public utility preferred stocks began to weaken. Northern States Power preferred sold as low as 94 in June. It gradually rose to 98 bid 99 asked during the early part of August. In the week ending September 20, when news of the proposed dissolution of the syndicate spread and the general market declined, the preferred stock lost ground and at the time of the oral argument before the Commission the quotation was around 81 bid 82 asked.

The company asked permission to amend the preferred stock contract to make it obligatory for it to reimburse the owner of stock for any taxes (other than estate, succession, income, and inheritance) that might be imposed under the laws of Pennsylvania or upon a resident of that state, not exceeding a tax of 5 mills upon each dollar of taxable value of the stock; it also proposed that the preferred stock be reclassified into a like number of shares of stock to be convertible on or before

September 2, 1947, at the option of the holder into four shares of common stock.

The alleged justification for obligating the company to reimburse the Pennsylvania taxes, which would cost it between $12,800 and $21,000 annually, was that the addition of the reimbursement feature would enable the underwriters to sell from 20,000 to 30,000 shares in Pennsylvania, and a stock that is well received in Pennsylvania achieves a certain standing with investors in other states.

The more important consideration was the proposed reclassification. The corporation claimed that the conversion feature would raise the current market price of the preferred stock and tend to mitigate any dissatisfaction that might exist among investors who had purchased it at higher prices. It was also claimed that any increase in the market price of the preferred would have a similar beneficial effect on the preferred stocks of the parent company. Thirdly, it was maintained that the addition of the conversion privilege would facilitate future financing through the issuance of common stock.

The Commission found none of these arguments persuasive and held that the issuance of the security in question was "not necessary or appropriate to the economical and efficient operation" of the business of the corporation within the meaning of the statute.

The corporation had already received the proceeds from the sale of the securities. The benefit from the proposed conversion feature was conjectural and remote and the financial structure would not be substantially improved. The Commission perceived that the real party in interest was the underwriters, who had a large loss and had not been able to sell stock since the end of July. They had unfortunately misjudged the market or paid too high a price in the beginning and were seeking a method of ridding themselves of a bad bargain. This phase was touched upon by the Commission: "These conclusions are reached without deciding whether it would be proper to give any consideration to the benefits which the underwriters might derive from the proposed addition of the conversion privilege and to the close relationship which exists between certain of the principal underwriters and the issuer. The latter circumstance has caused us to be especially careful to determine whether the proposed changes meet the statutory standards."[8]

In the abovementioned case the principle to be maintained was probably more important than possible injury to the interests of the corporation. The Commission might have commented on the novelty of a public utility operating company preferred which is convertible into common stock. A straight 5 per cent preferred stock is not looked upon as burdensome. That the underwriters had sustained a substantial loss was unfortunate. The annals of corporations show many instances when events proved that the company offering its securities might have obtained better terms. Underwriters have not been called upon to modify the terms of a contract that turned out to be unexpectedly profitable.

The Commission sometimes imposed conditions in approving applications for exemption from the provisions of Section 6 (a) of the Public Utility Holding Company Act. The exemption applies in a number of circumstances, one of which is the sale of a security by a subsidiary of a registered holding company if the security is issued and sold solely for the purpose of financing the business of the subsidiary, and it has been expressly authorized by the State Commission of the state in which the subsidiary is organized and doing business.

Virginia Public Service Corporation is a direct subsidiary of Eastern Power Company, a registered holding company, and an indirect subsidiary of Southeastern Electric and Gas Company, General Gas and Electric Corporation, Associated Gas and Electric Corporation, and Associated Gas & Electric Company, all registered holding companies. It proposed to issue and sell $677,000 principal amount of bonds of Newport News and Hampton Railway Gas and Electric Corporation (a constituent company). The proceeds were to be used to retire an equal amount of bonds assumed by it in a merger effected in 1926; the bonds were to be sold privately. The Commission made a study of the financial structure of Virginia Public Service, as a result of which it concluded that the provisions

[8] Securities and Exchange Commission, Holding Company Release No. 874.

for retirement reserve had been inadequate. The exemption was conditioned on an increase of the annual charges to operating expenses from 12 to 16 per cent of the gross gas and electric revenues. This would result in an annual increase in the credit to the reserve of approximately $240,000.

It also found that the net property account was $45,249,443 and the ratio of long-term debt thereto was 80.8 per cent. Eliminating the estimated remaining write-up of $3,141,560 in the property account, the ratio would be 86.8 per cent. In addition, the Commission found that the company had an urgent need for betterments and additions to its property account. The extremely unfavorable ratio of debt to property indicated the need for increasing the common equity. Consequently, the order granting the exemption was conditioned also by the requirement that no dividend be declared or paid on the common stock except with the Commission's approval.[9] These conditions buttressed the position of the senior security holders whose investment represented over four times the investment of the holders of the equity. Ultimately all the security holders including those of the holding company, will benefit. This is a commentary on the charges that the Holding Company Act was inspired by the desire to ruin the holders of public utility securities.

A case that attracted some attention was that involving the Kansas Electric Power Company. One of the questions concerned the conflicting interests of the trustee of a proposed bond issue of the company. The Commission's investigations led to the introduction of several bills concerning corporate trustees, one of which was called the "Trustee Indenture Act" by its sponsor, Senator Alvin W. Barkley. The underwriting arrangements for the proposed bond issue were handled by the Middle West Service Company, which is organized to furnish advice of this character. The Service Company is a wholly owned subsidiary of the Middle West Corporation. Its finance committee consisted of four directors, two of whom represented the trust company named as trustee. Indirectly, this trust company was the largest single stockholder of the

[9] Securities and Exchange Commission, Holding Company Act Release No. 1296, October 31, 1938.

Middle West Corporation. This stock had been received as a result of a reorganization and the trust company could hold its stock only until an acceptable purchaser was found. When it learned of the Commission's opinion that the dual relationship was improper, the trust company resigned from the trusteeship. The Commission emphasized its belief that there are dangers in such a situation. To be sure, the Commission held, it was possible that the trustee's officers in this instance possibly might "have enough character and pride in carrying out their fiduciary obligations so that they have sunk, and will continue to sink, all questions of the individual interest of their company in their desire to be of service to the prospective purchasers of this issue." The principle that the corporate trustee, on whom the bondholders must depend in great measure to protect them in the drawing of the trust indenture, and through later vigilance so that its terms are not violated actually or in effect, should have, in the words of the Commission's opinion, "a single and undivided interest in the welfare of the bondholders"[10] is a sound one. The reader who is interested in the importance of solving the problem will find a number of illuminating case studies assembled in the Commission's Report on "Trust Indentures." This study is Part VI of the "Report on the Study and Investigation of the Work, Activities, Personnel and Functions of Protective and Reorganization Committees."

Voluntary Reorganizations

The International Paper & Power Company[11] proceeding, in which the result was different from that in the case of the Northern States Power Company, has become something of a *cause célèbre*, and created sharply divergent opinions among the Commissioners. The question of jurisdiction does not concern us. The possible influence of the Commission on corporate practices and finance in more clearly defined cases under the Holding Company Act or the Chandler Bankruptcy Act is illustrated by this case.

[10] Securities and Exchange Commission, *Decisions*, Vol. 1, No. 3 (pamphlet), pp. 891 ff.

[11] Securities and Exchange Commission, Holding Company Releases Nos. 641, 642, 770.

International Paper & Power Company is one of the largest paper companies through ownership of 98 per cent of the stock entitled to vote of the International Paper Company. It also owned about 97 per cent of the voting stock of the International Hydro-Electric System. This company, in turn, owns about 88 per cent of the common stock of the New England Power Association, which through subsidiaries owns, controls, and operates important public utility properties in New England. The International Hydro-Electric Corporation, Ltd. is a holding company for public utility properties in Canada. The company had expanded rapidly in the years preceding 1929, when 62 per cent of the capital assets of over $650,000,000 was represented by properties and investments in the utility field. The policy of expansion under the management of A. B. Graustein, not without some criticism, had resulted in a complex capital structure through the formation of the top holding company and reclassification of the capital stock of the International Paper Company pursuant to a plan declared operative in November, 1928.

Owing to the poor condition of the newsprint business and the fact that the company had overextended itself in the public utility field, operations from 1931 to 1935 were unprofitable, its losses for this period aggregating $23,120,000. Stock capitalization was as follows as of December 31, 1936:

		Number Shares Outstanding
7% cumulative preferred ($100 par)		914,746[1]
6% cumulative preferred ($100 par)		3,708
Class "A" common	(no par)	832,596
Class "B" common	(no par)	821,805
Class "C" common	(no par)	2,122,839

[1] Including 4,891 shares held by International Paper Co.

STOCK PROVISIONS

Seven per cent cumulative preferred—has first preference as to assets and dividends: entitled to par and dividends in liquidation, whether voluntary or involuntary; callable as a whole or in part on any dividend date or at least thirty days' notice at 115 and dividends; has one vote per share.

Common Stock—the class "A," "B," and "C" common,

and after such classes shall disappear, the common stock shall be subject to the prior rights of the holders of the 7 per cent and 6 per cent preferred (because of the small amount outstanding provisions of this issue are omitted). After dividend requirements on the preferred stocks have been complied with, further dividends will be applied as follows: (1) dividends aggregating $12 a share shall from time to time be declared and paid or set apart for payment in respect of the class "A" common; (2) thereafter the class "A" and the class "B" common shall constitute one class (designated class "A" common) and further dividends aggregating $12 a share shall from time to time be declared and paid or set aside for payment in respect of such combined class "A" common; (3) thereafter the separate classes of common stock shall disappear and all shares originally constituting classes "A," "B," and "C" common shall be shares of one class (designated common stock) and shall have the same rights in respect to dividends. Each class has one vote per share.

Dividends unpaid and accumulated on the 7 per cent preferred on December 31, 1936, amounted to $40.25 a share. An initial dividend of $.60 was paid in February, 1929, on the class "A" stock; none was paid thereafter. No dividends were paid on the "B" and "C" common stocks.

During 1936 earnings improved; the company ended the year with a profit of slightly over $5,000,000, and the estimate for 1937 was over $9,000,000. Under the company's declaration of trust no distribution of profits was possible as a dividend so long as there was a deficit on the company's books. Since the heavy undistributed profits tax was in effect, it was feared that the estimated earnings would subject the company to a tax of over $5,000,000. Consequently, the management decided to submit a plan of recapitalization to the stockholders at the annual meeting.

The plan provided that one share of 7 per cent preferred would receive one new share of 5 per cent convertible preferred, and one share of new common stock. Each share of preferred stock would be convertible into 2½ shares of new common stock.

Exchange for each share of common stock was to be made on the following basis:

Class "A"—8/20ths of a share of common and a warrant for 12/20ths of a share

Class "B"—6/20ths of a share of common and a warrant for 9/20ths of a share

Class "C"—3/20ths of a share of common and a warrant for 9/40ths of a share

Assuming the exchange was made by all stockholders, the resulting stock capitalization would be as follows:

	Number of Shares
5% cum. conv. pfd. ($100 par)	918,454
Common stock ($ 15 par)	1,815,465
Common stock purchase warrants	1,346,907

The board of directors selected a committee of five members, with whom a sixth director collaborated, and entrusted this committee with the responsibility of preparing the plan. The committee, it appears, through the holdings of interests represented by its members owned 43 per cent of the total stock outstanding of all classes. This total was divided as follows:

	Per Cent
7% preferred	14.5
Common Stock	
Class "A"	43.1
Class "B"	61.6
Class "C"	48.1

The plan was submitted to the board of directors, who unanimously approved it. Holders of the preferred stock had less than 1,000,000 votes and holders of the common over 3,700,000 votes; accordingly, the common stockholders had the dominant voice in the selection of the board of directors.

The proponents of the plan urged that the common stockholders would refuse to consent to elimination of the deficit by reduction of the stated value of the common stock and that, in consequence, failure to adopt the plan would result in the payment of $5,000,000 by way of undistributed profits tax. Only by the concessions from the preferred stockholders involved in the plan would it then be possible to eliminate this heavy payment. The prompt resumption of dividends on the senior stock was contingent upon the elimination of the deficit. The Commission, however, pointed out the remoteness of the common stock as to dividends under the existing capital structure. If the elimination of the deficit were not effected, earnings of almost three years at a $10,000,000 annual rate would be necessary before dividends could be restored on the preferred stock. A 6 per cent return on the added working capital of $20,000,000 would earn $1,200,000 annually. Dividend payments on the preferred stock required about $6,-400,000 annually. Out of the total available earnings of $11,200,000 only $4,800,000 could be applied to the arrears in dividends on the preferred stock. At that rate it would require eleven years to pay off the existing arrears of $36,-708,000 plus the additional arrears which would accumulate! In other words, almost fourteen years would elapse before payments could be resumed on the class "A" common stock. It would then take another 1½ additional years before the class "B" stock could receive dividends, assuming the average annual earnings of $11,200,000. It would then require almost four more years, or almost twenty years, before the class "C" stock would be entitled to dividends. After this period, all classes of common would be merged into one class.

From the standpoint of book value the common stocks were also remotely situated. Net book value as of December 31, 1936, was $128,531,000. The preferred stock was entitled to receive before any distribution could be made on any other stock, its par value of $100 a share and all accrued and unpaid dividends; this preference on December 31, 1936, amounted to $128,026,000. Deducting this sum from the net book value would leave $505,000 applicable to the small 6 per cent preferred stock and the three classes of common stock. This would be equivalent to only 60 cents a share on the preferred and class "A" common, and no equity remained for the other two classes.

The preferred stockholder was asked to relinquish his prior claim to accumulated dividends of practically $40 a share, and to accept a reduction from 7 to 5 per cent in the dividend rate. In return, he was to receive one new share of common stock and the right to convert his share of new preferred into two and one-half shares of common stock. Several calculations of earnings were made to determine the position of the various stocks under the new plan, taking into consideration whether or not the preferred stock was converted, the exercise of the warrants, etc. These calculations at various levels of earnings were, of course, entirely theoretical. At $10,000,000 per year, and prior to the exercise of the warrants and the conversion of the preferred, there would be available on the preferred per share earnings of $7.98, or slightly less than $1 a share above the former dividend requirements. There would be applicable $1.19 in respect of the fractional share of new common issued in respect of a share of class "A," 89 cents in respect of the fractional share of class "B,'" and 45 cents in respect of the fractional share of class "C."

The balance sheet would show a book value for the new preferred stock of $120 against $140 per share for the old "preferred," the holder of class "A" with a book value of about 60 cents would receive a fractional share of new common with a book value of about $8, and the class "B" and "C'" stocks would obtain a fractional share of new common with a book value of about $6 and $3 respectively, whereas their present holdings had no equity. The new preferred stock, it is true, was made convertible without time limit into two and one-half shares of common, or at $40 a share. The warrants granted to the common stockholders would entitle them to buy stock at $25 or $15 per share lower than the conversion price of the preferred, for about four and one-half years. As to voting power, prior to the conversion or the exercise of the warrants, preferred stockholders would have 33.6 per cent of the total voting power.

The majority of the commission, while recognizing that the proposed plan represented a "bargain" between common and preferred stockholders, refused to describe the plan as unfair. The opinion rested on the advantage of the plan in simplifying the capital structure and the consequent possibilities of further financing by the company as a result of this simplification. Commissioners Healy and Douglas dissented; the opinion of the former was couched in scathing terms.

The Commission's own statement of the facts seemed to make inevitable the conclusion that the plan was unfair. Commissioner Healy doubted the advantages to the prior stockholders in receiving stock on which immediate dividends were possible and which had a book value. Payment of the excess profits tax would injure them as well as the preferred stockholders. The priorities of the preferred stockholders—contract rights—were to be modified or eliminated now that for the first time in many years the company was on a profitable basis and had a good prospect of increasing profits. He said: "Those buying common stock deliberately took an inferior position, well knowing the rights of the preferred and it seems wholly wrong that they should use obstructive and dog-in-the-manger tactics to force unfair concessions from the preferred stockholders. The latter went without returns for several years because of poor earnings, and now upon the first sign of returning profits they are asked to cancel their claims for arrearage of dividends for a consideration the value of which is so greatly uncertain, involving as it does future earnings, which may or may not be realized.

"It is difficult to observe without some concern the extent to which stockholders, in many companies, who in good faith believed they were paying their money for a genuinely preferred position, have, through reorganization of perfectly solvent companies, such as this, through the bargaining leverage of common stockholdings, been euchered, cajoled, coerced, elbowed, and traded out of their legal rights. Although we must recognize that often, especially in failing enterprises, various charges in stockholders' rights and various concessions become necessary, nevertheless, it seems to me, there should be an emphatic recognition that the terms of preference stated in preferred stock certificates mean what they say. If not, it should not be permitted that they be called 'preferred.' "

Commissioner Douglas later held that "It is my judgment that as a general rule cumulative preferred stock should not be countenanced, under conservative standards of finance, in situations such as these, unless it has at least the modicum of protection which flows from the right to elect a majority of the directors in case of dividend defaults. The absence of such protective clauses sets the stage for the common at a future time to serve their own personal ends at the expense of the preferred—a practice which, as shown by the annals of finance, has been duplicated many times. Even more important is the matter of the warrants—a hybrid form of securities which add only a speculative element."

It is interesting to note that later the plan was approved by the stockholders. Only 8.8 per cent of the preferred stockholders voted against the plan, a tribute to the persuasiveness of the sponsors. As a footnote, it may be observed that the preferred dividend was omitted in the first quarter of 1938. Net profit for 1937 was $9,134,701, but in the first three months of 1938 a deficit of $332,241 was reported, against a profit of $1,746,577 in the same period of 1937. This stock and its predecessors have had interesting careers. The preferred stock of International Paper Company exchanged share for share for International Paper & Power Company preferred received only part of the dividends called for from 1908 to 1916 and a controversy arose over the plan of liquidating the arrears which was not accepted by all the preferred stockholders. In 1925 an offer was made and accepted by the shareholders who had not consented to the plan of March, 1917.

Another case of significance in which the Commission's part arose out of a different statute was that concerning Consolidated Film Industries, Inc. This company is the leading developer and printer of film for the motion-picture industry. It also produces nontheatrical films through subsidiaries. Capital stock outstanding at the end of 1936 was as follows:

$2 cumulative preferred ($20 par)........... 400,000 shares
Common stock ($1 par).................... 524,973 shares

The preferred stock is entitled to receive cumulative dividends at the rate of $2 per share per annum, after which the common stock is entitled to receive dividends in excess of $2 per share per annum. When the common stock has received $2 dividends, all additional distributions in any year are payable to the holders of both classes, share for share. The preferred stock is redeemable at $35 per share per annum and accumulated dividends.

The preferred stock is entitled in liquidation or sale of the assets to $35 per share and dividends. It has no voting power except only after and during default in four consecutive quarterly installments of the fixed dividends, in which case it is entitled to one vote per share equally with the common stock. The original offer of preferred stock was at $26.50 per share, each ten shares carrying a bonus of two shares of common stock. In passing, it may be noted that the common stock could retain voting power as a class in any event and the preferred could be rendered voteless by the payment of one dividend out of four, since the senior stock obtained voting privilege only if four *consecutive* dividend payments were omitted.

The certificate of incorporation also contained a provision that no dividends shall be paid on the common stock so long as the preferred stock is outstanding if the net current assets of the company at book value are in amount, or by such dividend on the common stock would be reduced to, less than $2,400,000.

A brief summary of the company's financial record prior to the recapitalization plan follows:

	Net Income (in millions)	Earned per Share		Dividends Paid Per Share	
		pfd.	com.	pfd.	com.
1936	$ .9	$2.39	$ .23	$1.75	None
1935	1.0	2.69	.53	1.25	None
1934	.9	2.29	.22	2.00	None
1933	.9	2.27	.21	None	None
1932	.8	2.16	.12	1.	None

As of December 31, 1935, land, buildings, etc., were carried at $5,300,000, after reserve for accrued depreciation of $2,211,371. Accumulated dividends on the preferred stock when the plan was submitted were $5 per share.

The letter of the president outlined the reasons why the plan should be approved at a meeting to be held on October 9, 1936. As both classes of stock are listed on the New York Stock Exchange and registered pursuant to Section 14 of the Securities Exchange Act and the regulations promulgated by the Commission thereunder, the company must file at the time of soliciting proxies a copy of its soliciting material. The regulation requires that such material contain no statement which at the time and in the light of the circumstances under which it was made is false or misleading with respect to any material fact. Upon examination of the proposed plan the Commission suggested that the company recircularize the stockholders, which the company refused to do. In the meantime, the meeting of the stockholders had been deferred. Finally the Commission decided to make public its observations on the president's letter. This it did in a statement under date of October 22, 1936, which attracted considerable notice.[12]

The plan proposed by the management provided that the charter be amended so that the $2 cumulative participating preferred stock be reclassified as 500,000 shares of $1 cumulative participating preferred stock and $100,000 shares of new common stock; and that the outstanding 524,973 shares of common be reclassified as 349,982 shares of new common stock. Upon adoption of the plan, a dividend payment of $1 a share would be paid on each share of preferred stock on account of accumulated dividends.

The letter of the president, it appeared to the Commission, might be misleading in the following particulars:

1. The letter did not point out that the redemption price and liquidating value of the preferred was $35 a share plus accrued dividends, so that at the corresponding figure of the new preferred, $28 a share, the 14 shares to be received would have only the same liquidating and redemption price, exclusive of the amount of accumulated dividends.

2. The letter stated that holders of the common stock gave up one-third of their present holdings. Although the common stockholders were to receive two shares for each three held, common stockholders would still hold practically seven-ninths of the new common stock.

3. The letter stated: "The corporation has not been able to pay the full quarterly dividend on the presently outstanding

[12] Section 21A provides that the commission may make such investigations as it deems necessary to determine whether any person has violated any provision or rule or regulation and may publish information concerning such violation.

Preferred stock since April 1, 1932, although payments on account have been made from time to time." As indicated above, the reported earnings were in excess of the annual dividend requirements in each year from January 1, 1932, to December 31, 1935. Working capital requirements were apparently responsible for the failure to pay the full dividend, but the company's statement was susceptible to an entirely different interpretation.

4. The letter emphasized the advantages under the new plan if earnings exceeded $800,000. The statement ignored the fact that under the existing capitalization the excess would be paid entirely to the preferred stock until the aggregate of accumulated dividends had been paid; omitting consideration of the accumulated dividends, the annual requirements on the old preferred stock were $800,000 against $683,300 under the plan.

5. Under the proposed plan the certificate of incorporation would be amended so as to reduce the minimum net current asset requirement set forth above to $1,500,000.

The plan of the company was approved by the stockholders. The president's best defense, it appears, was that the Commission's statement said that the letter of explanation "might be misleading" but did not say that it "was misleading." He also added that he did not intend to submit to the business judgment of any outside interest, including the Commission. The plan was opposed by a committee of preferred stockholders who successfully carried the case to the courts. In December, 1937, the Supreme Court of the State of Delaware decided that the proposed plan was invalid.

Ordinarily the details of a plan of recapitalization are complex. In the above example the preferred stockholders might have concluded that the management—ostensibly their management as well as that of the junior stockholders—would propose a fair plan and explain it fairly. The comment of the Commission, while guarded, leaves little doubt as to its conclusions. Its action probably fortified the opposing stockholders' committee which was ultimately successful. The court, too, another "outside" interest, had its misgivings about the plan from a purely legal standpoint.

While the voluntary plans of solvent corporations generally involve the rights of preferred stockholders, the interests of the Commission are by no means confined to the protection of any one group. The ease with which preferred stockholders' contract provisions have been devitalized has given the Commission a special interest in these cases. In the summary of its special report on recapitalization and other reorganization plans effected by managements without the aid of protective committees, the Commission stated:

"Serious conflicts of interests may also result from the management's usual identity with the common stock. The report finds that where the management owns any securities of the company, its holdings more often than not consist exclusively or predominantly of common stock. Moreover, in cases where the management does not itself hold common stock, its allegiance and loyalties, according to the report, often run to the common stockholders who, in the typical case, elect the management and are responsible for its continuation in office. Nevertheless, as the report points out, these voluntary plans often demand drastic sacrifices on the part of the senior security holders with correspondingly liberal treatment of the common stock. In this connection, the report states: 'The vice of the situation arises in part from the frequent failure of the management to make adequate disclosure of their dominant and substantial pecuniary interest in junior securities. But the difficulty does not end even though the management makes such disclosure. The fact remains that the management is purporting to act for the benefit of the whole group of security holders. It alone conceives and formulates the plan. In so doing it has to decide what the fate of its own investment will be. Self-interest will urge lenient treatment of that investment. Self-interest likewise will inspire an interpretation of the plan to the senior security holders in such a way as to allay their doubts or fears and to condone or conceal the liberality of the treatment of the junior interests.' "[13]

In 1935 a large public utilities system filed a registration statement containing a balance sheet which showed that the

[13] Securities and Exchange Commission, Securities Exchange Act of 1934 Release No. 1699, May 10, 1938.

company had a capital surplus of approximately $111,000,000 and an earned surplus of about $12,000,000. Appended to this balance sheet were a great many pages of footnotes relating to the balance sheet; these disclosed that many improper accounting and financial practices had been followed. The footnotes were long and complicated. The company was required to compute the effect in dollars and cents, as far as possible, of the improper accounting practices, and to set up a balance sheet in a form permitting comparison with the balance sheet as originally filed. The adjusted balance sheet indicated that if the proper accounting and financial practices had been followed the company's assets would have been $153,000,000 less than those shown on the original balance sheet, and that in place of the capital surplus of $111,000,000 and earned surplus of $12,000,000 the company would have a corporate deficit of $30,000,000.

THE CHANDLER ACT

Under the Chandler Act the duties of the Commission have been broadened in a manner that may eliminate many of the aspects of corporate reorganization condemned in its studies. After the filing of a petition in bankruptcy, the court must fix a time for a hearing to be held not more than sixty days after the approval of the petition. Notice of the hearing must be given to the Commission and the trustee must submit to it a brief statement of the financial condition of the debtor, the operation of its business and the desirability of the continuance thereof. A trustee is appointed in every case in which the indebtedness of the debtor is $250,000 or over.

Every plan concerning a debtor with indebtedness not exceeding $3,000,000 may be submitted to the Commission for examination and report, and must be submitted to it if the liabilities exceed $3,000,000. Such report shall be advisory only, but the opinion of the Commission is certain to have great weight with the courts. It is further provided that the judge shall not enter an order approving a plan submitted to the Commission until after it has filed a report thereon or has notified the judge that it will not file a report, or until the expiration of such reasonable time for the filing of the report as the judge has fixed.

After a plan has been accepted, a hearing is set following notice to the Commission for the consideration of the confirmation of the plan and of such objections as may be made to the confirmation.

Following the hearing and the filing of the Commission's report (unless it has notified the court that a report will not be filed) the judge shall enter an order approving the plan or plans which in his opinion are fair, equitable, and feasible. Upon the judge's approval, the trustee is to transmit the plan or plans and summaries thereof, together with the opinion of the judge and the report of the Commission or a summary thereof.

The very fact that an independent survey and analysis will be made should have a salutary effect. Minority security holders and creditors, reposing confidence in a plan approved by the Commission, may be expected to indicate their support more rapidly. It will not be easy for groups to consummate plans pursuant to which the interests of one class of security holders is unjustifiably sacrificed to those who have advantages not available to the dispersed mass of security holders, who are also the victims of their own inertia. That the Commission will scrutinize a plan should in itself induce greater care in the formulation.

As compromise of legal rights is often essential in corporate reorganizations if the business is to continue, it is hoped that the Commission will administer the law without aiming at an attainment of the ideal in every respect. Particularly when a plan calls for the investment of new capital the terms may appear onerous to an observer, but businessmen trying to obtain additional capital for an enterprise that is bankrupt know the difficulties involved. The services of the Commission will probably be welcomed by none more than by the judges, many of whom feel that the intricacies of finance are outside their field and belong properly to the financial experts and not to jurists. Often Adam Smith and Sir William Blackstone do not mix well. When the next depression takes its toll of industry, the process of reorganization should be smoother and be effected in a more satisfactory manner than in the past.

ADMINISTRATIVE PROBLEMS

Overshadowing any specific grant of power to the Commission under the Securities Act of 1933 or the Securities Exchange Act of 1934 is the administration of these acts. Hostility to commissions or boards with broad powers, a tradition in Anglo-American law, flares up from time to time. The multiplication of such agencies under the New Deal has renewed the struggle, with members of the bar prominent in their attacks on possible star-chamber proceedings, the alleged absence of due process of law, and the exercise of judicial functions by administrative experts who are political appointees. The loss of constitutional rights abroad and the spread of totalitarianism give added strength to the dissent, but the principal lines of thought were developed many years ago.

The dangers of administrative agencies were well described by Frederick J. Stimson in 1910 in a chapter discussing American legislation on "Property Rights," in his book entitled, *Popular Law Making*.[14] He wrote: "I believe this to be the most dangerous tendency that now confronts the American people—government by commission, tenfold more dangerous than 'government by injunction.' Not only is there no liberty, no right of appeal to common right and the courts, but all permanent 'boards' tend to become narrow and pedantic, or worse, to be controlled by the works they are created to control. The constitutionality of such boards is, of course, always questionable, but the tendency to create them is perhaps the most striking thing in modern American legislation. Not only do we find them in enormously increased numbers in all the states, but even a late President of the United States seriously recommended that the contracts and affairs of all corporations at least (and the bulk of modern business is done in corporate form) should be so submitted to the control or dictation, or even the nullification, of such an administrative

[14] Reprinted in *Readings on the Relation of Government to Property and Industry*, by Samuel P. Orth (1915), which contains a number of excellent papers on commissions and boards.

board or commission, and this again with no appeal to the courts." This proposal the author denounced as the most audacious ever "attempted in the history of the English people, not even by the Stuart kings, who were most of all disposed to interfere in such particulars." The impetus given to the establishment of commissions or boards during the war, and more recently by the depression, is known to every serious observer of public affairs. The Lord Chief Justice of England called it the "new despotism" and the phrase has been echoed in our legislative bodies, in the courts and at bar association conventions.

In a brief survey of a perplexing problem we must content ourselves with a few general remarks. The complexity of modern affairs definitely seems to call for administrative agencies. To exercise their powers without swamping the courts, these agencies must exercise quasi-judicial powers. They must not be looked upon as an excrescence on the body politic. They have developed as an attempt to meet the needs of the times both in countries whose legal systems are based on the common law and in countries where other legal systems prevail. Their form in this country has been molded by the Anglo-American conception that government and law stand opposed to each other, and the constitutional doctrine of the separation of powers. The zeal to protect the rights of the individual will probably protect us from the dangers of commissions. The right of judicial review may be broadened where Congress is convinced of administrative abuse.[15] In every agency, from the local zoning board and health department to the national government's Immigration Department, Federal Trade Commission, or Internal Revenue Department, and the Securities and Exchange Commission, a constantly higher standard of public service will help reconcile the public to the functioning of these agencies and promote their efficiency and ability to make a democracy work.

What about status of the Securities and Exchange Commission? Both acts provide for court review of the Commission's

[15] *Administrative Justice and the Supremacy of Law in the United States*, by John Dickinson (1927), pp. 32 ff. This is a learned treatise showing the pitfalls of dogmatic generalization.

orders.[16] The petition by anyone aggrieved by an order issued by the Commission is heard before the Circuit Court of Appeals of the United States within any circuit wherein the person resides or has his principal place of business or in the Court of Appeals of the District of Columbia. The judgment and decree of the court affirming, modifying, and enforcing or setting aside an order of the Commission is finally subject to review by the Supreme Court as provided in the Judicial Code. The court may stay an order of the Commission upon the commencement of proceedings for a review of the Commission's order. The findings of the Commission as to the facts in a proceeding, if supported by substantial evidence, are made final. As a rule, the courts have given similar administrative bodies wide latitude in the determination of facts concerning matters brought before them, but the right to review the facts and determine whether they are supported by "substantial evidence" is a safety valve.

In its daily work an agency like the Securities and Exchange Commission may be cooperative or obstructive. Judgment is not to be guided merely by the number of times that its rulings are reversed or nullified. Acts entirely within the provisions of the law may be made unnecessarily obnoxious, tardiness can be costly, and in the numberless contacts with business and finance the work may be conducted so as to annoy, exasperate, and wear out those affected. Fortunately even critics of the law are almost uniform in praising the spirit in which the Commission has performed its work. Consultation has been invited so as to iron out, as far as possible, questions that may arise concerning interpretation of the statute and the Commission's rules. Helpfulness, not antagonism, has been the main approach. Arthur H. Dean, a member of the law firm of Sullivan and Cromwell, has stated: "On the whole, I believe the merits of The Securities Act, especially as it has been administered by the Securities and Exchange Commission, definitely outweighs any possible demerits." The examiners who hear evidence in behalf of the Commission are not assigned to other duties. Otherwise, an official of the Commission en-

[16] Section 9(A) of the Securities Act of 1933, and Section 25(A) of the Securities Exchange Act of 1934.

gaged part of the time in the preparation of cases for violation of the manipulation sections of the act, or in administering the Holding Company Act, or other work involving qualities other than that of judicial balance and restraint, might sit as examiner exercising a judicial function.

Carefully guarding against the possible conflict of an individual acting as a judge at one time and at other times as an administrator, the Commission added to its staff of examiners to avoid injustice to parties whose rights and duties are in question. In only one notable instance has the Commission been overruled—the J. Edward Jones case.[17] Here the Commission refused to permit the withdrawal of a registration statement. The United States Supreme Court held that the commencement of a stop-order proceeding in respect of beneficial interests in an oil royalty trust to be created by Jones had prevented his registration statement from ever becoming effective. The Commission, therefore, had erred in denying an application to withdraw the statement. None of the securities sought to be registered had been offered or sold, hence there could be no public interest to be prejudiced by the withdrawal, which, under the circumstances, was an unqualified right. When the motion to withdraw was made, the stop-order proceeding had lapsed. A subpoena which had been issued later was held invalid, not having been issued in a properly pending proceeding under the act. Justices Cardozo, Brandeis, and Stone dissented. The Circuit Court of Appeals had rendered a decision favorable to the Commission. The scope of the Supreme Court's decision was limited.

In another case the finding of the Commission was delayed for an extremely long period. Uncertainty, where the finding may affect a large organization as well as the principals involved, creates worry and hardships. It is axiomatic that delayed justice is injustice. The Commission, it must be said in fairness, was confronted with an unusually difficult set of facts in the case referred to; on the whole it has acted as promptly as one could expect.

What is "substantial evidence" admits of no clear statement or fixed definition. The decisions as to what is a question

17 298 United States, p. 1.

of law and what a question of fact show that there will always be differences of opinion among the judges reviewing the determination of administrative departments. An able Commission and a competent staff, on the one hand, and a bar eager to challenge every encroachment of the Commission, on the other, may be relied on to avoid the extremes of inept administration and the sacrifice of personal and property rights.

The administrative official and the businessman, as a rule, are of different temperaments. The businessman is primarily a man of action, impatient, a stout protagonist, and by reason of his business experience inclined to brush aside anything that seems to stand in his way. The administrative official, especially the large number in jobs below the highest rank, usually is a critic and analyst in the first instance, a student who is accustomed to weigh the facts before him impersonally, and in the light of what he believes to be larger considerations. The clash is not softened by the differences in income that usually exist. The administrator, accustomed to review alleged violations of a statute, or acts of malfeasance or misfeasance, begins to lose sight of the small, often insignificant number of such cases, in contrast to the total number of acts or transactions. On the other hand, the executive smarts at the need of justifying his actions before an official or board. These attitudes apply to all administrative agencies. The value of the critic and analyst is not to be gainsaid. Criticism may reach the heights of creative effort. Except in a special sense, however, the critical faculty can operate only where the creative spirit has sown; that is, an able constitutional critic may not have the qualities that would enable him to be one of the chief spirits in forging a constitution. So, too, Thorstein Veblen could not be a Henry Ford. Both made a contribution to American life; our civilization needs both, and a mutual regard for and recognition of their respective places. If administrators were also executives and executives had previous experience in public service, the differences might be entirely resolved, but that is an expectation similar in its unlikely happening to kings being philosophers and philosophers kings.

Happily, the situation is not hopeless. Primarily, we need

a higher type of public servant and more enlightened business-men. Young men and women of education and good social back-ground can be taught not to disdain public service. Business-men in growing numbers are being recruited from the ranks of the universities and will look at business with cultivated minds through the eyes of Mr. Justice Brandeis: " 'Big busi-ness' will mean professionalized business, as distinguished from the occupation of petty trafficking or mere money-making. And as the profession of business develops, the great industrial and social problems expressed in the present social unrest will one by one find solution."[18] The opportunity is greater than it was in 1912 when these words were uttered.

Chief Justice Hughes, in warning of the consequences of even petty encroachments on the rights of individuals by administrative bodies and commissions, recognized that they are "necessarily called and being called into existence by the increasing complexities of our modern business and political affairs."[19] In so far as Wall Street is affected, the essential steps toward resolving the difficulties has been taken: the Commis-sion's willingness to move slowly and to listen to the case of those in the securities business and the acceptance by Wall Street of the objectives of the Commission spell cooperation.

The Interstate Commerce Commission repudiates the con-tention that it is an "irresponsible" body not definitely answer-able to any superior authority. That it combines legislative, executive, and judicial functions, and that at times the inde-pendent establishment may have the office in the same cause of both prosecutor and judge is of itself without meaning. "The independent establishment is a natural development in response to practical necessities of the legislative branch of the government. There was need for the legislative control of certain matters by the Congress, but the field was so exten-sive and complex that it was impossible for the Congress to undertake such control in detail. The Congress has solved this difficulty, where it has arisen, by enacting certain general principles or rules, and then creating an independent agency for the application of these rules to particular circumstances

[18] *Business—A Profession*, p. 12 (1933 edition).
[19] Jones Case, pp. 82, 265.

or situations."[20] The Interstate Commerce Commission "is in fact responsible to three authorities." Congress, to which it reports annually, may at any time change the general rules which the Commission applies. The Federal Courts can set aside action of the Commission, if they find that it has misconstrued its powers, or if it acts arbitrarily; finally, the President selects the membership of the Commission with the advice and consent of the Senate and has authority to remove members for inefficiency, neglect of duty, or malfeasance in office. These remarks apply equally to the Securities and Exchange Commission. Whatever defects there may be in its organization and whatever defects remain to be cured by legislation, the frequent use of the word "irresponsible" as a descriptive term is more proper in forensic argument by participants in litigation than in comments by fair observers.

The administrative process and its difficulties, problems, and opportunities are best described by an illustration of one of the numberless questions that may arise. Section 2, paragraph 10, of the Securities Act of 1933 defines the term "prospectus." It reads in part that "a notice, circular, advertisement, letter or communication in respect of a security shall not be deemed to be a prospectus if it states from whom a written prospectus meeting the requirements of Section 10 may be obtained, and, in addition, does no more than identify the security, state the price thereof, and state by whom orders will be executed." The purpose of this provision as it relates to advertising is to make it possible to advertise a security without giving the entire contents of the prospective or the summary called the "newspaper prospectus." At the same time, by limiting what may be stated in such an advertisement, the investor is protected against circumvention of the statute and thwarting of the intent that the investor be fully informed. In June, 1937, the common stock of Air Associates, Inc. was registered and duly offered by a prospectus.[21] In the prospectus, below the name of the issuer, appeared the following words:

[20] Fifty-second Annual Report of the Interstate Commerce Commission, November 1, 1938, pp. 25 ff.

[21] The facts recited are within the writer's own knowledge.

"Distributors and Manufacturers of Aeronautical Equipment."

Later, the underwriters wished to advertise the security and use the same phrase in the advertisement. The question arose: Did the phrase violate the provision above cited, by containing more than the subsection permitted? The reason for using the phrase was to avoid confusion with companies with somewhat similar names and to identify the company better than was done by the corporate name. In the opinion of an official of the regional office of the Commission the use of the words "distributors and manufacturers of aeronautical equipment" would constitute a violation of the act. The attorneys for the underwriters then took the matter up with the authorities in Washington. An official replied, permitting the advertisement. The letter carefully qualified the official's opinion by restricting it to the case in point and by observing that the views expressed were not an official ruling.

Now, the administrative process, if it is not to cripple action, must be flexible; for instance, authority for the letters of deficiency issued when an attempt in good faith has been made to meet the registration requirements, but the statement submitted is faulty in some respects, is nowhere to be found in the statute. It was exercised to prevent the statute from working an unintended and pointless hardship. The authorities must adopt reasonable rules of interpretation, rules that will facilitate underwriting and carry out the intent of Congress.

Reverting to the illustration, it is common knowledge that securities at present are not bought solely because an advertisement appears. From a business standpoint, the underwriters properly hoped to attract the attention of those interested in aviation securities. Air Associates, Inc., from its name, might be an investment trust, an air-conditioning company, a finance company, or a promotional enterprise formed to exploit patents applying to anything relating to the air. The words in question, it seemed, "identified" the security. They were used to attract those whom it was desired to reach and to avoid the possibility of misconception. I think that, if anything, the advertisement without the phrase was less in harmony with the spirit of the act than with it. One meaning of "identify," in the definition of the Century Dictionary and Cyclopedia is "to mark or characterize in such a way as to show what the thing marked is, serve as a means of identification for." To identify may mean more than to name. When a question is so close as to create divergent opinions among experts, the administrative authority might well give the benefit of the doubt to those seeking its favorable opinion, as it did in this instance. To adopt a new name more descriptive of a company's business is to give up the value of a name known and recognized within the industry. A legal contest over the use of the identification may have an adverse effect on investors, who are likely to remember that there was some difficulty with the Commission without recalling the exact nature of the controversy. It is true that the ruling can be contested and taken to the courts, but this takes time, involves the expenditure of money, and if the result is a victory over the Commission, it leaves the government agency open to criticism for its officiousness and obstructive tactics. Mayor La Guardia may have intended his epithet on "semicolon boys" to refer to lawyers both in private practice and in government agencies.

The same underwriters later offered the common stock of Kirkham Engineering and Manufacturing Corporation. The prospectus, under the name, carried the phrase "Manufacturers of Aircraft Parts." They wished to use the phrase in the advertisement announcing the offering. The consent of the Commission was denied in an unofficial opinion, although the phrase did no more than identify the security. The corporate title might have referred to a company building railroads in Abyssinia, a hydroelectric power plant in Saskatchewan, or a new type of prefabricated house. The securities of General Plastics were offered by an advertisement in which the word "Durez," trade name for its products, was prominently displayed. How the advertisement in the form for which permission was requested could be of disservice to the investor it is hard to determine. This, of course, is not the test; proposed action must come within the terms of the statute. But surely what may "identify the security" issued by Standard Oil Company of New Jersey or by Consolidated Edison Company of New York does not necessarily identify the security of a small enterprise. Technically the words "new issue," often used by underwriters, have no warrant if the language of the act receives a literal interpretation. At a time when all the agencies of government are straining to foster the investment of private capital, every step within reason should be taken to help underwriters. There is more to administration than contentment with saying, "No, you can read the statutes." Many provisions are susceptible of different interpretations, any one of which may be rationalized if the will be present. An authority on the modern state has called the power to make exceptions "nine-tenths of administration."

CHAPTER V

Stock Exchange Reforms

Organization

VARIOUS groups in New York Stock Exchange circles were friendly to the idea of internal reorganization, but the weight of precedent and unwillingness on the part of members to lead in a movement for change which would necessarily embrace a redistribution of power retarded progress. The report of the Securities and Exchange Commission on "The Government of Securities Exchanges" gave the movement an impetus and encouraged the dissenters within the Exchange, since they now had a powerful ally.

The report of the Commission was made pursuant to Section 19 (c) of the Securities Exchange Act of 1934, which directs the Commission to "make a study and investigation of the rules of national securities exchanges with respect to the classification of members, the method of election of officers and committees to insure a fair representation of the membership, and the suspension, expulsion and disciplining of the members of such exchanges." At the time the report was made to Congress, 34 stock exchanges were in operation in the United States. Because the New York Stock Exchange transcends all other exchanges in the volume of security trading, it was selected for specific treatment. The report dealt with three broad subjects: the classification of members; the method of election of officers and committees; the machinery of discipline.

Members were and still are classified as:

Commissioner brokers: a member who is engaged primarily in the business of effecting transactions in securities for the account of customers among the general public.

Floor brokers: a floor broker is a member engaged principally in the business of effecting transactions for the account of other brokers, usually for commission brokers. A floor broker is sometimes referred to as a "two dollar" broker, derived from the commission that was at one time paid him for the execution of a 100-share order. The floor broker receives a fixed percentage of the regular commission paid by the customer to the commission broker with whom the customer has an account.

Floor traders: a member who effects transactions in securities on the floor of the Exchange primarily for his own account.

Specialists: a member whose activities are confined primarily to securities in which he specializes. He accepts and executes orders from other members and also trades substantially for his own account in these securities. He is thus a broker as well as a dealer.

Odd-lot members: a member who specializes in effecting transactions in lots of less than 100 shares under an arrangement with the Exchange that he will buy and sell odd lots at any time within a fraction of a point (one-eighth to $100 a share) of the last transaction in that security. The odd-lot dealer's transactions are not directly with the public, but are limited, except in negligible instances, to transactions with other members, usually commission brokers.

Bond brokers and dealers: members who specialize in bond transactions, acting as brokers for the account of customers, or as dealers for their own account.

Inactive members: members who have retired from active business; who purchased their seats to receive the benefits of reduced commissions on their personal dealings or who are members of investment banking firms which employ the seats to execute security transactions on the Exchange as registered firms.

Members are not registered in any particular functional class or limited to act in any particular capacity. The floor privilege is personal to the owner of the "seat" and may not be delegated to a nominee.

DEFECTS OF ORGANIZATION

The Governing Committee of 50—40 governors, 8 governing members, the president, and the treasurer—was confined to members. It had the powers necessary for the government of the Exchange, the regulation of the business conduct of its members, and the promotion of the welfare, objects and purposes of the Exchange. Generally this committee had the authority to appoint and dissolve all standing committees, as well as other committees, except the nominating committee; to define, appoint, and regulate the jurisdiction of all committees; to exercise original and supervisory jurisdiction of all subjects referred to all committees; and to direct and control the actions or jurisdiction of such committees at any stage. To all intents and purposes the Governing Committee was the Exchange.

At the end of 1934 the Governing Committee of the New York Stock Exchange included 14 governors who represented commission houses, whereas 26 members consisted of specialists, floor traders, or odd-lot dealers. At that time 52 per cent of the total seats were owned by commission houses. The situation was an anomalous one, since the commission broker did not have representation that was equitable. Firms outside New York had little voice in determining the policies of the Exchange. The commission broker to a greater extent than the other classes represented the outside speculator and investor, who often felt that the rules and practices favored the floor trader and specialist. Furthermore, the "floor member" partner of a commission house, the only member of the firm eligible for participation in the government of the Exchange, was often of lesser importance than the "office" or executive partner, who was responsible for the conduct and management of the entire business.

The method of election of the Governing Committee also came in for criticism. The term of governor was four years; of the 40 governors 10 were elected annually. The nominations were made by a nominating committee of 5 members. According to the report of the Commission, which was concurred in by many members and confirmed by the recommendations of the committee for the study and organization of the New York Stock Exchange: "The method of election itself is, however, subject to just criticism. The results of its operation have been the perpetuation of the 'in' group. The power of the nominating committee to nominate its own successors tends to prevent open discussion of change.

"The remedy of an independent slate by petition is ineffective, because petition connotes open revolt, and subtle forms of pressure make its use in practice infrequent. Thus, 75 per cent of the governors of the New York Stock Exchange have been renominated at least once and 50 per cent at least twice." Through their hold on the governing committee, the "old guard" resisted any important change in the constitution of the Exchange. The method of election of the president was also criticized. The examination of the Arbitration Committee and the powerful Business Conduct Committee is devoted to matters of chief interest to members and the Commission's conclusions are indicated in its recommendations, all of which are briefly summarized below:

1. A better numerical representation of the commission broker who possesses direct contacts with the public should be had on the governing committee.
2. Office partners of registered firms should be eligible for membership on the governing committee.
3. Nomination to the governing committee should be by petition and not by the device of a nominating committee.
4. One-third of the membership of the governing committee should be elected annually.
5. Nomination of the president should be by petition and he should be elected by the full membership.
6. Nonmembers of the Exchange should be allowed to be candidates for the office of president and the other executive officers.
7. Membership on the standing committees should not be restricted to members of the governing committee.
8. The expenses of arbitration should be reduced.
9. The arbitration tribunal, in cases to which a nonmember is a party, should not be a mere committee of the Exchange, but should either be composed of nonmembers, or, if members serve upon it, representation between members and nonmembers should be equalized.
10. Adequate and effective appeals should lie from the business conduct committee to the governing committee.
11. Customers preferring complaints against members should be furnished with the answer made by the member to the cus-

tomer's complaint, and should be entitled to appear before the committee. Both parties in these cases should have the right of appeal to the governing committee.

Discussion created by the Commission's report bore fruit slowly. The statement of Commissioner Douglas on November 23, 1937, in which he referred to the organization of exchanges as "private clubs" and declared that such organizations had become "archaic," brought into the open differences between the Commission and the Exchange. He also stated that the public aspects of the exchanges, especially the New York Stock Exchange,* had come more and more into the ascendancy and that their organization must keep pace with the evolution from small groups of traders and brokers, to small membership associations, to great public market places. The report of the Commission was brought to the attention of the financial world. The Commission desired to avail itself of the already existing machinery and was ready to encourage the self-rule of the Exchange, but "operating as private membership associations, exchanges have always administered their affairs in much the same manner as private clubs. For a business so vested with the public interest this traditional method has become archaic. The task of conducting the affairs of large exchanges (especially the New York Stock Exchange) has become too engrossing for those who must also run their own businesses. And it may also be that there would be greater public confidence in exchanges (and the prices made thereon) which recognized that their management should not be in the hands of professional traders but in fact, as well as nominally, in charge of those who have a clearer public responsibility."

Shortly thereafter the president of the Exchange appointed a committee, of which Carle C. Conway was chairman, to study the organization and administration of the Exchange. The so-called Conway report, dated January 27, 1938, was of far-reaching importance. It recommended revolutionary changes which were almost entirely adopted through amendments of the constitution and revisions of the rules of the

* Note: "Exchange" refers to the New York Stock Exchange. The other important exchanges have followed the lead of the New York Stock Exchange.

Board of Governors, both of which became effective May 16, 1938, opening a new era in the history of the Exchange.

The most striking recommendation was that the president should be a fully paid executive devoting all his time to the task and that no restriction be placed upon the field from which a president could be chosen. The power of the president in the appointment of committees should be broadened. The Board of Governors should be reduced in numbers and should be selected with due regard to the various interests represented in the membership. The Advisory Committee, the inauguration of which had been a forward-looking innovation, should become full members of the Board with voting privileges to represent the public viewpoint more effectively. The need for an advisory committee as such would no longer exist. The report raised the question of a number of important problems in addition to advising how the organization of the Exchange should be revised in accord with changing times and conditions.

The influence of A. A. Berle, Jr., a member of the committee, may be traced in the pointed discussion of liquidity. Between 1900 and 1938 the increase in supposedly liquid assets rose from 18 to about 38 per cent of the national wealth. It has been stated that no large holders of securities had a right to expect that they could be marketed on a moment's notice. Others have taken the position that there should be at all times a speculative market sufficient to give liquidity to the $82,000,000,000 or more of assets represented by listed stocks and bonds. Small holders of securities are more likely to suffer from the absence of liquidity than large investors. Perhaps it has not been sufficient to restrict the speculative element.

The function of carrying securities from an investor who wishes to sell to an investor who wishes to buy has been performed by a great number of people. The report further states: "They include daylight traders, brokerage houses trading for their own account, specialists, large speculators, small speculators, operators on large and small margin accounts and the like." While the restrictions such as cutting out shoe-string margin trading have value, "there has been little thought devoted to who shall perform the function of those groups in case they or a substantial part of them are eliminated." It was found necessary to observe at some length that a large part of the public has little understanding of what the Exchange does. In some quarters the Exchange itself is held responsible for the movement of security prices. By broadening the scope of operations, either through associate memberships or the admission of additional securities, these misunderstandings could be minimized. The committee properly commented on the fact that there is little realization that the initial steps toward maintaining the quality of securities on the Stock Exchange came from the Exchange itself, which pioneered the whole problem of standards of accounting, of fair disclosure, and so forth. Parenthetically we may add that the position of the Exchange would have been immeasurably strengthened had its leading representatives at that time, emphasized this work and the intention of further efforts in this direction instead of showing constant opposition to proposed changes.

The New Constitution

The present organization of the Stock Exchange reflects the recommendations of the committee and the earlier report of the Commission.

The Board of Governors consists of 32 members, all of whom except the president and three public representatives are elected by the Exchange membership. It is comprised of the chairman and president; 15 members of the Exchange, 6 nonmember partners of New York member firms, 6 partners of out-of-town member firms; and 3 representatives of the public, who are appointed by the Board itself on nomination by the president. This arrangement adopts the suggestion of the committee, so that the Board is designed to effect adequate representation of members and partners who come into daily contact with the public, plus the addition of public representatives. On May 9, 1938, the first election of the new Board was held and the slate elected virtually constituted a new management as only 13 of the old governing committee have places on the new Board. The Board is vested with all powers necessary for government of the Exchange, the regulation of the business conduct of Exchange members, the promotion of the welfare objects and purposes of the Exchange. In the exercise of its powers it may adopt such rules, issue such orders and directions, and make such decisions as it may deem appropriate. Among its most important duties is the election of the president of the Exchange and the fixing of his compensation. The president serves at the pleasure of the Board. To secure proper rotation of members no governor except the chairman, who has served part or all of two consecutive terms, is eligible for re-election except after an interval of one year. The chairman, in addition to presiding at meetings of the Board of Governors and of the Executive Committee, is an ex officio member of all standing committees. The chairman appoints the members of three committees:

The Executive Committee consists of 7 members—chairman and president and 5 governors, at least one of whom is a nonmember partner. Its duties are the safeguarding of the interests of members and the property and assets of the Exchange; the examination of the accounts and vouchers of the Exchange; to advise the president and Board of Governors; to make recommendations and reports as to financial policy, and to examine the gratuity fund.

The Committee on Admissions consists of 9 members of the Board of Governors. Its duties are to pass on applications for membership and for reinstatement of suspended members and to pass on all partners of member firms.

The Arbitration Committee consists of 5 members, at least 3 of whom are governors, other members, or partners. Its duties are to hear cases between members or member firms and to select arbitrators for nonmember claims.

The number of standing committees authorized has been reduced from seventeen to seven, and the president will take over some of the functions hitherto handled by the various committees.

Despite the retention of the Board of Governors, the new organization has transferred from it to the president such broad powers as to raise the cry that a dictator has been created. This is not an accurate description of the office. The shift of authority, established after careful deliberation, is merely part of a plan to provide for more democratic representation and at the same time to make the executive head the chief official in fact as well as in name. Greater responsibility and full-time devotion to duty, as well as reasonable compensation, should enable the Exchange to select executives second to none in ability. Only a decade ago the choice of an official from the outside would have been regarded as unthinkable, but the wisdom of having the widest range of choice is obvious. It is not uncommon for the most important industrial organizations to pick a president from outside the enterprise and even the industry. Mr. William McC. Martin, the first president of the Exchange under the new constitution, was regarded as an excellent choice despite his youth, as he had been a leader in the reform movement. The selection of an outsider might have been construed as a reflection on the Exchange membership or as an admission that none had the necessary qualifications.

The president of the Exchange, as its chief officer and executive, represents the Exchange in all public matters. He appoints, subject to the Board of Governors, the general counsel and other officers such as the treasurer, secretary, etc., and has general jurisdiction over employees of the Exchange. He appoints all the committees aside from those discussed above, who are appointed by the Board of Governors. These committees are:

Floor Procedure, consisting of not less than 5 members, at least 3 of whom are governors; the others may be members or partners. This committee has general supervision of the dealings of members of the Exchange, supervises activities of specialists and odd-lot dealers; supervises elections, and has jurisdiction over deliveries on exchange contracts.

Member Firms is a committee of 5 members, at least 3 of whom are governors and the others members or partners. The duties include general supervision of registered exchange firms; examination of business conduct and financial condition of members; supervision of partnership arrangements, quotations, and wire services between members and nonmembers. The committee requires observance of the provisions of the constitution relating to commissions.

Public Relations consists of 5 members, at least 3 of whom are governors. The duties are to advise the president with regard to relations between the Exchange and the public. It also supervises the advertising of members and registered Exchange firms.

Stock List also consists of 5 members, at least 3 of whom are governors. Its duties include supervision over questions pertaining to listed securities affecting issuers and the listing or removal of securities.

It will be noted that the Board of Governors constitutes the majority of each committee appointed by the president, making for a sound balance between the president and the Board.

No description of an organization limiting itself to the bare statement of the charter provisions gives a lifelike picture of its functioning. A description of the national government derived from the Constitution alone would give inadequate attention to the vast part of the Supreme Court or of the importance of the President's Cabinet; the great powers at one time in the hands of the speaker of the House of Representatives would be entirely lost. The new organization of the Exchange, more than any study of its make-up can portray, probably marks the passing of the "private club" theory. The Exchange has made the all-important concession, to use the words of a report of its own committee, "that the public interest is the paramount consideration." And in determining what is in the public interest the nation is to have a voice through representation in the Board of Governors. The three public representatives chosen under the new constitution were Carle C. Conway, chairman of the board of Continental Can Company; Dr. Robert M. Hutchins, president of the University of Chicago; General Robert E. Wood, president of Sears, Roebuck & Co. The choice, announced in October, 1938 was applauded by the Commission and the entire financial world. Later Dr. Hutchins resigned in a controversy arising out of the Whitney case.

On pages 100-102 will be found a list of some eighteen reports required to be filed by members and member firms. These range from the report on the safekeeping of securities, by firms not carrying margin accounts, to the report on short positions of each customer and that relating to transactions for foreigners. Member firms, considering the clerical work involved in these reports, in addition to the ordinary tax reports, monthly statements to customers, occasional questionnaires on other matters from the Exchange or the Commission, look back with understandable longing to the simpler ways of doing business twenty years ago, or even ten. Too great care cannot be exercised in assuring the absence of financial scandals. A more constructive attitude would be the attempt, through advertising copy, to acquaint the public with the measures taken for their protection and the work entailed after the seemingly simple execution of an order.

DELISTING STOCKS

The Exchange does not guarantee the value of the securities listed. Hence, the traditional viewpoint concerned itself little with the problem of securities which for one reason or another had become valueless, yet continued to be dealt in: *caveat emptor* still prevailed.

One of the earliest steps taken by the Exchange to delist a security was in the case of the stock of the Minneapolis & St. Louis Railway. This 1,600-mile railroad was capitalized as follows:

Funded debt. (app.)	$46,000,000
Capital stock (par $100)	25,792,600

A receiver was appointed in 1923. Less than 25 per cent of the interest charges was earned in the decade 1923-1932. Occasionally nothing was left for bond interest after operating expense, taxes, hire of equipment, and joint facility rents. No plan of reorganization was made effective and dismemberment of the road was proposed. Except for a small issue of bonds secured on the mileage with a fairly heavy traffic density and on terminal centers, the various bond issues sold at 10 or less. Obviously the stock's position was hopeless. From time to time it had flurries either because of general discussion of railroad consolidation, of speculative activity, or a few months of increased earnings from a wretchedly low point. The delisting of the stock in October, 1936, created widespread comment.

REPORTS TO THE NEW YORK STOCK EXCHANGE

Members and member firms, unless specifically exempted, are required to file with the Exchange periodical reports as follows:

WHEN REQUIRED PERIODS COVERED	NATURE OF REPORT	TO BE SENT TO
1. Initially before completion of transaction.	*Initial* report on every joint account for dealing on the Exchange in which a member, firm or partner is a participant before any transaction for such account is completed. (Rule 535 and C-5575.)	Committee on Member Firms
2. Weekly, covering previous Monday to Saturday, inclusive, to be filed as soon as all entries are completed.	Report by each member of firm carrying margin accounts of daily record of every case in which initial or additional margin must be obtained in customers' accounts. (Rule 552 and circular letters of 2/17/37 and 2/26/37.)	Stock Clearing Corporation (Night Branch) 52 Broadway Room 112 on court
3. *Weekly, before noon each Monday, covering transactions made during week ending preceding Wednesday night.	Report covering security transactions executed in the United States for account of "foreigners," security transactions abroad for domestic accounts, transactions in joint foreign arbitrage accounts in securities and foreign debit and credit balances. (C-5491 and letter of 5/5/36.)	Stock Clearing Corporation (Night Branch) 52 Broadway Room 112 on court
4. *Weekly, each Monday for the activities of preceding week.	Report of Temporary Relief Specialist, indicating: dates and hours during which he was Temporary Relief Specialist, name of stocks, and name of Registered Specialist whom he relieved.	Committee on Floor Procedure
5. **Weekly, at or before 12 noon, on fourth business day following close of reporting period specified on ticket or Form.	Reports by Clearing Members and Clearing Firms of daily aggregate of all full lots and odd lots of stocks sold on Exchange cleared or settled by them. Rights and Warrants are not to be reported. (Circular letters of 9/25/36 and 12/22/36.)	Stock Clearing Corporation (Night Branch) 52 Broadway Room 112 on court
6. *Weekly, each Friday, by 12 Noon, covering previous week.	Reports of aggregate daily share total of purchases and sales of stocks, upon Exchange, for account of members, firms, and all partners, including special, as principals, omitting transactions effected as brokers. Reports to be made each week even though no reportable transactions took place. (Circular letters of 2/25/36, 5/5/36 and 12/22/36.)	Stock Clearing Corporation (Night Branch) 52 Broadway Room 112 on court

No.	Report	Frequency	Reported to
‡7.	Report on every joint account which has substantial commitments in listed securities or which trades actively upon the Exchange in which a member, firm or partner is interested or has knowledge by reason of transactions executed by or through them. (Rule 536 and C-5575 and C-5769.)	*Weekly, on reportable information, by 12 o'clock noon each Friday, as of the close of business the preceding Wednesday.	Committee on Member Firms
‡8.	Report on all options relating to listed securities (including purchase warrants and puts and calls) in which a member or his firm is directly or indirectly interested or has knowledge by reason of transactions executed by or through them. (Rule 537 and C-5222, C-5575 and C-5769.)	*Monthly, on no reportable information, by 12 o'clock noon, the 5th day of the month following.	Committee on Member Firms
9.	Report on customers' debit and credit balances and short positions and on money loaned and borrowed. ("Seven-Question Questionnaire.")	Monthly, at the call of the Committee, as of close of business last day of preceding month.	Stock Clearing Corporation (Night Branch) 52 Broadway Room 112 on court
10.	Report of money borrowed in New York on collateral, including statements of the amounts of United States Government securities pledged against such borrowings. These figures relate only to loans involved in the security business. (Rule 534.)	*Monthly, on the 1st day of each month (2nd for out-of-town firms) as of the close of business the last day of the preceding month.	Stock Clearing Corporation (Night Branch) 52 Broadway Room 112 on court
11.	Report on short positions in each listed stock for each account or customer.	Monthly, as of close of business of last settlement day of each month, due not later than noon on second full business day thereafter.	Stock Clearing Corporation (Night Branch) 52 Broadway Room 112 on court
12.	Report on aggregate dollar amount of sales of securities made on Exchange and settled by member or firm, together with total number of shares of stock and total principal amount of bonds. This report must be accompanied by a check for the Securities and Exchange Commission Registration Fee. (C-5427, C-5435, letter of 3/28/35, C-5455, C-5467, and letter of 12/22/36.)	*Monthly, before 10:30 A.M. on the 10th of each month, covering all sales cleared or settled in preceding calendar month.	Committee on Floor Procedure
13.	Report on discretionary transactions in listed stocks executed or caused to be executed by a member while on Floor, under the provisions of Rule 252. (C-5615.)	*Quarterly, covering three-month periods ending January 31, April 30, July 31, and October 31 of each year, due not later than 10th day following end of period covered by report.	Committee on Floor Procedure

REPORTS TO THE NEW YORK STOCK EXCHANGE (*Continued*)

WHEN REQUIRED: PERIODS COVERED	NATURE OF REPORT	TO BE SENT TO
14. *Quarterly on January 1, April 1, July 1 and October 1 of each year, beginning April 1, 1938, covering previous three months.	Report by members carrying international arbitrage non-member correspondent (vostro) accounts, as to whether or not they have received monthly statements from each non-member vostro arbitrage correspondent and whether or not they have found that all transactions effected through them in such accounts have been countered or offset within five full business days, as specified in Circular C-5706. (C-6393, 12/7/37.)	Committee on Member Firms
15. Semi-annually at call of the Committee.	Report of employment after hours by members or firms of employees of Exchange or affiliated companies, indicating salary paid and nature of services rendered. (Rule 605.)	Committee on Member Firms
16. Not less than twice in each year at the call of the Committee.	Report on the financial condition of each member firm in the form of an answer to a financial questionnaire. (Rule 530.)	Committee on Member Firms
17. Not less than once in each year at the call of the Committee.	Report by each member or firm not carrying margin accounts as to whether such member or firm holds securities for safekeeping. When such securities are held, a statement must be filed that they have been checked and found intact. (Rule 533.)	Committee on Member Firms
18. At call of Committee.	Reports covering expense incurred by employees in entertainment of persons not employed by reporting member or firm. Reports to show date, amount, name of employee, name of person entertained, nature of entertainment and name of member or partner authorizing expenditure. (Rule 445 and C-5794, 3/12/36.)	Committee on Member Firms

* If the date indicated falls on a Sunday or holiday, reports will be due the following business day.

† Until further notice no weekly reports need be filed when participants [in joint accounts] are neither members nor registered firms nor partners thereof, and in which total transactions for week are less than 1,000 shares of stock or $10,000 principal amount of bonds. (C-5769, 2/7/36.)

‡ No options need be reported for less than 1,000 shares of stock or $10,000 principal amount of bonds. (C-5769, 2/7/36.)

** Odd-lot dealers and specialist odd-lot dealers will also report upon special form 121-A.

More recently a number of applications were made by the New York Stock Exchange for the delisting of securities. The reasons varied and are of general interest.

In the case of the Mother Lode Coalition Mines Company, an Alaskan mine in which the Kennecott Copper Corporation had an interest, the basis of the application was advice from the company to the effect that no new copper deposits had been uncovered. Some stockholders opposed the proposal. They contended that the stock should remain listed until the mines were actually abandoned, so that the shareholders would continue to have a market. Representatives would continue to have a market. Representatives of the Exchange asked for delisting to protect the interests of persons who otherwise might purchase the stock without full knowledge of the status of the mines and liquidating value. It was even intimated that the Kennecott Copper Corporation or other interests might have an improper motive in reporting to the committee on stock list that the mines had become depleted. No independent investigation was made by the Exchange but there was no reason to doubt the honesty of the management's representations. In granting the application to strike from listing and registration thereon of 2,500,000 shares of common stock, the Commission rejected the contention of twelve objecting stockholders who were suspicious of the company's motives. It was held that the indirect ownership by Kennecott of 25 per cent of the issuer's outstanding stock and the fact that certain officers and directors were common to both corporations did not in themselves justify the imposing of any terms or conditions as necessary for the protection of investors.

In February, 1938, the governing committee approved a recommendation of the committee on stock list that the Securities and Exchange Commission be asked for permission to strike from listing and registration the securities of three companies. These were:

Duluth, South Shore & Atlantic Railway common and preferred stocks

Fairbanks Company common stock

National Railways of Mexico 4 per cent noncumulative first preferred and 5 per cent noncumulative second preferred.

It was remarked that a new attitude was shown in the statement: "It is in the interest of the investment public to terminate listing." Supporting its claim with respect to the Duluth, South Shore & Atlantic securities, the committee pointed out that as of January 31, 1936, the company's accumulated deficit was $22,243,787 and that the market value of all its securities at the beginning of 1938 was only $95,000.

The report of the committee follows in part:

"The Duluth, South Shore & Atlantic Railway Company was organized in Michigan in 1887. It operates approximately 550 miles of railway, chiefly a through route from Sainte Marie, Michigan, to Superior, Wisconsin.

"The accrued deficits in the company's profit and loss account as of December 31, 1936, amount to $22,243,787. Total assets at the figures shown in the company's balance sheet as of December 31, 1936, amounted to approximately $48,000,000, against which there was outstanding $20,684,000 of funded debt (part of which has since matured) and $25,247,780 of current liabilities, including $24,693,135 of unpaid matured interest. The book deficit indicated for the 6 per cent noncumulative preferred stock was approximately $200,000 ($2 a share) and the book deficit indicated for the common stock was approximately $10,200,000 ($85 a share).

"The company's income accounts for the last ten years indicate that there have been substantial deficits each year, before provision for dividends on the preferred stock. Deficits a share on the common stock, after provision for current unpaid dividends on the preferred stock, were as follows:

1927	$ 7.25	1932	$17.45
1928	8.83	1933	13.26
1929	8.39	1934	11.89
1930	12.13	1935	9.68
1931	13.95	1936	7.47

"Market quotations for the preferred stock from 1927 to January 1, 1938, ranged from a high of 11¼ in 1927 to a low of ¼ in 1932. During the same period, market quotations for the common stock ranged from a high of 7⅞ in 1927 to a low of ⅛ in 1932. The last sale in January, 1938, for the preferred stock was at ⅝ and for the common stock was at ¼. The approximate total market value as of February 1, 1938, amounted to $65,000 for the preferred stock issue and $30,000 for the common stock issue."

More recently the Exchange, on its own initiative, took steps to delist the stock of an investment trust. For some years the stock had no net asset value, and there was no reason to believe that its portfolio would rise to a point giving the junior equity participation in the company's assets. The action of the Exchange is to be commended and the principle is sound. The volume of trading is reduced by delisting and possible commissions are likewise reduced. In the long run the confidence of the public will be gained by these sacrifices. The problem will not always be simple. Perhaps an industrial company whose stock has been removed will become the owner of a tremendously valuable patent, or unexpected ore bodies will be discovered in the properties of the mining company. The Exchange authorities can be governed only by the information available and must reach their decisions accordingly. Since they will be reluctant to take such drastic steps, the remote possibility of error is a chance that must be accepted. It is obviously to the interest of the Stock Exchange to have as many securities traded in as meet the requirements set up.

Occasionally corporations have delisted their securities and withdrawn them from registration, reversing the usual process of removal from the over-the-counter market to one of the stock exchanges. The reasons advanced are that registration compels the publication of information that the corporation wishes to keep confidential. Consent of the Commission to keep such information confidential, when refused, has been followed by request for permission to withdraw, which removes the requirement of registration.

The capital stock of Jonas & Naumburg Corporation was delisted from the New York Curb Exchange because of differences of opinion between the officials and the Commission. The company refused to publish certain information, contending that none of its competitors had registered and that it would not be to the company's interests to have the information made public. This information probably related to gross sales and operating expenses, from which could be obtained the corporation's profit margin and inventory turnover, if considered in conjunction with the balance sheet. In another instance, concerning a corporation whose stock was listed on the Cleveland Stock Exchange, it was contended that competitors furnished information to important customers derived from the Commission's files to show that the company had made large profits in one year. Customers cited the large profits and complained that the company was charging too much for its product. Later financial statements were shown to salesmen, with the inference that the company's position was not sound.

The Commission has no power to deny an application to delist, but has indicated that it could impose conditions, such as requiring the company to obtain consent from a majority of the stockholders to delist.

INFORMING THE STOCKHOLDERS

Two recent contributions of the Stock Exchange in its effort help the investor who is outside, looking in, furnish proof of its ability to raise the standards of the market place. The laissez-faire principle applies only when equals are concerned. The differences between unequal groups—such as minority stockholders, on the one hand, and officials, directors, and controlling interests, on the other—can be removed or at least modified only by positive action until the golden rule prevails.

The Stock Exchange, by circular letter addressed to corporations whose securities are listed, suggested that each corporation should advise its stockholders whether or not it was its practice to enter into commitments for the future purchase of raw materials. Corporations were also requested to disclose in their financial statements the approximate amount of any realized loss existing on the date of the report. The immediate occasion of the request was the rapid decline in commodity prices beginning in the fall of 1937, which was bound to have important effects on earnings, particularly of those enterprises with large commitments for raw materials. The investor may be aware that such contracts in important amounts are necessary in the operation of some businesses, but often, when the business world is influenced by fears of inflation or the repercussions of large-scale preparations for war, a general buying movement is generated in which some executives are swept from their ordinary course, with resulting large profits or losses, as the commodity market rises or falls. The Stock Exchange sought and obtained the advice of the committee in cooperation with stock exchanges of the American Institute of Accountants. A typical statement relative to inventories was made by the Ex-Cello Corporation: "Steel, castings, standard nuts, bolts, pipe fittings, etc., account for substantially all of the corporation's purchase of raw materials and a large part of the corporation's commitments for such raw materials, are based on customers' orders." As to its inventory of raw materials, "reference is made to this item in the balance sheet submitted in support of this application, indicating less than $100,000 of raw materials as at December 31, 1937, and less than $70,000 as at December 31, 1936, and December 31, 1935, respectively. The purchase of commodities, such as rubber, cotton, wool, sugar, wheat, etc., does not enter into the corporation's inventories."

The pamphlet annual report of the Continental Can Company for the year ended December 31, 1937, contained the following comment in regard to the company's inventory: "Certain commodities principally tin, required by the Company in its operations, must of necessity be imported. Our general practice is to have at least six months supply of such commodities on hand or on forward purchase commitments. With respect to the quantities of such commodities on hand at December 31st, inasmuch as the market price was over $400,000 less than the company's cost, the inventory has been written down to the market which is in accordance with the company's practice of valuing its inventories at the lower of cost or market."

In addition to the raw materials carried in the inventories, the company also had certain forward purchase commitments as above referred to, for future delivery. The drop in commodity prices in 1920, far more precipitate than that which impelled the recent action of the Stock Exchange, created heavier losses, since commodity speculation was far more prevalent in the postwar period. The spirit of reform, however, was not strong enough to bring about this helpful step.

Early in 1938 the Stock Exchange extended its requirements concerning the depreciation policies of corporations. For some years each listing application contained the following statement: "The corporation will not make any substantial change, nor will it permit any subsidiary, directly or indirectly controlled by it, to make any substantial change in accounting methods, or in policies as to depreciation and depletion, or in bases of valuation of inventories or other assets, without notifying the Exchange and disclosing the effect of any such change in its next succeeding interim and annual report to its stockholders." The Exchange has now gone further. Corporations are required to make a clear-cut statement of depreciation policy in all new listing applications for securities of industrial companies. Pressure has been brought to bear on the companies already listed to recognize the benefits of establishing such a policy. The Exchange makes no attempt to determine what amount should be charged against earnings, or which of the several methods or systems should be adopted. The executive secretary of the Committee on Stock List, John Haskell, in an address described the policy of the Exchange in the following words: "It *does* believe that a corporation eligible to have its securities on the New York Stock Exchange, with the implied invitation to the public to invest and trade in them, should have some depreciation policy which, in its essential particulars, follows one of the several policies which are commonly regarded as finding general acceptance among engineers and accountants, or which, if novel, is sound and logical."

That for more than a decade the investor has not been offered nonvoting common stocks is the measure of the effectiveness of the opposition to this form of security by the Stock Exchange. In 1926, when such valiant crusaders for a square deal in corporation finance as Dr. William Z. Ripley (see his *Main Street and Wall Street*) were describing the abuses inherent in the issuance of nonvoting common stocks, the Exchange went on record in opposition to the practice several years before the investment bankers virtually refused to underwrite these issues. In the same year, and since that time, the Exchange has urged its listed companies to publish quarterly earnings. This applies chiefly to industrial corporations, as the Interstate Commerce Commission requires that railroads issue monthly reports. With few exceptions, the larger public utility corporations issue reports quarterly, and in some instances monthly. In 1929 a special report of requirements and recommendations was issued with respect to stock dividends. During the twenties stock dividend payments were popular. To prevent deception on the part of the investor, the Exchange required applicants for listing to sign the following agreement: "not itself, and not to permit any subsidiary, directly or indirectly controlled, to take up as income, stock dividends received at an amount greater than that charged against earnings, earned surplus or both of them by the issuing company in relation thereto." Greater publicity for investment trusts was demanded in the special requirements adopted by the Exchange for the listing of investment trust securities. These called for the publication of the portfolio and a high degree of disclosure of other pertinent data. Since then much water has flowed over the dam. Investment trusts regularly publish such information, but when the Exchange took steps in this direction some trust managers felt that it had exceeded its rightful authority.

Early in 1932 the Exchange required that companies seeking to list their securities agree to have qualified independent accountants audit the financial statements contained in future annual reports to their stockholders, thus anticipating in a measure the requirements embodied in the Securities Act of 1933. Later the Exchange recommended to its listed companies a form of auditor's certificate which had been put forward by the American Institute of Accountants. All companies applying for listing must execute an agreement not to make any change in depreciation policies or rates without notifying the Exchange and calling attention to the change in the next published report, and this applies to any other substantial change in accounting methods.

Reforms

The Committee on Stock List applied these advanced principles in 1936. A number of oil companies were changing their methods of accounting for intangible drilling costs. Previously such costs had been treated as an expense and charged against current earnings, but a movement developed from this practice to that of capitalizing and thereafter amortizing such costs. One of the reasons for the change was that under the proration laws only a small part of the potential output of wells was produced. The effect of the change was in some instances substantial, increasing the indicated earnings. Comparison with previous years was distorted and comparison between the earnings for the same year of different companies following different methods became extremely complicated. In February, 1936, the committee addressed a letter to listed oil companies asking them to publish in their annual reports the following information: first, whether it was the company's practice to charge the intangible drilling costs to expense or to capital; second, in case the company's practice was to capitalize the costs, then the date when such practice began and the basis of the amortization employed; third, whether (in case a company had changed from the expense method to the capitalization method) it capitalized the intangible drilling costs pertaining to producing wells and costs incurred prior to the change.

Not so many years ago statisticians attempted to arrive at an estimate of the earnings of various Standard Oil companies that published only a brief balance sheet annually. Surely the progress in the recognition of the stockholders' right to information, for which the Exchange is partly responsible, has been great. As stated by J. M. B. Hoxsey, of the Committee on Stock List of the New York Stock Exchange, whose unremitting efforts in behalf of the public have been one of the brightest spots in the work of Wall Street: "The Exchange is interested in the accounts of companies as a source of reliable information for those who deal in stocks. It is not sufficient for the Stock Exchange that the accounts should be in conformity with the law or even that they should be conservative; the Stock Exchange desires that they should be fully and fairly informative." Mr. Hoxsey's address, "Accounting for Investors," delivered before the American Institute of Accountants in September, 1930, remains a brilliant and thought-provoking guide to accounting practice. He did not hesitate to disagree with the decision rendered by a majority of the Supreme Court in the case of *United Railways and Electric Company of Baltimore* v. *West et al.* In that case the court held that the proper basis of depreciation was the present value of property. Mr. Justice Brandeis, in an opinion concurred in by two other justices, opposed this view, and Mr. Hoxsey asked that accountants follow sound principles of economics and accounting where the law was apparently in conflict with these. The Exchange has supported the substitution of the natural business year for the calendar year, as, for instance, department years, many of which now close their books January 31, instead of December 31.

The foregoing summary of constructive measures adopted by the Stock Exchange is not complete, but serves to illustrate some of the valuable steps taken to safeguard the public. A. A. Berle, Jr., co-author of *The Modern Corporation and Private Property* and a severe critic of some aspects of finance capitalism, has had opportunity to study the legal aspects of finance and as a member of the Advisory Committee gained additional firsthand knowledge of Wall Street. From this source we should not expect more than a forthright appraisal of the Stock Exchange. Candor and an open mind prompted the following tribute: "The most forward looking steps in finance taken during the 1925-1929 boom were not taken by government, but by that most maligned institution, the New York Stock Exchange. I speak from experience. As a seeker after clean finance, the only friendly shoulder I found to weep on was that of the expert staff of the New York Stock Exchange and the listing committee of that Exchange made more forward steps during that period than any other body in the United States. They are continuing and accelerating that work now. I mention this as an illustration to show what can be done when business men themselves decide to protect their public. Other businesses can do likewise. This is a moral responsibility. Incidentally, safety lies that way."

COMMITTEE ON STOCK LIST

One of the clearest condemnations of holding company evils dates back to 1926 and was prepared in Wall Street. In fact, the memorandum was written by an official of the New York Stock Exchange for the Committee on Stock List. It was pigeonholed in the files of the Exchange until its contents were made public during the course of the investigation of railroads, holding companies, and affiliated companies by the United States Senate.[1] J. M. B. Hoxsey placed his finger on the dangers of holding company finance in this statement: "It lies in the attenuated degree of equity in the earnings of the constituent operating companies which may be represented by some or all of the securities of the holding company." In the campaign against the Public Utility Holding Company Act of 1935 irrelevant statements were made to show that the United States Steel Corporation, General Motors Corporation, and hundreds of other soundly operated and financed corporations were holding companies. These companies own directly and operate subsidiaries. They own all or practically all the securities of these subsidiaries. The other extreme is represented by the holding company "which acquires voting control through ownership of a greater or less majority of the voting stock of heterogeneous and unrelated companies, such subsidiary companies being overloaded with securities bearing fixed or preferential charges, in addition to which the holding company itself may issue a large proportion of securities bearing fixed or preferential charges." The attempt to confuse the issue by disregarding the differences among holding companies did not deceive students of the subject; the energy—and expense— might have been utilized in an effort to make constructive suggestions.

In another memorandum prepared in April, 1930, Mr. Hoxsey wrote prophetically of the public's reaction: "In regard to what I have termed the 'social danger,' if corporations of this type are multiplied, there is likely to be a strong public protest. This protest will, I think, occur if it should

[1] Hearings before a subcommittee of the Committee on Interstate Commerce, United States Senate, 74th Congress, Part 5, pp. 1801 ff., and pp. 1945 ff.

become apparent that any large part of the industry of the country is virtually controlled through minority holdings." Mr. Whitney, president of the Exchange during part of this period, did not recall these studies when questioned regarding them. We have as yet to consider the listing requirements of the Stock Exchange. John Haskell, secretary to the Committee on Stock List, has warned the public of the limitations on the protection that can be given the investor. He states: "The greatest disservice that can be done to the investing public is to soft pedal the old saying, 'Let the buyer beware.' Let us hope that in making the seller beware we will not lull the buyer into any sense of false security nor lead him to forget to use common sense and prudence in selecting his investments. More information is available with respect to listed securities today than ever before—let the prospective buyer take advantage of it before he buys." Having duly impressed the investor with the need of intelligence and rejected the notion that the Exchange can be charged with the duty to maintain prices at a given level or with guaranteeing purchasers against loss, the comprehensive requirements for listing may be examined as an indication that the Exchange does not rest on its lack of responsibility for losses.

The Exchange requires as conditions precedent for listing:

1. That the applicant be a substantial going concern;
2. That the management have a good reputation and agree to be bound by the standards of the Exchange with respect to the responsibility to security holders;
3. That the company be legally organized and the securities validly authorized and issued;
4. That there be sufficient volume and distribution of the securities to warrant a national market;
5. That the company comply with the Exchange's requirements as to accounting, periodic reports, and disclosure of corporate information.

J. M. B. Hoxsey, in a statement before the subcommittee of the Committee on Banking and Currency of the United States Senate, named ten recent examples of the constant stiffening of the requirements demanded by the Exchange:

1. The refusal of the Exchange to list nonvoting common stock.
2. The disclosure of ultimate corporate control of subsidiary companies.
3. The disclosure of options and the reacquisition of the corporation's own stock.
4. The disclosure of any change in the collateral securing listed bonds.
5. The refusal to list fixed investment trusts and the requirement of periodic disclosure by other investment trusts of securities held.
6. The requirement that corporate statements be audited by independent public accounts, with certain exceptions as to companies whose accounts are regulated by public authority, and the continued improvement of the methods of corporate accounting.
7. The disclosure of depreciation policy and the prohibition of any change without notice.
8. The adoption of a uniform form of auditor's report certifying that corporate accounts are kept in accordance with accepted accounting principles consistently maintained.
9. Prevention by the Exchange of the taking of stock dividends as income to the recipient corporation in an amount greater than that charged against the earned surplus of the issuing corporation.
10. Strengthening of the requirements regarding corporate trustees and the form of bond indentures.

The Exchange does not list purely promotional enterprises. Substantial assets or earnings, or both, are required. Earnings of at least $500,000 and assets of $5,000,000 are generally insisted upon, although substantially larger earnings might offset smaller assets. It may be that the Exchange should lift the barriers and permit the listing of smaller enterprise if all other requirements are met satisfactorily. There are many meritorious corporations with earnings and assets of perhaps half the present minimum. If the distribution of securities is broad enough and the corporation meets the other requirements, no good reason for exclusion seems to exist. If the Exchange considered such applications favorably, smaller corporations might be able to enter the capital markets more frequently. The listing of a security is of some advertising value, and makes it easier for security holders to borrow from the banks on their securities. The Exchange has necessarily been careful to avoid listing securities with so small a distribution as to facilitate the likelihood of a corner, or a disorderly market from an insufficient supply of securities. The Exchange has no hard and fast rule. Each case has to be examined with regard to the special facts disclosed.

Modifying its previous attitude, the Stock Exchange now emphasizes, in place of earnings and assets, such considerations as the standing of the company in its particular field, the character of the market for its products, its relative stability and position in its industry, and whether or not the industry is an expanding one with prospects of maintaining its position. The criterion, instead of any mathematical measure of earnings and assets, is whether or not a clearly developed national interest exists in a corporation and its securities. The distribution of holdings, nevertheless, must be such as to offer reasonable assurance that an adequate auction market will prevail so that listing will not represent merely a device for registering occasional quotations. The new policy also embodies a difference in the method of fixing the fees for listing privileges. The single fixed initial fee has been supplanted, as to stocks, by a substantially reduced initial fee coupled with a continual annual fee.

Information concerning reacquisition of any previously issued and listed stock or subsequent sale of previously acquired stock is published monthly by the Exchange. Until the Exchange instituted this requirement, few corporations advised security holders of these activities except in their annual reports. The business of a corporation is not trading in its securities. At times such trading may be extremely profitable—in 1937 the Lima Locomotive Works showed a larger profit from security transactions in its stock than in operations. Yet these are exceptional transactions open to many possible abuses, and the Exchange has shown good judgment in requiring that they be made public.

Many of the other requirements are now accepted without argument, but only a few years have elapsed since one of the most important industrial companies, which had large outside investments, stubbornly resisted the demands of the Exchange that the securities portfolio be made public. Nothing contributes more to needless doubt and false rumors than secrecy. Every step in the direction of fuller information promptly released should be supported by security holders. In addition to the other pledges that an applicant makes, the company must agree to furnish the Exchange on demand such information regarding the company as the Exchange may reasonably require. This comprehensive agreement enables the Committee on Stock List to revise its requirements whenever it is convinced that some benefit to investors will result.

THE EXCHANGE AND THE COMMISSION COOPERATE

The Richard Whitney case is closed. The disclosure fell on a discouraged, dazed Wall Street. To the rank and file the story was comparable only to the treason of Benedict Arnold in the dark days of the Continental Army of 1780. The tragic details need not be related here. But the episode prompts a number of observations, since it hastened the reform measures announced November 1, 1938.

The betrayal of confidence could be so shocking because it was exceptional. Men of rectitude, reviewing the facts, were bound to condemn the attitude of those close to Whitney, who had reason to suspect the truth or at least suspect irregularities but did not report the facts to the proper Stock Exchange authorities. Upon examination, they refused to admit that silence was an injustice to the public or that a duty to speak existed. The rebuke contained in the Commission's report is merited. Nevertheless, in their relations men are not governed by a simple formula. A great judge said that hard cases make bad law. Likewise a hard set of facts, in which family relations and close friendship conflict with larger responsibilities, makes for bad judgment. Those who have read or seen a performance of the late John Galsworthy's *Loyalties* will remember that the characters recoiled from the correct course of conduct, plain enough to the reader or observer, because of the grip of fixed notions of loyalty to their group or class. However strong the conviction that society was the loser and that a new code of morals must supplant the old, the playwright's understanding of human beings left one with sympathy for the weaknesses portrayed. Finally, the Commission did not use the incident as a weapon to bludgeon Wall

Street into submitting to a set of rules hurriedly adopted and presented to a dispirited community. Instead, the Commission cooperated with the new leadership in the Stock Exchange in working out a comprehensive program to provide additional protection to the public in dealing with member firms of the New York Stock Exchange. Many of the rules will be extended to other exchanges and to the over-the-counter market. Taken as a whole, the program is one of the most far-reaching developments in the history of Wall Street.

The program is outlined in Appendix III. It revolves around the disclosure to the authorities of every detail of the activities of members and member firms; the insistence on the eventual establishment of a trust institution to hold customers' credit balances and securities; and the beginnings of segregation of broker and dealer functions. Gradually the Commission is expected to retire to a "residuary role" in the regulation of the security markets, permitting the exchanges to police themselves.

CHAPTER VI

The Commission and Speculation

The Commission's Trading Rules

THE sixteen rules for the regulation of trading on exchanges recommended by the Commission on April 16, 1935, for adoption by national securities exchanges are intended to provide additional safeguards against certain activities which lend themselves to manipulative tendencies. A number of these rules are similar to existing practices or regulations of the New York Stock Exchange or represent codification of these rules. Bonds, arbitrage, and odd-lot transactions are exempted from the operation of some of the rules.

1. Members, their firms, and partners are prohibited from effecting transactions which are excessive in view of the market for such security or in view of the financial resources of the member, firm, or partner. What is "excessive" becomes a matter of fact dependent upon the circumstances in each case.

2. No member, while on the floor of the exchange, shall without prior notice to it, initiate the purchase or sale of any security classified for trading as a security by the exchange for any account in which he, or the firm of which he is a partner, or any partner of such firm, is directly interested with any person other than such firm or partner. This rule does not apply to joint accounts maintained solely for arbitrage transactions or to transactions by an odd-lot dealer or a specialist for any joint account in which he is expressly permitted to have an interest. The Senate investigation disclosed that members participated in joint accounts to a large extent, and that manipulation was based on a combination of a member's manipulative skill and trading ability with the financial backing of outsiders jointly interested in the account.

3. Joint accounts must be reported. This rule is supervisory in intent and approximates an exchange regulation in force before the issuance of these rules.

4. A member handling a discretionary account for a customer is forbidden, while on the floor, to execute orders for such accounts which are excessive in size or frequency in view of the financial resources of the account. The purpose is twofold. It is designed (1) to eliminate trading for discretionary accounts which is primarily motivated by the broker's desire to increase his commissions and (2) to eliminate any opportunity for a member to effect transactions by means of discretionary accounts for the purpose of stimulating activity or raising or depressing prices.

5. A broker, while holding a customer's unexecuted market or limited price order, is prohibited from competing with his customer by trading for his own account in the same security in the same side. This rule is declaratory of prior New York Stock Exchange practice.

6. Members, firms, and partners are prohibited from making purchases at successively higher prices or sales at successively lower prices for the purpose of creating a misleading appearance of activity, or making a price which does not reflect the true state of the market in any security. A favorite device of pool operators has been prohibited. Tape readers and board room habitués were prone to be attracted by such buying or selling. Immediately rumors sprang up and discussion became rife. This, of course, was exactly the intent of the pool operators. If they had knowledge of the specialist's book they could often calculate how much stock would have to be bought or offered within certain price limits.

7. A member, while on the floor of the exchange, may not initiate a transaction for his own account or for that of his firm or partner in which he or the firm or partner holds or has granted any put, call, straddle, or option. The Senate investigation disclosed that options were used frequently in connection with manipulative activities.

8. Records of orders must be kept. The New York Stock Exchange provides that such records be kept. This rule simply embodies accepted good practice.

9. Specialists are required to register. Although functional classification has long differentiated between commission bro-

kers, floor brokers, floor traders, bond brokers, etc., the specialist who combines the functions of dealer and broker occupies a unique position and registration was required as a supervisory measure.

10. Specialists are required to restrict their dealings for their own account in securities in which they specialize to those reasonably necessary to maintain a fair and orderly market. An interpretation of this rule is discussed below.

11. Specialists may carry a joint account in any security classified by the exchange as a stock only with a partner, a member of the exchange, or a firm of which a member is a partner. This rule was adopted for the same reasons as Rule 2.

12. This rule provides for the keeping of records by specialists and was always considered good practice by the exchanges.

13. Odd-lot dealers are required to register.

14. This rule covers the conditions under which odd-lot dealers may carry joint accounts in the same way as the eleventh rule does for specialists.

15. Odd-lot dealers or specialists, like other members, are prohibited from holding or granting options in any security classified for trading purposes as a stock.

16. This rule relates to short selling.

An interpretation of the tenth rule was issued by the director of the Commission's Trading and Exchange Division. The interpretation stated that the phrasing of the rule prohibits all transactions for the account of a specialist in the security in which he is registered, excepting only such transactions as are properly a part of a course of dealings reasonably necessary to permit the specialist to maintain a fair and orderly market, or to act as an odd-lot dealer. Therefore, each transaction by a specialist for his own account must meet the test of reasonable necessity. A comprehensive affirmative statement of the criteria of reasonable necessity was considered inadvisable, but certain negative tests were set forth.

Certain types of transactions were described as having a detrimental effect upon the market, and as being therefore commonly unjustifiable. The following were placed in this category:

1. A purchase above the last sale price.
2. The purchase of all or substantially all the stock offered on the book at the last sale price.
3. The supplying of all or substantially all the stock bid for on the book at the last sale price.

The rules regarding specialists have been severely criticized. They are said to place an unreasonable burden on the specialist. If the specialist system has a valid place in the mechanism of the market, the specialist must not be so restricted as to eliminate any chance of profiting by his being a specialist. The New York Stock Exchange has extended the Commission's rulings and has issued a number of instructions to specialists with reference to dealings on the floor of the Exchange in stocks in which they are acting as specialists. These instructions impose positive duties on the specialist:

1. The function of a member acting as specialist on the floor of the Exchange includes, in addition to the effective execution of commission orders entrusted to him, the maintenance, in so far as reasonably practical, of a fair and orderly market on the Exchange in the stocks in which he is so acting.

2. The maintenance of a fair and orderly market implies the maintenance of price continuity and the minimizing of the effects of temporary disparity between supply and demand.

3. In connection with the maintenance of a fair and orderly market, it is commonly desirable that a member acting as a specialist engage to a reasonable degree under existing circumstances in dealings for his own account when lack of price continuity or disparity between supply and demand exists or is reasonably to be anticipated.

4. Transactions on the Exchange for his account effected by a member acting as specialist must constitute a course of dealings reasonably calculated to contribute to the maintenance of price continuity and to the minimizing of the effects of temporary disparity between supply and demand, immediate or reasonably to be anticipated. Transactions not part of such a course of dealings are not to be effected.

5. A specialist's quotation, made for his own account, should be such that a transaction effected thereon, whether having the effect of reducing or increasing the specialist's position, will bear a proper

relation to preceding transactions and anticipated succeeding transactions.

6. Transactions on the Exchange for his own account of a member acting as specialist are to be effected in a reasonable and orderly manner in relation to the condition of the general market, the market in the particular stock and the adequacy of the specialist's position to the immediate and reasonably anticipated needs of the market.

In the course of the violent decline of October, 1937, the specialist in the capital stock of Nash-Kelvinator violated these instructions, especially the first two. On October 19 the specialist bought for his own account 8,300 shares of stock at $5 a share. On the previous day transactions took place between $10 and $12½ a share. It was charged that for approximately twenty-three minutes after the purchase he failed to make stock available in the market, although during the period the stock market advanced rapidly. The next day the price range was $10⅛-12⅞. The Board of Governors held that the specialist had failed to fulfill his duty. They did not believe the failure willful but the specialist was suspended for a three-month period from acting in that capacity.

The specialist's activities, besides being restricted to safeguard the public, are now supervised closely by the Committee on Floor Procedure. In the event that the committee is dissatisfied with the way a specialist's book is handled it may cancel his registration as a specialist or relegate some of his stocks to another post. The committee has also formulated minimum capital requirements to ensure that capital will be available at all times to enable the specialist to maintain a fair and orderly market in his stocks.

Occasionally the general trading rules and regulations concerning specialists may work a hardship. Yet, members have told the writer that many of the rules, some of which were instituted by the Exchange, have been accepted after the original outcry that they would stifle the market and that the earlier practices have been almost forgotten as floor traders and members have adjusted themselves to the new order. Confidence in the Exchange and in brokers by the general public should be promoted by widespread publicity given the new rules. This should be the Street's policy instead of grudging obedience on the assumption that perhaps the changes are merely temporary.

CONCERNING INSIDERS

The shocking disclosures of the activities of "insiders" crystallized in a demand that Congress take affirmative steps to prevent, so far as possible, the acts described in the Securities Exchange Act as the "unfair use of information which may have been obtained by such beneficial owner, director or officer by reason of his relationship to the issuer." All directors, officers, and owners of 10 per cent or more of any registered "equity security" are required to file with the Commission a monthly statement of their purchases or sales of such security. Such persons are required to turn over to the corporation issuing the security all profits derived by them from the purchase and sale of such security within six months, if during that period they shall have been directors, officers, or owners of 10 per cent or more of the equity security in the corporation. "Equity securities," in addition to preferred and common stocks, include bonds convertible into stock and bonds carrying stock purchase warrants. The leading New York newspapers now publish excerpts from the reports of the Commission. Changes in ownership must be reported within ten days after the close of the month following the change. The holdings of large owners, directors, and officers are reported originally at the time of registration on a national securities exchange. Short sales are prohibited, as well as short sales "against the box." Profits arising from the transactions described inure to the corporation. Suit may be instituted within two years of the date such profit was realized either by the corporation or in its name by any owner of the security if the issuer has failed or refused to bring suit within sixty days after request or has failed diligently to prosecute the suit thereafter.

Part of a typical report appears on pages 124-125.

This provision, it is asserted, has actually worked to the disadvantage of the general stockholder by tending to eliminate informed buying in periods when the market is in a state of semipanic. "Protective buying by insiders," in the words of

DESCRIPTION ISSUER SECURITY REPORTING PERSON INDIRECT	RELATIONSHIP SEE PAGE 2	DATE OF TRANSACTION	OWNERSHIP AND TRANSACTION KEY	TRANSACTIONS DURING MONTH "NC" = NET CHANGE DURING MONTH	HOLDINGS REPORTED AS OF END OF MONTH
AUTOMOBILE FINANCE CO COMMON					
DECEMBER 1937 REPORT WM R BARRICK PITTSBURGH PA	0	23	C	100 100 NC	100
B					
BALDWIN RUBBER CO COMMON					
JUNE 1938 REPORT HARRY M PRYALE PONTIAC MICH	0 D	22 23 24		400 - 600 - 69 - 1069 - NC	2000
BALTIMORE TRANSIT CO COMMON VTC					
JUNE 1938 REPORT BANCROFT HILL BALTIMORE MD	0 D	3	E	60 60 NC	60
1ST 5PC PREFERRED VTC					
JUNE 1938 REPORT BANCROFT HILL	0 D				125
W H BARBER COMPANY $1 PAR COMMON					
W W STONE MINNEAPOLIS MINN	0	1	G N	100 - 100 - NC	
BICKFORDS INC COMMON					
HELD FOR CORRECTION EDWARD C KING NEW YORK CITY	D	1		100	384

*First Column No Key-direct ownership. "1" direct ownership, with ship, etc.) where no disclaimer is made and the total holdings of the in-ownership where no disclaimer is made but proportionate interest of re-where no disclaimer is made and it is not indicated whether total or claimer. "8" nature of ownership (direct or indirect) not reported and no Second Column "G" shares acquired or disposed of by GIFT. "S" an in-through BEQUEST or INHERITANCE. "C" receipt of securities as COM-(called, matured, retired). "T" TRANSFERRED or ACCRUED. "D"

FORM 4 REPORTS FOR JULY, 1938, UNLESS OTHERWISE INDICATED   **11**

DESCRIPTION ISSUER SECURITY REPORTING PERSON INDIRECT	RELATIONSHIP SEE PAGE 2	DATE OF TRANSACTION	OWNERSHIP AND TRANSACTION KEY •	TRANSACTIONS DURING MONTH "NC" = NET CHANGE DURING MONTH	HOLDINGS REPORTED AS OF END OF MONTH
BOHN ALUMINUM & BRASS COMMON					
JAMES M HUTTON JR CINCINNATI OHIO	D		N		
W E HUTTON & CO		21 25	2 2 N	200- 300- 500-NC	
HELD FOR CORRECTION FRANK C ROOT GREENWICH CONN	D	21		1000- 1000-NC	4156
BOYD WELSH INC COMMON					
JUNE 1938 REPORT HELD FOR CORRECTION FRIEDA H GRIFFITH ST LOUIS MO	OD	22		30 30 NC	2630
SEPTEMBER 1936 REPORT FRIEDA H GRIFFITH RECD FROM ESTATE	OD	3 3	T	350 1750 2100 NC	2600
GEO C GRIFFITH EST		3	2 T N	3500- 3500-NC	
BREWSTER AERONAUTICAL CAPITAL					
HELD FOR CORRECTION JAMES WORK LONG ISLAND CITY N Y	OD 	26 28	G G	5000- 4000- 9000-NC	118104
COMMON WARRANTS					
JAMES WORK	OD	19	G	2300- 2300-NC	22700

beneficial interest disclaimed. "2" indirect ownership (as through partner-
termediary are reported. "3" same as "2" with disclaimer. "4" indirect
porter is shown. "5" same as "4" with disclaimer. "6" indirect ownership
proportionate indirect holdings are reported. "7" same as "6" with dis-
disclaimer made. "9" same as "8" with disclaimer.
crease in holdings through STOCK DIVIDEND. "B" a change in holdings
PENSATION. "E" EXCHANGE or CONVERSION. "R" REDEEMED
DISTRIBUTION. "N" NO EQUITY SECURITIES HELD.

W. W. Aldrich, chairman of the board of directors of the Chase National Bank, "lessened the losses of other stockholders who might be obliged to sell at a time when the market for the stock was disorganized and undoubtedly operated to steady the market as a whole and make it capable of absorbing sudden unexpected selling." In an excited bull market the sales of the informed insider who saw his stock rise to unreasonable heights also acted as a stabilizing influence, and prevented less informed buyers from making purchases at even higher prices.

Several suggestions have been made for changes in the law. The activities harmful to others are in cases where the insider has initiated a price movement. The consummation of an important contract or the sale of certain assets at favorable prices are examples of how the insider may obtain unjust enrichment. Hence, it is suggested that the Commission exempt transactions by insiders which follow a break or rise of a certain per cent, say 5 or 7 per cent, which takes place within two days. Once the abrupt market change has taken place by reason of transactions of others, the purchase or sales of insiders would tend to allay fears, dampen enthusiasm, and provide a more orderly market. Publication of the transactions is held to be sufficient protection against the threat of "inside operations." The insider can still obtain advantages as the result of his favored position if a serious development is impending, or an exceptionally favorable development has come to his knowledge. Experience with the law probably has been too limited to prove conclusively whether or not amendment may be advisable. Private expressions of opinion of large owners, directors, and officials tend to indicate a reluctance to purchase stocks which they might formerly have bought as a matter of pride or out of a sense of responsibility.

Evasion of the law is comparatively simple with respect to purchases. I doubt that circumvention has been prevalent. The statute seems to give the Commission authority to suspend the provisions or to exempt transactions and to relieve officers, directors, and stockholders of their obligation to surrender their profits where unfair use has not been made of confidential information. In a period of violently declining or advancing prices a general exemption might be authorized for a short time on the assumption that purchases and sales within this period did not arise from the unfair use of inside information. The results might enable the authorities and the financial community to make a fairer appraisal of the provisions of Section 16, although the difficulty of isolating cause and effect in such cases is ever present. That some brake on the ability of the insider to profit at the expense of other stockholders has been necessary no longer requires discussion. That the large security holder, director, or official is generally better informed than the small investor is a truism. The statute cannot remove this inequality; indeed, there is no reason why it should make the effort. I am of the opinion that sizable stockownership by directors and executives is the surest guaranty of sound management. Widely scattered ownership often makes for mediocre results. The sale of the stock by the individual or family responsible for the creation and growth of a business often marks the beginning of a decline in its place in the industry.

MANIPULATION AND THE COMMISSION

The vast field covered by the work of the Commission justifies an entire volume. One has only to receive the releases of the Commission to gain an insight into the quantitative aspects of its work and the complexity of the problems to which its attention is directed. By comparison the Interstate Commerce Commission, despite its supervision over the 230,000 miles of railroad and widening control over other means of transportation, deals with a homogeneous problem. The subject of this book, however, is not the Commission. It has functioned for a comparatively short period and important monographs and special studies have appeared in the legal and economic periodicals. It will be some time before a comprehensive study like that of Professor Sharfman on the Interstate Commerce Commission is possible. For our purpose it will suffice to use as an illustration of the work of the various divisions a few instances of their activities. In the chapter on "New Financing," examples of the work of the Registration Division are set forth.

The Trading and Exchange Division has few more important or difficult tasks than the prevention of manipulative practices. The Securities Act of 1933 applies primarily to the disclosure of information by the registration of new securities about to be sold to the public. Section 17 (a) deals with fraudulent interstate transactions and is broad enough to cover transactions in already outstanding securities. Mr. A. A. Berle, Jr., points out that it is under this provision that the Commission usually proceeds. It is made unlawful to sell securities by the employment of any device, scheme, or artifice to defraud; to obtain money or property by means of any untrue statement of fact, or to engage in any transaction, practice or course of business which would operate as a fraud or deceit upon the purchaser. This probably does little more than to codify the existing substantive law. One of the primary reasons for the Securities Exchange Act is tersely described in the statute itself: "Frequently the prices of securities on such exchanges and markets [securities exchanges and over-the-counter markets] are susceptible to manipulation and control, and the dissemination of such prices gives rise to excessive speculation, resulting in sudden and unreasonable fluctuations in the prices of securities." The consequences mentioned in the act are alternately unreasonable expansion and contraction of the volume of credit, the hindrance of the proper appraisal of the value of securities, the prevention of the fair valuation of bank collateral, and the obstruction of the effective operation of the banking system. The omnibus catalogue of evils, sweeping as it is, represents an indictment supported by the evidence. Recent studies establish the importance of price movements of securities as a causal factor in business cycles. The traditional conception was that the changes in price are wholly a reflection of phases of the business cycle. The ever-growing degree to which enterprise is publicly owned as distinguished from the single proprietor or family-owned business makes recorded prices of added significance. The tendency toward "liquidity" has been observed for many years, but its implications are still to be fully explored. The volume of loans on securities probably will remain within proper bounds because of the present banking laws and the additional powers vested in the Board of Governors of the Federal Reserve System. Yet, security loans occupy a permanently important place in the banking structure. Manipulation leaves in its trail unnecessary losses and unearned gains.

The numerous pools and the method of operation were disclosed to an aroused public by the investigation into Stock Exchange Practices. If the act seems to be severe, one must remember the provocation. The pool in the stock of American Commercial Alcohol Corporation[1] which operated in 1933 became a telling weapon for national legislation.

The act refers to registered securities but by regulation of the Commission the prohibitions now apply equally to unregistered over-the-counter securities and securities admitted to unlisted trading on national securities exchanges. It is made unlawful for any person to use the mails or any other instrumentality of interstate commerce or the facilities of any national securities exchange for the purpose of "creating a false or misleading appearance" with respect to the market in any of the following ways:

A. Wash sales
B. Matched orders
C. Market "rigging"
D. Dissemination of information that market operations will raise or depress prices.
E. False or misleading statements.

The New York Stock Exchange, with varying degrees of effectiveness, had long condemned "A," "B," and "E," but could reach its members only through disciplinary action. The law now reaches not only brokers and dealers and exchange members acting for themselves or others, but anyone using the facilities of an exchange or the mails or other means of interstate commerce.

The broadest section of the act makes it unlawful in the manner described "to effect, alone or with one or more other persons, a series of transactions in any security registered on a national securities exchange creating actual or apparent active trading in such security or raising or depressing the price of such security, for the purpose of inducing the pur-

[1] See *Security Speculation*, by John T. Flynn, pp. 189 ff. (1934).

chase or sale of such security by others." Enforcement of this provision, which was intended to prohibit both pool activity and every other device used to persuade the public that activity in a security is the reflection of a general demand instead of a mirage, depends in part on a subjective test that is hard to prove, that is, the illegal purpose of the transactions. The purchase or sale of a substantial number of shares of stock by a large speculator, especially if his activities become public, are bound to influence others. This, however, is not the test, nor is the fact that this consequence is an agreeable one. "In the instance of manipulation, the principal object, the immediate end to which activity is directed is the inducing others to trade."[2] At one time, as in the days of the famous Radio pool, market operators did not object, when it suited their purpose, to have such activities discreetly publicized. Now that heavy damages and criminal liabilities may be incurred, the task of uncovering manipulative activities requires skill in detection, dogged perseverance, and a knowledge of the methods of manipulators.

That Michael J. Meehan was a product of the "new era" is plain; unfortunately, he could not believe that the period had come to a close. The popular magazines lost good material in the passing of Gould and Drew, and at a later date when the spectacular operations of Gates and Keen were brought to a close. The titans and their imitators had picturesque careers. In their day, manipulation often related to an attempt to gain control of a corporation which had peculiar value, as the strategic position of a railroad if properly managed. The manipulation of the twenties was devoid of any saving grace.

"In the matter of Michael J. Meehan"[3] a specific violation of the Securities Exchange Act of 1934 is followed through to the finding that the respondent be expelled from the national securities exchanges of which he was a member.

Bellanca Aircraft Corporation was formed in 1927.* As of April 5, 1935, 168,495 shares of common stock ($1 per value)

[2] *Yale Law Journal,* Vol. 46:624 pp. Comments on "Market Manipulation and the Securities Exchange Act."

[3] Securities and Exchange Commission, Securities Exchange Act of 1934, Release No. 1331, August 2, 1937.

* Note: No reflection on the present management is intended.

were outstanding. The corporation manufactured a plane which had achieved a considerable reputation in aviation for its efficiency in lifting and carrying large loads at reasonable speeds with low fuel consumption. The business had not been financially successful. Up to July 31, 1935, it showed a net loss of $1,240,000.

	Sales	Net Profit or Loss
1929	$564,500	$109,000 net loss
1930	740,000	324,000 " "
1931	590,000	397,000 " "
1932	396,000	100,000 " "
1933	682,000	53,000 " "
1934	538,000	139,000 " "

By 1935 the corporation was in need of additional funds and in March an application was made to the Reconstruction Finance Corporation for a loan of $150,000. The loan was refused because the collateral was inadequate and because it was felt that this amount would be insufficient to put the corporation on a sound operating basis. Late in 1928 a syndicate was formed for the sale of 104,000 shares of stock, which were distributed on the New York Curb Exchange at $23.50 a share at a gross profit to the syndicate of $800,000 and a net to the company of $1,625,000. Michael J. Meehan was one of the members of the syndicate and his interest in the company derived from that transaction. Through another member of the syndicate, L. Sherman Adams, who was a director of the company until the Reconstruction Finance Corporation application to which he was opposed, had been turned down, the respondent kept in close touch with the affairs of the company. An attempt to interest an investment banking firm in the new financing failed to obtain the approval of the president of the company, G. W. Bellanca. Through the efforts of the respondent, a "finder" of deals, Raymond De Voe discussed with him and Bellanca the possibility of De Voe's buying 50,000 shares from Bellanca, the latter to lend half the money received to the company. It appears that the respondent and De Voe had agreed to make this a joint venture. Half the stock was to be bought at $4 a share, and half at $6 a share. This conference took place May 17, 1935. The contract was signed by Mrs.

Meehan. On May 15, the stock had closed at 2½. The market for the stock between January 1 and May 15 had been limited. In no month had a thousand shares been traded; the dealings in all had aggregated only 3,100 shares. Immediately the stock became active with the following closing prices:

May 16	3⅝
May 17	4¼
May 18	4½

Dealings on May 17 were 1,800 shares. The Commission was not able to find that the purchases which were made by associates of De Voe and Meehan, or others who directly and indirectly had heard of their interest through the so-called grapevine method, were traceable to the respondent. That they raised the price of the stock was clear, but this of itself was not enough without proof that the rumors circulated were attributable to Meehan. The agreement of May 17 was not carried out. On June 13 an agreement was made between Bellanca, Hammons & Co., and the respondent for the purchase of 18,000 shares of stock from Bellanca, half the proceeds to be advanced to the company. The Commission found nothing illegal in Meehan's orders between May 20 and June 7 to buy stock at 4 and under, apparently as support for the stock, or in the purchase of the stock for the discretionary account of a friend.

Through Mr. Meehan's holdings, directly and otherwise, he had an interest in Bellanca stock of 30,550 shares, but 29,150 shares were sold by him between June 10 and June 18. Liquidation was accomplished in nine trading days during which the market rose from a low of 4 to a high of 5½, and during which a total of 40,900 shares were traded. The Commission found that in this period the respondent had not followed the simple type of manipulation. There the pattern was buying that would raise prices and stimulate others to buy at advancing prices. The manipulator might buy occasionally after selling on a rising market, but was careful to sell on balance. With regard to the trading in Bellanca a different set of facts was present. Here buying was generated by others than Meehan. He used the buying power in a discretionary account;

stimulated buying by urging others to come in; added buy-ing power through his own floor representative and as Mee-han expected, the activity resulted in the specialists taking speculative positions for their own account. Matched orders also were used to give a misleading appearance of strong buy-ing support to the market. The Commission found that "no unstimulated market could have attracted to it the purchas-ing that developed during these days."

On June 17 an underwriting agreement was executed be-tween the Bellanca Aircraft Corporation, the president, G. M. Bellanca, Hammons & Co., and Meehan. In brief, it provided for the purchase of 100,000 shares of stock at $4 a share, to be distributed by Hammons & Co. through dealers who were to receive a commission of 50 cents a share. Warrants for 72,-000 shares were to be issued entitling the holders to buy stock for three years from the date of issuance at $5 a share. Op-tions at $4 a share were to be issued for a 60-day period for 25,000 shares. A new board of directors was to be elected, and a president satisfactory to Hammons was to be elected. War-rants for an additional 52,500 shares were to be issued to the new president, Bellanca, and other officers for the purchases of stock at $5 a share for a five-year period. Bellanca was to trans-fer the patent rights in his name to the company—previously he had refused to make this assignment. Bellanca agreed not to sell his stock for a period of 144 days after the underwriters had taken down their stock. The Commission's comment on the underwriting contract follows:

"The terms of this agreement, which had substantially been assented to by June 6, are of interest. It calls for the take-down of stock by underwriters at a price almost 25 per cent in ex-cess of its book value in a corporation whose earnings for the past six years have shown a deficit of $1,016,000. The take-down price, moreover, on June 6 was an eighth above the mar-ket price, which, already without support, after the flurry of May 16 to 18, seemed to be ready to subside to the lows pre-vailing prior to that time. To be at all profitable to the under-writers, the market price would have to rise to the neighbor-hood of $5 per share (the contemplated offering price), and, indeed, beyond that if the underwriters were to realize upon the majority of their warrants. Added to this, we find that for 144 days the holdings of the largest stockholder (Bellanca) are immobilized by agreement, a factor of no mean significance. That an agreement of this character provides not only an incentive to manipulate the stock on the market but also assistance to that end, is undoubted. The price at which distribution of the stock offered away from the market can be made, is, of course, dominated by the price of the stock on the market."

During this period, Meehan also sold 16,000 shares over-the-counter at $5 per share. The story of the manipulative activities are vivid reminders of the ease with which activity may be created by a large speculator. In the days preceding the Securities Exchange Act the whisper that "Mike Meehan is in —— stock" was a far more potent influence than a thorough analysis of a corporation's financial record and prospects. The Commission seemed to be astonished at the character of the following Meehan succeeded in developing. It declared: "The naïveté of all the purchasers is almost beyond belief. They purchased on the mere say-so of respondent and without even the semblance of an intelligent inquiry into the stock. To a president of a bank and to a betting commissioner alike, the mere word of respondent seemed sufficient." Between June 19 and October 26, 1935, the interest of Meehan in attempting to keep the price around 5 was obvious, as the underwriting could not be profitable otherwise. The same general pattern was followed.

The Commission found: "On the face of this record it is not difficult to assay that nature of respondent's activity in Bellanca stock during the period from June 19 to October 26. We see him active in bringing new buying power into the market, encouraging his friends to buy, inducing persons in the brokerage business to recommend the stock to their customers. We see his associates, such as Wigmore, trading heavily in the stock on narrow price fluctuations. We find a market, when weakness in the stock developed, supported and banked by heavy scale buy orders placed sometimes directly by respondent for M. J. Meehan and Company, at other times by respondent for the account of his alter ego, Mrs. Meehan, and occasionally by the Dore and Wigmore account. The record leaves us in no doubt that respondent during this period was actively responsible for a series of transactions in Bellanca stock, the purpose of which was to maintain its price at or about the level that the stock had reached on June 18."

Weakness cropped out October 25 and the following day the stock collapsed, and sold as low as 2¾ after several months of activity during which most transactions had taken place at 5 or fractionally lower.

The mere rumor of an investigation by the Commission into the trading in a stock often creates weakness in the price. Investigations are instituted as a result of the observation by representatives of the Commission of the ticker, disclosures in the reports of registered security holdings, and upon complaint of the public.

The desirability of eliminating manipulative practices of the type described is generally admitted. Not all cases, however, are as clear-cut. It is well known that the securities of secondary companies often suffer because of a limited market or because the corporation is not well known. X Corporation is a supplier of equipment in an important industry and has been successful. Last year the company earned $2 a share on the common stock, and the average earnings for several years have been satisfactory. There are approximately 200 shareholders. Officers and directors hold approximately 60 per cent of the 200,000 shares of common stock. General market conditions have been unfavorable and we find that the stock is selling around $8 a share. In the face of a business slump the company's progress has continued to the point that additional capital is required. Bank credit has been fully utilized and the total authorized preferred stock is already outstanding. Sound financial practice suggests the advisability of issuing 50,000 additional shares of common stock to raise about $600,000. The management and the investment banking firm responsible for the company's previous financing do not regard the market price of $8 as at all a fair appraisal of the value of the stock. There has been little market activity in the stock and the purchase of possibly 2,000 to 3,000 shares probably would move the stock to between $12 and $14 a share, a level more in keeping with its value. Sale of the stock at a price under $8 a share would dilute the equity and net the company less than $400,000. The situation can be varied to describe the same difficulty by assuming all the facts are the same, except that the banking firm has an option from the company on 50,000 shares of stock at $12 a share. In these cases purchases of the stock with the thought that these purchases would lead to an advance sufficient to enable the company to finance, or make it profitable to exercise the option, would be dangerous.

The law is couched in language indicating that the market price before such purchases are effected is assumed to be a reasonable measure of value. In many instances this is not true. Inactive stocks are not attractive to the speculator who is more interested in the possibility of making a "quick turn" than in buying an underpriced stock unresponsive to general market conditions. Only a limited number of cases have been before the Commission under the prohibition against manipulation of security prices. Perhaps, as varied types of manipulative practices are condemned, the financial community will gain a clearer view of what transactions come within the scope of the statute. At present, fear of violation of the law seems to be working a hardship on corporations and stockholders where facts exist similar to those in the illustration used above.

The existence of the law and the surveillance of the authorities of the leading stock exchanges, without doubt, have curtailed manipulative activities to a far greater extent than the few cases reported by the Commission tend to indicate. Until recently the Commission seemed to be dissatisfied with the efforts of the stock exchanges. In its third annual report the Commission remarked that the national securities exchanges had not as yet demonstrated the capacity themselves to police their markets effectively against manipulative and deceptive practices. "In consequence," the Commission frankly stated, "the burden of detecting and instituting proceedings against such practices has rested almost entirely upon the Commission." At the end of June, 1937, a total of 2,778 exchange issues were under regular observation and price and volume records of approximately 225 securities traded in over-the-counter markets were made. During that year 420 reports dealing with the probability of manipulation on exchange markets and 72 preliminary investigations, 18 new formal investigations were authorized, 60 were closed or completed, and 48 were in process as of June 30, 1937. Twelve formal investigations were authorized without preliminary investigations. In the over-the-counter markets, the Commission authorized 15 preliminary investigations. When a formal investigation develops evidence which makes it appear to the Commission that any person is violating or is about to violate any provision of the act, appropriate legal proceedings are instituted. Such proceedings may take the form of a suit for injunction; they may take the form of a reference to the Department of Justice for criminal proceedings; and they may take the form of a proceeding by the Commission to suspend or expel the offender (if the offender is a member of a national securities exchange) from the exchange of which he is a member—as in the M. J. Meehan proceeding; also proceeding against Harry A. Dart *et al.*, etc. Proceedings have been instituted sparingly and only when the Commission has good reason to believe a violation of the law has been or is about to be committed. It is significant that no appeals from the Commission's rulings under Section 9A of the act have been successful.

Short Sales

The short sale affords an interesting study of the change in the mechanism of the market. At the same time it illustrates concretely the resistance to change, and the fallacies that may underlie a generally accepted belief. Statistical evidence unavailable until recently has battered away the conventional viewpoint, leaving little of the conclusions found in the earlier studies of Wall Street and markets. In the *American Mercury* I suggested that the entire subject be reexamined.

For the traditional viewpoint we may turn to a pleasant book by W. C. Van Antwerp, *The Stock Exchange from Within*. The chapter on "The Bear and Short Selling," without a single detailed reference to the markets, ends as follows: "The bear has come to stay. As a spectre to frighten amateurs, he may continue for a time to stalk abroad o'nights;

as a necessary and useful part of all business he is a substantial reality. And he is not 'immoral.' "

The author, a member of the New York Stock Exchange, quoted with satisfaction from the report of the so-called Hughes Commission.[4] The report, dated June 7, 1909, stated: "Short sellers endeavor to select times when prices seem high in order to sell, and times when prices seem low in order to buy, their action in both cases serving to lessen advances and diminish declines in price. In other words, short selling tends to produce steadiness in prices, which is an advantage to the community. No other means of restraining unwarranted marking up and down of prices has been suggested to us." For thirty years or more these words were quoted as if they expressed the eternal verities. The report cited no data such as was obtained in the Senate investigation or by the Securities and Exchange Commission, and so far as we know made no effort to obtain evidence to sustain its dogmatic judgment. How unrealistic this study was may be understood when we remember that the Hughes Commission asked the governors of the Stock Exchange if a change in the practice of dealing on margins would be desirable. To ask the principal beneficiaries of a business arrangement if a change be desirable is naïve.

The discussion in the *American Mercury* was one of the first that raised the questions that finally led to the rules adopted by the New York Stock Exchange. One of the arguments that I advanced has not been generally offered: "The short sale is compared with the sale of a house by a builder even before a foundation is laid, or with the sale of a crop by a farmer before it is planted. Texts illustrate the short sale by a comparison with the miller or textile manufacturer who hedges against the purchase of his raw materials. The analogies are weak. In these cases an economic process has taken place. The short sale is incidental to a primary transaction."[5] The writer is now prepared to go further. One has no right in the nature of things to sell the Woolworth Building because

---

[4] The report is reprinted in S. S. Pratt's *The Work of Wall Street*, pp. 377 ff. (1919 edition).

[5] *American Mercury*, Vol. XIX, No. 76, April, 1930. "The Short Sale," by R. L. Weissman, pp. xxx ff.

he believes that he will be able to repurchase it at a lower price. Short selling has been made possible only by the existence of foreign exchange markets, commodity markets, and securities markets, where the unit of trading is similar to every other unit, i.e., francs, crude rubber, or shares of common stock of the United States Steel Corporation. Consequently, the short sale should be under the control of the markets.

In the same article I referred to a forgotten episode. During our participation in the World War it was feared that weakness in the stock market might retard war financing. The governors of the New York Stock Exchange called upon the members in November, 1917, for a statement of all stocks sold and bought on the previous day. Commenting on the measure, the conservative *Commercial and Financial Chronicle* stated: "Short selling in the ordinary way, with the risk it involves, is one thing. Throwing stocks over by the ream with the sole view of breaking the market, and then covering on the break, is a totally different thing. Those who argue that short selling is legitimate and really constitutes an element of safety in the situation, too frequently fail to bear this distinction in mind. One class of operation is unobjectionable and may really serve a good purpose. The other class must be unqualifiedly condemned. If such acts are wicked in normal times, they are positively criminal when the country is engaged in a great war." Not until the panic in the fall of 1929 did the New York Stock Exchange feel it necessary to take any steps with regard to short selling. At that time short selling was inferentially discouraged.

Finally, I questioned the contention that short selling stabilizes the market. A brief examination convinced me that the long-accepted opinion was probably in error. "Instead of stabilizing prices, short selling often intensifies both the fall and the rise. I have examined the price records during the last break and find no support for the theory that price changes were broader in stocks which did not harbor large short interests. The changes in successive dealings in more inactive stocks, less likely to be sold short, are often more than an eighth or a quarter away from the preceding sale, but to investors the differences are not decisive."

In the light of the foregoing it is interesting to summarize the conclusions of the careful study of the problem in the survey of *The Security Markets,* of the Twentieth Century Fund, Inc., which was fortified by the information made available by the Hearings on Stock Exchange Practices, and the New York Stock Exchange, as well as the Twentieth Century Fund's research staff. The staff included a day-to-day study from May 23, 1931, to December 31, 1932, of individual stocks and a longer term study of the averages of fourteen active leading stocks compared with the averages.

The summary of findings follows:[6]

1. The practice of short selling finds universal application in all fields of economic endeavor where credit is used. Viewed purely as a technical device it should not be condemned unless it is proven to be inherently harmful wherever applied.

2. Whether short selling is desirable or not as applied to securities must be judged on the basis of its effect upon the security price structure. Other and collateral effects of short selling in securities are of minor moment.

3. In its relation to the trend in security prices, short selling is likely to appear after prices have started downward and to grow in volume as they continue downward, to be covered through purchases either at lower price levels or after prices have turned upward. Short selling cannot, therefore, have any appreciable effect in limiting the extremes to which prices may rise. Its tendency is to accelerate the downward trend of prices during the early and middle phases of the movement, and either to check the price trend in the lower phase or heighten its movement after prices have turned upward.

4. In its relation to the small price cycles extending over periods of a few weeks, short selling again appears after prices have started downward, to be covered at a lower point or after recovery is under way. Its tendency as a stabilizing influence is similar here, only on a smaller scale, to that in the longer trend movements.

5. In its relation to particular issues of stock or at particular points in time, short selling appears in widely varying amounts and types. In its relation to the prices of individual stocks, short sales appear most frequently as prices move downward and are covered as a rule while they continue downward. This is particularly true

[6] *The Security Markets,* Twentieth Century Fund, Inc., pp. 397 ff. (1935).

of the larger transactions. For the smaller transactions covering is more likely to occur after prices have turned upward.

6. On the basis of points 3, 4 and 5, one might conclude that the tendency of short selling is to cause price instability. This raises the question of how stable prices should be. The best single guide to answer this question is the earning power—net—of corporations. Judged by this standard it does not appear that short sales are out of place during periods of declining prices. They would, however, be much more valuable if made in volume during the latter phases of upward movements in price.

7. While the tendency of short sales is to add weight to the downward trend and to the minor downward swings in prices, judged by recent years they have not been in sufficient volume to warrant the belief that their actual effect is at all material. During the past four years, they probably did not at their maximum point exceed 15 per cent of the positions or sales for long speculative account for all stocks. For most of this period they ranged between 5 and 10 per cent. In so far as trading of itself is a market factor, therefore, much greater importance is to be attached to the positions and trading on the long side of the market.

8. The observation just made was with reference to all stocks considered as a group. While the total volume of short sales was comparatively small, in particular issues it rose to relatively large amounts. The exact size of these individual short positions, relative to the total speculative interest in each stock, is not known, however, due to the fact that the long speculative interest for individual stocks is not known. It is with reference to particular issues and particular points in time that close supervision over short selling is needed. There is considerable evidence to support the belief that in these individual issues short selling does at times exert an artificial influence. This belief is supported by more exhaustive evidence on short selling in the commodity markets. It is likely that the most pronounced influence is to be found in instances where short sales are made by a single interest in large quantity during comparatively brief periods of time.

As a result of the criticism leveled at unrestricted short selling, the New York Stock Exchange on October 5, 1931, through its Business Conduct Committee forwarded a circular to the members directing that before executing any selling orders members shall ascertain and notify their floor brokers whether such orders are for long or short account. Members were also warned to notify their customers that short stock would not be sold at a lower price than the last preceding transaction. No rule was adopted that short sales could not be made at a price below that of the last sale. The general regulation against trading tending to demoralize the market was regarded as sufficient.

Until the collapse of the market in September and October, 1937, further regulations were not deemed necessary. In January, 1938, the Securities and Exchange Commission promulgated its rules on short selling together with a statement on the results of the investigation of the situation. The adoption of these rules, important in themselves, was of added significance as the Securities and Exchange Commission had been reluctant to impose rules, leaving it to the stock exchanges to govern themselves so far as possible. Chairman Douglas only a few months previously, in a formal statement, declared: "As is well known, the commission has in the past made a practice of permitting the exchanges to adopt as their own the rules governing the trading practices of their members. This method appeared to have two distinct advantages. First, it would permit the necessary elasticity required because of varying conditions on the various exchanges. And second, it was thought that it would add the weight of the Exchange itself as an enforcement agency having jurisdiction over its members." It was thought that the government might avail itself of this already established enforcement machine. Foreshadowing an "immediate and more pervasive administration directly by the commission," Mr. Douglas expressed his doubts as to the desirability of assigning to exchanges such a vital role in the nation's economic affairs until they had adopted programs of action designed "to justify their existence solely upon their value as public market places."

For the purposes of the rule the term "short sale" was declared to mean "any sale of a security which the seller does not own or any sale which is consummated by the delivery of a security borrowed by, or for the account of the seller." The rules became effective February 8, 1938. In addition to providing that no selling order shall be executed without first being marked either "long" or "short," the new regulation provided that a short sale must be made at a price above the price at which the last sale, regular way, was effected. In other words, a short sale must be made at a price one-eighth above the preceding sale. The data on which the ruling was based was taken from a study of short selling on the New York Stock Exchange and will be considered.

The data covered two weekly periods September 7-13 and October 18-23, 1937. The movement of the averages during these periods is summarized and justifies the Commission's reference that they were characterized by a "large volume of trading, erratic price movements and intense liquidation."

The Commission secured a transcript of the positions and trades made in twenty representative stocks by all individual members of the New York Stock Exchange and their partners and firms, covering a total of 5,551 accounts. A detailed analysis was also made of every trade as it occurred in six market leaders for shorter periods to examine not only the origin of individual short sales but also the effect of their timing on the general market.

During the period September 7-25, 1937, short selling in five selected stocks constituted the following percentage of total sales in those stocks.

	Per Cent
American Telephone & Telegraph	31.9
General Motors common	20.4
New York Central	14.1
Standard Oil of New Jersey	5.6
United States Steel common	30.3
Average	22.37

Sales of these stocks actually owned were 1,609,000 shares; short sales added 473,300, and increased the total volume of selling by some 30 per cent.

The extent to which members of the Stock Exchange, general partners, and firms were sellers for short account in twenty stocks for the two periods combined and the ratio of their short selling in each stock to their total short selling in these stocks is shown below:

	Members' Short Sales Shares	Ratio to Total Per Cent	Cumulative Percentage
United States Steel	80,639	29.51	
General Motors	67,554	24.72	54.23
Chrysler	50,155	18.35	72.58
New York Central	15,705	5.75	78.33
Radio	11,100	4.06	82.39
Western Union	10,750	3.93	86.32
Montgomery Ward	10,200	3.73	90.05
American Telephone & Telegraph	7,625	2.79	92.84
Westinghouse Electric	6,125	2.24	95.08
Standard Oil of New Jersey	3,050	1.12	96.20
American Smelting & Refining	2,550	.93	97.13
International Harvester	2,500	.92	98.05
Atchison, Topeka & Santa Fe	1,680	.61	98.66
International Paper and Power pfd.	1,300	.48	99.14
Johns-Manville	600	.22	99.36
Loew's	500	.18	99.54
American Can	425	.16	99.70
Youngstown Sheet & Tube	350	.13	99.83
J. I. Case	281	.10	99.93
Douglas Aircraft	200	.07	100.00

Total members' short position:
273,289 shares

For the week September 7-13 the member groups accounted for 40 per cent of the short sales of United States Steel, and over 44 per cent of the short sales of specialists are included. Short selling by Stock Exchange members, partners, and firms was highly concentrated in the hands of a few individuals. Of the 4,551 member accounts studied, only 54 showed short sales in United States Steel during the week of September 7-13. A total of 60 per cent of the short selling done by this group originated with only five individual members. The majority of members' short selling was concentrated in only eleven individuals. The Commission concluded: "The preponderance of available evidence points to the conclusion that in a declining market certain types of short sales are seriously destructive of stability."

In the Senate investigation of Stock Exchange Practices, Mr. Richard Whitney, president of the New York Stock Exchange at the time, strongly upheld unrestricted short selling. He termed it an integral part of speculation, and contended that speculation, together with investment, makes up the markets.

If one part of either were taken away, the market would lose its equilibrium and stability. He did not believe that short selling depressed the market. Such statements do not coincide with the facts adduced by recent investigation. The present regulations may not be the last word in dealing with the problem, but as yet there is no conclusive evidence that the restrictions have added to the market's disequilibrium or instability. Defenders of unrestricted short selling cite the equally great declines in stocks in which little or no short selling took place. Market observers know how often well-timed short selling creates general uncertainty and weakness, leading to the liquidation of other securities. This liquidation might not occur except for the impetus provided by short sales in the accepted market leaders. Further experience may show that the Commission's rules are too severe. The Commission should be open minded if the evidence suggests the advisability of modifying the present restrictions.

A further step in the direction of disclosure of pertinent information was taken when, for the first time, the Stock Exchange released the amount of the short interest in each of sixty-five stocks as of May 31 and June 30, 1938. Subsequent figures have been released monthly in stocks in which a 5,000-share short interest exists or in which a change of 2,000 shares has taken place during the month. The Exchange has made available for inspection all its data on individual stocks as far back as 1931.

MARGINS

The power of curbing undue speculation through the excessive use of credit has been vested in the Federal Reserve System. The Board of Governors fixes margin requirements and thus determines the extent to which securities may be carried on margin by brokers. It is also vested with authority that, taken together with the present banking laws, should be effective in preventing bank loans on securities from becoming excessive.

At one time it was possible to purchase equity securities on a 10 per cent margin. That speculative trading was stimulated by the ease with which the purchase of stocks could borrow is not debatable. Whatever the reasons may be, the overwhelming majority of margin accounts result in ultimate loss. Investigations made early in the century and since then, as well as observation, confirm this conclusion.[7] As early as 1909 the report of the Hughes Commission, which was conservative in its general tone, although rejecting the prohibition of margin trading or legislation, urged "upon all brokers to discourage speculation upon small margins and upon the Exchange to use its influence, and, if necessary its power, to prevent members from soliciting and generally accepting business on a less than 20 per cent." The brokerage business flourished and expanded on margin trading and it was too much to expect severe restrictions from the Exchange authorities. The expansion of speculation in the "new era" period is so well known and has been described so fully that we need not discuss it at length. Prior to the issuance of the rules of the Federal Reserve Board the exchanges' own margin requirements applicable to fair-sized accounts stood at a little less than 24 per cent of the market value of the securities carried.

The Federal Reserve Act, by amendment adopted in 1934, gave the Board of Governors the right to lower margin requirements "as it deems necessary or appropriate for the accommodation of commerce and industry, having due regard to the general credit situation of the country" and to raise the requirements "as it may deem necessary or appropriate to prevent the excessive use of credit to finance transactions in securities." No other central bank has specific power over margin requirements. The central bank viewpoint is set forth in the Board's annual report for 1936: "By raising margin requirements the Board is in a position to restrain the demand for credit from speculators in the stock market without restricting the supply available for other borrowers. This method differs from other means of credit control in that it affects directly the demand for credit rather than the available supply or cost, thus exercising a restraint on speculation without limiting the supply or raising the cost of credit to agriculture, trade, and industry."

[7] *Pitfalls of Speculation*, Thomas Gibson, 1909, Chapter X; *The Margin Trader*, Kemper Simpson, 1938.

THE COMMISSION AND SPECULATION

The Board adopted the formula stated in the law (but not required) for the initial extension of credit by brokers and dealers in securities. This standard provided that a loan on a security must not be greater than whichever is the higher of:

(1) 55 per cent of the current market price of the security, or
(2) 100 per cent of the lowest market price of the security since July 1, 1933, but not more than 75 per cent of the current market price.

Federal regulation relates to initial margins. After the purchase the margins to be maintained are governed by the stock exchanges. The New York Stock Exchange has required 30 per cent of the debit balance on long transactions.

The statutory margin formula was based on the theory that it was wise to provide for a constant increase of restraining influences as the prices of stocks advanced above their lows. So long as the price of a stock was less than 133 per cent of the low price in the period prescribed a customer might borrow from a broker as much as 75 per cent of its market price, because up to that point 75 per cent of the market price would not exceed 100 per cent of the low price. When the price of a security advanced above 133 per cent of its low price the amount that could be borrowed on it did not increase and the percentage margin requirement, therefore, increased as the price advanced. Under the stationary formula this condition continued until the price rose above 182 per cent of its low, when a constant 45 per cent margin requirement became effective. The reason that the situation changed at the 182 per cent line was that 55 per cent of 182 is 100, so that at prices above 182 per cent of the low a loan of 55 per cent of the market price would be more than a loan of 100 per cent of the low point and would, therefore, be the alternative chosen as the basis of calculating margin requirements and loan values. When the regulation went into effect on October 1, 1934, the average of stock prices was relatively low (Dow, Jones & Co. industrial stock average stood at 90.4) and the general effect of the regulation was slight as it increased the margin requirements on the average to only about 28 per cent.

One effect of the formula was that during the rise of the

price of a security from 133 to 182 per cent of the low price, no additional amount could be borrowed on the security, and consequently the profits arising out of the rise would not be withdrawn or used as margin for additional borrowing. In other words, profits could not be pyramided, and the stretch of value between 133 and 182 per cent of the low price of a stock came to be known as the "antipyramiding zone." By "pyramiding" is meant the use of paper or unrealized profits in stock transactions as margin for further commitments. When a rise in the price of a stock carried it above 182 per cent of its low, however, each additional advance of $1 enabled the borrower to withdraw 55 per cent of his profits or to use that amount as margin for additional borrowing. Profits could once more be pyramided. As a result of the advance in stock prices during 1935 it was estimated that at the end of that year, when the Dow, Jones & Co. industrial stock averages were at 144, margins required on active issues averaged about 40 per cent. This automatic increase as stock prices advanced represented the effects of the operation of the statutory formula. During a part of the advance pyramiding of profits was not possible for most stocks, but the rise in prices brought an increasing number to the level at which pyramiding with a 45 per cent margin was again possible. Largely because of this situation the Board announced that, effective February 1, 1936, the margins required on securities which had risen most in price would be raised from 45 to 55 per cent of the current market price. As of April 1, 1936, the Board of Governors abandoned the double option, antipyramiding standard aňd adopted a flat 55 per cent requirement on all stock purchases. No change was made during the course of the rising market of 1936 and part of 1937 because it did not appear that the rise was being financed in great degree by either loans to brokers or loans on securities to others than brokers and dealers. With the collapse of the stock market in the fall of 1937 the Board decided to lower the margin requirements to 40 per cent.

The governors of the Stock Exchange, when asked by the Hughes Commission "Would a change in the practice of dealing on margins be desirable?" replied in part: "The practice of dealing on margins is absolutely essential to the conduct of many transactions, whether in stocks or bonds. To prohibit it would be to deny to a man the right to invest his funds and to purchase property upon such terms as he pleases. As well might the purchase of real estate, where a portion of the consideration is left on mortgage, be prohibited." This has been the traditional answer to all past attempts to limit margin trading and in one form or other has been repeated. The movement away from *laissez faire* since 1929 has covered a manifold variety of activities and the dominant view of the nation has included margin trading as a proper subject for social control. Where the limitation should be set is a somewhat different question; to find a satisfactory standard is a difficult task. What makes a 40 per cent requirement proper? The 55 per cent requirement was not condemned until the violent decline in the markets in the fall of 1937. It now appears that the Board of Governors is likely to vary the requirements between an upper 55 per cent and lower 40 per cent level in accordance with its view of the price structure. This standard has the virtue of simplicity, an element of no little importance in view of the large and growing number of listed securities. Many firms do not lend on securities selling at less than $5 a share, and refuse to accept accounts with an equity of less than $1,000. A few conservative bankers like the late Melvin A. Traylor have advocated that buying for small accounts be restricted to a cash basis. The president of the New York Stock Exchange has gone so far as to express the wish that the person of small means would avoid trading on margin. Definite restrictions, formulated either by the Exchange or by the Securities and Exchange Commission, however, would arouse the opposition of many and provoke the comment that the wealthy security buyer has privileges denied to the small buyer.

Other standards have been suggested. A formula that would be related to earnings has much to recommend it. In other words, the requirements might be 30 per cent of the average earnings per share of the past three fiscal years multiplied by ten. The margin required would increase if the price represented a higher multiple of earnings. This would mean that on a stock with average earnings of $3 a share the buyer's minimum margin would be $9. If a stock sold at 12 times the average per share earnings the requirements would be 35 per cent; and at 15 times, 40 per cent. Above this level the margin would jump to 50 per cent. On the earnings used, $3 per share, the requirements would be as follows:

Price as a Multiple of Earnings	Margin Required Per Cent	Price per Share	Margin Required per Share
10 times or less	30%	$30	$ 9.00
Over 10 and to 12	35	36	12.60
Over 12 and to 15	40	45	18.00
Over 15 and assuming a price of	50	60	30.00

A plan of this type would tend to restrain the advance or fall of a stock: as it rose to a high level the requirements would increase, and as it fell the funds needed to purchase or carry it would automatically decline. The difficulty, other than the mechanical details, is that earnings of various industries are subject to different degrees of change. The form of capitalization is also to be taken into consideration in approving the value of a stock. The stock of an electric power and light operating company is likely to have more stable earnings than a highly geared holding company issue with a large "leverage" factor. Nevertheless, a standard related to earnings seems to be less arbitrary than a flat uniform standard. Banks in 1928 and 1929 were not guided entirely by market quotation. For loan purposes, notoriously speculative stocks like Radio Corporation were marked down materially from prevailing market prices.

In connection with the influence of higher margins on the narrowing of the market, Winthrop W. Aldrich made an interesting point. A 55 per cent margin, he declared, was really a margin of 122 per cent as brokers calculated it. If a man buys $10,000 worth of stock he must supply $5,500 in cash and he may not borrow more than $4,500. Consequently, the margin is 122 per cent of the loan of $4,500. If the new control were to operate fairly, prompt action when prices are falling should take place and the reductions "should not be grudging and limited." It was also suggested that increases apply initially to new borrowings and to new accounts, and to existing borrowings and accounts at a substantially later date.

The final word on margins and margin trading cannot be pronounced at this time. The choice is not between unrestrained trading on small margins or the elimination of all borrowings. Judged in the light of all the circumstances, and at least until more conclusive evidence be available as to its harmful effects, the present requirements may be regarded as reasonable. The contention that banks have found loans against securities safe does not go to the heart of the problem, which is not the experience of banks with security loans but the harmful effects of excessive speculation on the national economy.

The Banking Act of 1933 provides that no member bank shall act as a medium or agent of any nonbanking corporation or individual in the making of loans or securities. This provision was enacted to prevent the possibility of large loans for the account of others. The magnitude of these loans created in effect an invisible banking system over which the Federal Reserve authorities had no control. The Banking Act of 1935 empowers the Board of Governors upon the affirmative vote of not less than six members to fix from time to time for each Federal Reserve district the percentage of individual bank capital and surplus which may be represented by security loans made by member banks in such district. No loan shall be made by any bank to any person in an amount in excess of 10 per cent of its unimpaired capital and surplus, but this does not apply to limited state government obligations or fully guaranteed obligations. The Board also has the power to direct any member bank to refrain from further increase of its loans secured by stock or bond collateral for any period of one year under penalty of suspension of its rediscount privileges. It is made the duty of the Board to establish such percentages with a view to preventing the undue use of bank loans for the "speculative carrying of securities." In addition, if any member bank to which an advance has been made on its note secured by government obligations, during the life of the advance and despite official warning of the reserve bank of its district or the Board to the contrary, increase its outstanding loans secured by stocks or bonds other than obligations of the United States, the advance shall become immediately due and payable; the member bank is also made ineligible as a borrower at the reserve bank of the district for such period as the Board may determine. These provisions have not been invoked, but so long as they remain in the Federal Reserve Act the evils of excessive security loans should be avoided without difficulty. A single but important method of escaping the restrictive measures available to the credit authorities in this country exists in the loans of banks on securities, which may disguise the growth of collateral loans for business men who are borrowing for commercial purposes on security collateral. Although the preference of the banks for loans on marketable securities over the old type of commercial loans is a regrettable tendency, little in recent banking statistics discloses an unhealthy expansion in this type of loan.[8]

SEGREGATION

Section 11 (e) of the Securities Exchange Act of 1934 directed the Commission to make a study of the feasibility and advisability of the complete segregation of the function of dealer and broker, and to report the results of its study and its recommendations to Congress.[9] Originally Congress gave consideration to the exclusion of a provision prohibiting any member of a national securities exchange or any broker transacting business through the medium of an exchange member from acting as a dealer in securities. The storm of protests aroused by the belief that immediate segregation would seriously disrupt the financial machinery and that sufficient information was not available to recommend such far-reaching legislation induced the deletion of this provision.

A "broker" is a person engaged in the business of effecting transactions in securities for the account of others. A "dealer"

[8] For contrary view see "Securities Markets and the Investment Process," Kemper Simpson, *American Economic Review Supplement,* March, 1938, pp. 41 ff.

[9] The report of the Securities and Exchange Commission on *The Feasibility and Advisability of the Complete Segregation of the Functions of Dealer and Broker* (1936) is the source of most of the factual material in this survey. The report was preliminary in character. Important changes in the operations of specialists and in the over-the-counter market have been made since the report was published.

is a person engaged in the business of buying and selling securities for his own account. A person buying or selling securities for his own account, either individually or in some fiduciary capacity, but not as a part of a regular business is excluded from the statutory definition. The broker acts as the agent of his customer and his remuneration is limited to his commission. The relationship is fiduciary and the broker is held to a high standard of conduct. An agent is not permitted to acquire an independent interest and without complete disclosure must not purchase the customer's securities or sell to the customer his own securities. A dealer, on the other hand, receives no brokerage commission and is compensated by the spread between the price at which he buys and that at which he sells, like any other dealer or jobber in merchandise.

It is easy to see how the functions of broker and dealer frequently came to be combined in the securities business. Turning to the early days of the republic, when trading was confined largely to the newly created government stock, we shall assume that Peter Bleecker acted as a broker for William Gates. The latter had bought from time to time $5,000 United States Government 6s. The arrival of the mail from Philadelphia brought reports of a stormy Cabinet meeting at which Jefferson seemed to have the support of President Washington in his opposition to Hamilton's financial measures. The new government 6 per cent bonds were offered down to less than 14s. (par 25s.) compared with the price at which Gates had made his last purchase, 15s. 8d. Bleecker, confident of the Secretary of the Treasury's ultimate victory, was able to buy $3,000 at the low price of 14s. At the time he had no specific buying orders from Gates or any of his other customers. In the next day's newspaper, which carried the quotations, Gates observed the fall in price and sought out his broker and friend, Bleecker, saying: "If I had known of the fall in stock, I should have purchased $2,000 additional." Bleecker might reply: "Well, I succeeded in buying some yesterday and will let you have part of my purchase, but instead of the usual commission, I think it is proper that you should pay me 14s. 6d. Last night at Fraunces Tavern, the opinion was general that the softening of prices was but temporary." Gates agreed. Bleecker had become a dealer as well as a broker. As a matter of fact, with the lack of rapid means of communication it is likely that in the early transactions the dealing and brokerage functions were often united.[10] Later when new enterprises were formed—mainly banks, with a few ambitious industrial undertakings like the Society for the Establishment of Useful Manufactures—the brokers and dealers acted as agents, although capital was principally obtained originally through subscriptions by the corporation itself. Underwriting was a later development.

With the development of the stock exchange machinery, especially in recent years, the complexity of the system increased. In addition to the fact that many firms were exchange members, dealers and underwriters, further classification developed and must be described before the reasons for segregation are discussed.[11] Along with specialization, which in a sense might have been a general influence making for segregation, the business developed so that several of the various functions were generally exercised by one individual or firm.

Definitions and Functions

Commission brokers are the principal means through which the public buys and sells securities on the exchange. These firms generally extend credit to their customers who have margin accounts; borrow and lend securities for customers; and act as depositories for the safekeeping of customers' securities. They may also act as principals in underwritings, in the distribution of securities, and in trading operations for firm account. They commonly furnish investment advice to customers and may manage discretionary accounts. Firm members may be managers or directors of investment trusts, although this is now less frequent than formerly. The interrelationships may be further complicated when such firms hold customers' securities in pledge and free funds on deposit. Partners of such

[10] For this period, the highly interesting chapter on "The Rise of Stock Speculation, 1784-91" in *Essays in the Early History of American Corporations*, by J. S. Davis, Vol. 1 is recommended.

[11] Full descriptions are contained in the report referred to on p. 155.

firms as a rule trade for their own account and are often directors or officers of corporations whose securities are listed on
the exchange.

The Commission's report, in discussing the dual nature of
many brokers, comments: "Where the broker and dealer functions are combined in a single person, his own interests may
conflict with the interests of those to whom he owes a fiduciary
duty. This conflict may react to the disadvantage of his brokerage customers in a variety of ways. A broker who trades for
his account or is financially interested in the distribution or
accumulation of securities, may furnish his customers with
investment advice inspired less by any consideration of their
needs than by the exigencies of his own position. The securities, equities and credit balances of his customers may be
endangered by the risks which he incurs in making excessive
commitments for his own account. A complicating factor in
these situations is that the average investor too frequently
is unaware of the distinction between the broker and dealer
relationships and hence takes no account of the possibility
that the advice and service proffered by a broker may be
affected with a powerful, independent interest at variance
with his fiduciary obligation. As a method of safeguarding
the investor from dangers of this type, complete segregation
of the broker and dealer functions has been proposed."

The floor broker has little direct contact with the public
and is engaged primarily in the business of executing orders
for other exchange members and member firms. He is also
known as a "two-dollar" broker, because his commission for
some time was $2 for buying or selling 100 shares of stock.
Usually he also trades for his own account. Therefore, he acts
both as a broker's broker and as a principal.

The floor trader is engaged primarily in buying and selling
securities as a principal for his own account on the floor of
the exchange. He has no contact with the public, although he
may act as a broker for a few personal customers and from
time to time may execute orders for other members or firms.

The Commission's conclusions concerning the floor trader
follow:

(1) Members who trade for their own account while on the floor enjoy certain competitive advantages over the general public in that (a) the cost of effecting purchases and sales is materially lower for them than for nonmembers; (b) they can trade extensively with less capital than nonmembers; and (c) their presence on the floor enables them to make and revise their market appraisals more promptly than nonmembers upon the first manifestation of any trend or shift in trend.

(2) Floor trading is predominantly of the in-and-out variety.

(3) Members on the floor, during the period studied, traded with the daily price trend more frequently than against it, and thus tended to accentuate the trend of market prices on a majority of the days considered. It is not clear, however, to what extent they merely followed such trends.

(4) Trading by members for their own account may fairly be said to contribute in some measure to the continuity of the market and to the liquidity of securities. The utility of floor trading in this regard was materially impaired during the period under observation by the fact that it was principally centered in active securities.

(5) Floor trading tended to stabilize the market during about one-third of the period under observation.

John T. Flynn, in *Security Speculation*, criticized the floor trader's alleged advantages in the following words: "Those who are fond of describing the Exchange as a free market will remember that there is a vast difference between the position of the floor trader with his freedom from commissions, his inside information, his intimate and immediate view of the course of the market, and that of the outsider who must wait for the ticker report, who must pay commissions to a broker and who must also pay financing charges no matter for how short a time he holds a stock. A game in which two groups occupy such unequal positions can hardly be called 'free.' "

Much of his illustrative material was based on incidents that took place before the Securities Exchange Act went into effect. Before eliminating the floor trader it would be interesting to learn what the average return on capital has been over the past several years. The impression that the floor trader is almost infallible in his trading is erroneous. There is probably less reason for eliminating the floor trader than for permitting members of commission firms to trade for their own account, whether the trading takes place on the floor of the Exchange or from the office.

The odd-lot dealer's business is that of filling orders in amounts of less than the unit of trading at a fraction above or below the effective round-lot price. The unit of trading on the New York Stock Exchange is 100 shares, except in certain inactive stocks in which it is 10 shares. It is not necessary for our purpose to describe the odd-lot system. The bulk of the business is handled by a few firms specializing in odd-lot business. These firms do not deal with the public directly, but obtain their business from commission houses which in turn act as agents for those desiring to buy or sell odd lots. Transactions of the odd-lot firms are confined to the purchase and sale of lots smaller than the unit of trading and the purchase and sale of round lots to offset such odd-lot transactions. As they do not conduct a general brokerage business, the combination of functions is not present. The odd-lot broker (as distinguished from the odd-lot dealer) is engaged primarily in executing orders for the account of the odd-lot house with which he is associated. He has no public customers.

The bond broker generally also acts as a dealer because the exchange market in bonds is less continuous than in stocks and a larger volume in listed bonds is transacted in the over-the-counter market than on the exchange. Firms specializing in bonds generally carry an inventory. The bond broker and dealer on the floor of the exchange functions as a commission broker when he acts for the customers of his own firm; as floor broker when he acts for other firms; and as a trader when he takes positions for himself or his firm.

The inactive members are made up of a miscellaneous group. They include those who hold memberships in order to derive the benefit of greatly reduced commission charges in their personal dealings; those who purchased memberships largely to profit by an increase in their market price; and those who are connected with investment banking firms which utilize the memberships to obtain the privileges of member firms. Only the last group would be affected by segregation.

THE SPECIALIST

The specialist characteristically combines the functions of broker and dealer. As a broker he effects transactions for the account of other members and their customers in a particular stock or group of stocks; as a dealer he effects transactions for his own account. Elsewhere has been presented an outline of the present rules governing the activities of the specialist.[12] The Commission, after a careful survey of the arguments of the champions of the present system and its opponents, and of a considerable amount of statistical data, concluded: "(1) The specialist enjoys competitive advantages over the general public similar to those of other members on the floor; in addition, by virtue of the great volume of trading in which he participates and by virtue of his exclusive access to the information contained in his 'book,' he enjoys the advantage of special knowledge of the market for the securities which he handles.

"(2) The specialist has exceptional opportunities to engage in manipulative activity, by reason of his exclusive information concerning the existence of bids below and offerings above the market. Since the enactment of the Securities Exchange Act of 1934, however, the Commission has found little evidence of such manipulative activity by specialists.

"(3) Specialists, during the period under review, traded against the daily trend more often than with it, and thus, on the whole, did not tend to accentuate price trends but contributed to the continuity and orderliness of the market. However, it should be observed that, insofar as they traded with their books, rather than with others, they tended to augment the spread between bid and asked prices and thus to diminish the continuity of the market.

"(4) During the period studied, specialists traded in moderately active and inactive stocks in relatively greater proportion than in stock stocks.

"(5) In the capacity of broker, the specialist renders a useful service in the execution of limited and stop-loss orders.

"(6) Although it is argued that the brokerage activity of

[12] Page 158, etc.

the specialist renders him peculiarly liable to loss through errors, for which he must find compensation in trading, the evidence is too inconclusive to justify giving any weight to this contention.

"(7) The specialist has an important incentive to maintain a stable and orderly market."

Between June 22, 1935, and October 16, 1937, except for the period from December 14, 1935, to February 28, 1936, during which the data were not assembled, Dr. Dolley's later study shows that the round-lot transactions of the specialists gradually rose from 9.6 per cent to 10.1 per cent of the stocks in which they were specialists. Since the regulations concerning specialists were widened in the interest of the public and the responsibility of maintaining on orderly market was imposed on them, few complaints have been heard as to the system. Commissioner Douglas appears to be convinced of the necessity, nevertheless, of forbidding specialists from acting as dealers or from trading for their own account or for firm account. At this writing it has been suggested that a trial period be instituted during which, in a selected number of listed stocks, specialists will act only as specialists executing orders; during this period they will be forbidden to trade for their own account as dealers and will have no responsibility for maintaining an orderly market or stabilizing prices. Such a test seems desirable. Assuming that stocks with various degrees of activity are chosen, and the test period includes active and inactive markets, sharply rising and declining markets, a more certain judgment as to the merits of the present system will be available.

When the Commission made its study it obtained from the New York Stock Exchange a functional classification of its members.

The Over-the-Counter Market

The over-the-counter market presents essentially the same condition, with some differences owing to its structure. Practically all over-the-counter firms combine the functions of dealer and broker, and many are engaged also in the underwriting business. Especially in communities outside the large

CLASSIFICATION OF NEW YORK STOCK EXCHANGE MEMBERS ACCORDING TO
PRIMARY FUNCTIONS AS OF OCTOBER 1, 1935

Primary function	Total exchange members	Member partner of firms	Individual members	Primary function	Total exchange members	Member partner of firms	Individual members
Commission broker.....	391	391	......	Specialist............	348	248	100
Floor broker ($2 broker).	158	30	128				
Floor trader...........	35	4	31	Active members.....	1,148	774	374
Odd-lot dealer.........	25	25	......	Inactive members.....	227	163	64
Odd-lot broker.........	115	6	109				
Bond broker and dealer .	76	70	6	Total..............	1,375	937	438

cities, segregation would mean a disruption of the securities
business as it has been conducted. The volume of business of
small firms and individuals is too small to support specialized
activity, and to remain in business, participation in all activities is necessary. Usually, when an order is solicited for the
purchase of a security, the dealer function predominates.
Ordinarily, the dealer tries to sell to his customers securities
in which he has a position or in which he is interested as a
member of the selling group. This is a merchandising job for
which he is entitled to a reasonable profit; or he may be
interested in the purchase of a security, using advertising or the
mails to obtain selling orders from owners. The dealer usually
specializes in a more or less limited number of securities, in
some of which he may make a market.

On the other hand, unless an order involves special difficulties, where the initiative is taken by the customer in giving the
order, an essentially brokerage function is performed, whether
the transaction is made "net" or a brokerage fee is charged.
If, as is often the case, a security is purchased from a customer
with the knowledge that it cannot be immediately sold, a different situation obtains. This illustrates some of the difficulties
attending a rigid splitting of the functions in the over-the-
counter market.

If the securities business were set up *de novo*, a more logical
arrangement probably could be formulated. Inconsistencies
and temptation for unfair practices could be reduced. But the
extension of the Commission's authority over additional areas,

the cooperation of the Stock Exchange, and the new Maloney
Act covering the over-the-counter market will moderate any
evils arising out of the present mingling of activities. The
effectiveness of the regulations against manipulation and the
use of options by market operators, the "daylight" trading
rules, the understanding by customers of the capacity in which
the broker-dealer acts in a given transaction by reason of
disclosure, have tended to eliminate some of the reasons adduced in favor of segregation. Evidence recently submitted
shows that in the comparatively profitable years, 1935 and
1936, three conservative brokerage-underwriting firms about
broke even from their commission and trading activities, and
that underwriting was the sole substantially profitable department.[13] Practically all financial activities are extremely un-
even and spasmodic, precluding such planning as is possible
in many divisions of industry and commerce.

Under the circumstances it is felt that great care should be
taken in making further changes. We are aware of the present
defects in the structure of the securities business and markets
and have admittedly made great strides in reducing them. On
balance, there is probably some advantage in a customer being
served by one firm. Segregation would make it necessary for
many investors to deal with two or more firms. If the professional aspect of the securities business is to be stressed,
the investor should have sufficient confidence in one firm to
familiarize it with his security portfolio. If it were in the
hands of three firms, we should have a constant tug of war,
based on the desire of the various firms to increase the customer's business with the broker, dealer, or underwriter. A
public with a better financial education will be alert enough
to make a change if the service rendered is unsatisfactory or
if the results are poor.

Although differences exist as to detail, the Commission itself set forth the statesmanlike attitude that will assure the
best results. It said: "The existence of abuses arising from the
combination of broker and dealer functions is recognized; the
intrusion of a substantial percentage of dealer activity, largely
of a speculative character, is also apparent. By one stroke, to

[13] Article by Burton Crane, New York *Times*, August 28, 1938.

divorce the dealer and broker functions or to suppress dealer activity, or both, would mean simply to stand on the faith that the elimination of certain abuses by such methods would automatically have the effect of reducing speculative activity to the extent that a safe and sound economy demands and no further. But that such an effect would result rests on conjecture.

"An evolutionary but direct approach, pointed toward abuses and toward the restriction of types of speculative activity, enables one to test the waters by gradual approaches rather than to dive headlong into them. By such an approach, effects upon liquidity, continuity, and stability can be measured and gaged as action is taken, and adjustments made in the light of the experience acquired. Emergencies may well justify a comprehensive course of action based more on moral and economic faiths than on rational deductions; but in the absence of such a compulsive demand for a comprehensive program of immediate action, the processes of trial and error seem the course of wisdom."

CHAPTER VII

Thin Markets

The Evidence Reviewed

BEFORE considering the effects of a less liquid market—a market more sensitive to a given quantity of buying or selling, with consequently greater price changes per unit of trading—the evidence that the market is thinner will be reviewed.

The insert on page 164 is a tabulation of the relationship between the volume of transactions and the price changes for thirty individual common stocks during the winter of 1936-1937 and the winter of 1930-1931, which was the most recent period when the general price level of stocks was similar to that prevailing when the report of the special committee of the New York Stock Exchange was made. For the twelve days of the first period during which the market prices as a whole experienced the greatest declines, the total amount of recession in the price of the common stock of Westinghouse Electric & Manufacturing Company, for example, was determined and the average volume of transactions per $1 and per 1 per cent decline was computed. Similar computations for twelve days in the early part of 1937 were also made. As the table shows, in 1930-1931 the market absorbed sales of 26,800 shares for each $1 decline, whereas in 1937 it absorbed only 800 shares for each $1 decline in price. Corresponding figures per 1 per cent decline were 21,300 and 1,100 shares. During advancing markets in 1930-1931, 16,900 shares were necessary to create an upward move of $1 whereas in the second period trading of 1,900 shares was accompanied by a simliar advance. Corresponding figures per 1 per cent advance were 16,600 and 2,800 shares.

Wide variations are reported in the thirty stocks covered. The average for thirty stocks did not show nearly so great

REPORTED VOLUME OF TRANSACTIONS PER ONE DOLLAR AND PER ONE PER CENT CHANGE IN PRICE

Name of Stock	Advancing Prices Average for Twelve Days				Declining Prices Average for Twelve Days			
	Thousands of Shares for Price Change of							
	One Dollar		One Per Cent		One Dollar		One Per Cent	
	1930-31	1936-37	1930-31	1936-37	1930-31	1936-37	1930-31	1936-37
Westinghouse Electric & Manufacturing Company	16.9	1.9	16.6	2.8	26.8	0.8	21.3	1.1
General Electric Co	41.8	16.2	20.0	8.1	64.8	8.5	29.6	4.8
General Motors Corp	65.4	34.3	26.7	24.6	94.8	22.4	34.3	13.8
Chrysler Corp	74.1	9.4	14.4	12.1	56.8	5.4	9.4	6.5
Anaconda Copper Mining Co	25.6	15.6	9.0	7.1	42.3	15.6	13.2	9.2
International Nickel Co. of Canada, Ltd	70.6	19.1	12.1	11.6	90.6	7.8	14.5	5.2
United States Steel Corp	23.5	14.5	34.0	10.6	32.8	9.8	43.4	11.3
Bethlehem Steel Corp. (Del.)	20.8	8.1	12.1	5.9	27.1	4.3	14.6	4.0
Montgomery Ward & Co. Inc	38.4	12.1	8.0	7.0	27.8	6.2	5.0	3.8
Woolworth (F. W.) Co	10.1	7.2	6.0	4.4	11.2	5.9	6.7	3.1
General Foods Corp	16.3	7.5	8.9	3.0	15.4	7.0	7.6	2.9
Corn Products Refining Co	4.3	3.5	3.8	2.6	3.5	2.3	2.4	1.4
Pennsylvania R. R. Co	8.6	12.2	5.1	5.1	7.4	6.7	4.3	3.0
Atchison, Topeka & Santa Fe Railway Co	0.8	3.5	1.5	2.8	2.2	2.9	4.1	2.4
Union Carbide & Carbon Corp.	14.2	3.5	8.7	3.5	22.2	1.8	12.1	1.8
American Tel. & Tel. Co	5.4	1.7	10.3	3.1	10.3	2.9	19.9	4.8
Standard Oil Co. of N. J	15.8	14.9	7.9	9.4	40.6	7.1	18.4	5.1
American Can Co	20.0	2.9	24.4	4.0	34.5	1.8	38.6	1.8
Johns-Manville Corp	4.7	0.4	3.1	0.6	4.6	0.4	2.6	0.5
Briggs Mfg. Co	57.1	4.7	11.1	2.9	23.6	2.7	3.4	1.3
Shell Union Oil Corp	15.6	7.9	1.4	2.0	52.1	1.8	4.1	0.5
Bendix Aviation Corp	17.2	10.5	3.6	3.1	13.8	7.1	2.3	1.8
American Radiator & Stand. San. Corp.	27.2	28.4	4.9	6.6	23.5	12.7	4.4	3.2
Texas (The) Corp	9.8	10.8	3.4	4.8	18.1	16.7	5.7	9.6
Reynolds (R. J.) Tob. Co. "B"	24.1	22.2	10.0	10.0	11.4	12.0	5.3	6.0
United States Rubber Co	9.3	11.0	1.3	4.5	8.8	3.8	1.2	2.2
Western Union Telegraph Co	1.1	3.8	1.5	3.4	1.1	1.7	1.4	1.2
Southern Pacific Co	1.1	9.4	1.1	4.1	3.1	4.9	3.1	2.8
Radio Corp. of America	58.0	96.4	9.9	11.3	81.6	129.5	13.7	13.6
Northern Pacific Ry. Co	1.6	12.2	0.9	3.3	2.1	7.6	1.1	2.5
Averages for 30 Stocks	18.5	10.1	11.3	6.9	23.1	6.7	13.1	4.7

The dates selected were those of larger price change for the market as a whole.

In the 1930-1931 period the dates of advancing prices were: 1931—Jan. 2, 3, 6, 16, 20, 22, 23; Feb. 7, 9, 10, 19, 20. The dates of declining prices were: 1930—Oct. 31; Nov. 5, 10, 17; Dec. 10, 16, 22; 1931—Mar. 27; Apr. 17, 21, 28 and 29. In the 1936-1937 period the dates of advancing prices were: 1936—Oct. 2, 3, 6, 16, 27, 29; Nov. 4, 5, 16, 17, 24 and 27; The dates of declining prices were: 1937—Mar 8, 11, 18, 22; Apr. 1, 2, 6, 7, 22, 23, 24, and 26.

susceptibility to price change as Westinghouse, but the averages were convincing. Here and there stocks were more sensitive in the earlier period (Atchison, Topeka & Santa Fe; Texas Corporation; United States Rubber; Western Union; Southern Pacific; and Northern Pacific) and in other instances only a moderate change is shown. For the thirty stocks as a whole, trading in 18,500 shares was accompanied by a price advance of $1 in the earlier period, and 10,000 shares was sufficient for an equal rise in the latter period; for each decline of $1 in the earlier period the market absorbed 23,100 shares, whereas in 1936-1937 it absorbed only 6,700 shares. Apparently the declines occurred on relatively smaller volume than the advances.

The data in the table recorded price declines in the earlier period for twelve days for each of thirty stocks, that is, 360 price declines. The average of these price declines was $1.25 for the earlier period and $1.33 for the more recent period. The average of price advances was $1.04 for the earlier period and $1.03 for the more recent period.

A study made after the price collapse in October, 1937, on a somewhat different basis produced similar results.[1] In the 1929 period industrial stock prices, as measured by the Dow-Jones average of prices at the close of the day, declined 27 per cent. There was on the average a 4.35 per cent change in prices for each 1 per cent of listed shares traded. In a similar 64-day period in 1937 (August 16 to October 30) the percentage of price change per unit of volume was 12.54.

Independent examination supports the facts submitted by the Stock Exchange.[2] In May, 1935, trading of 50,583 shares of General Motors common stock produced one point of average change in daily closing prices; 19,200 shares traded produced the same effect in May, 1937, a drop of 63 per cent. Corresponding figures for Chrysler showed a drop of 88 per cent. For other active stocks the decline ranged from 25 per cent in the case of Commonwealth & Southern to 82 per cent

[1] New York Stock Exchange *Bulletin*, November, 1937.

[2] The data in this and the following paragraph is based on the discriminating article on "Government Regulation of Stock Trading" by Dr. James C. Dolley in *American Economic Review*, March, 1938, pp. 9 ff.

for General Electric. A test of less active stocks, including all the common stocks the names of which began with the letter "A" (except American Express Company) and providing a sample of 85 to 90 stocks, showed that between May, 1935, and May, 1937, the average spread between the closing bid and ask quotations increased from .70 point to 1.19 points. The average spread in 1937 was 70 per cent above 1935, indicating a distinctly more discontinuous market in 1937. A change of two or three points in stock prices now has no more significance than a change of one point had several years ago. Member trading for own account has been particularly affected. Odd-lot trading has increased. Dr. Dolley concludes: "The security exchanges have become less continuous markets, and stocks correspondingly less liquid. The organized markets have become less able to absorb heavy liquidation and the danger of collapsing price declines has been accentuated. As security marketability has diminished, it has become increasingly more difficult and expensive to raise new capital funds through the flotation of stock and bond issues and business expansion has been retarded accordingly." With the last conclusion, the author is not entirely in accord.

Colonel Leonard H. Ayres has made a somewhat different test. He used the price changes per million shares traded. The line shows for each month from 1930 to September, 1937, the total volume of price changes measured in eighths that have been recorded for each million shares traded on the New York Stock Exchange.[3] These eighths are the totals of the plus and minus changes recorded each day in the stock pages of the newspapers after all the net changes have been reduced to terms of eighths of a dollar. The study includes all the trading and is therefore more comprehensive than the other examinations cited. The price changes varied sharply from month to month from 1930 to 1933. It was not until 1934 when the new regulations went into effect, followed by further restrictions in the following years, that the volume of price changes per million shares traded greatly increased. By 1937 the market was several times as sensitive as in the earlier years of the period reviewed, despite the fact that the average price of stocks was much lower in 1937 than in 1930.

[3] The Cleveland Trust Company *Bulletin*, Vol. 18, No. 9, September 15, 1937.

It is difficult to escape the conclusion that the new regulations have resulted in less activity; lessened activity, in turn, has created a more discontinuous market. There is no way of establishing that any one of the regulations, such as higher margin requirements, restrictions on short sales, regulations governing the activities of specialists, limitation of the activities of insiders, sanctions on manipulation, etc., has been more responsible than any other. The Stock Exchange Committee's report deals at length with the necessity of the short-term dealer, who by being ready to buy or sell at the going price bridges over the inconvenience of time and price and minimizes the risk of ownership. Convertibility into cash in the maximum degree is held to be a paramount requisite of a free market. The report states: "Artificial banning from the market of some of those desiring to purchase or sell securities clearly constitutes artificial restriction upon the ability of the holder to withdraw his savings and of the owner of savings to invest them." The argument for the removal of restrictions concedes that manipulation and the undue use of the nation's total bank credit are to be avoided. The second major line of reasoning is that the narrow market hinders the flow of capital into new security issues.

The inability of the market to absorb readily fairly large blocks of stocks, or to enable investors to acquire at once substantial blocks without causing a stock to rise, results in inconvenience. At times it may result in discouraging the buyer altogether. In the event of necessitous liquidation it may affect the average price at which a stock is sold. A result unanticipated by the authorities is addition to the volume of the transactions in listed securities in the over-the-counter market. Stocks like Union Carbide & Chemical and International Business Machine have been offered and have been distributed through the over-the-counter market. Such distribution is generally made at a price between the bid and ask quotation on the Stock Exchange, and the commission to the distributing firm is usually substantially higher than the stock exchange commission. Transactions of this type have multiplied within the past several years. Other large blocks have been offered to investment trusts and insurance companies. These deals, involving negotiation, are made in a manner contrary to the impersonal purchase and sale conducted in the open market of a maximum number of buyers and sellers. In addition to providing maximum convertibility, this also provides the most appropriate prices. The Stock Exchange Committee states its case in these words: "It is mutual competition in one market of the expression of the needs and desires of the greatest number of individuals which can reasonably be expected to produce at a particular moment the most appropriate price." In an address of the former chairman of the Commission, James M. Landis, the position of the Commission is stated:[4]

"Instead of the common concern that one constantly hears about the difficulty of liquidating at a moment's notice huge blocks of securities in the markets, should not the real concern be with the causes that place strains and stresses of this character upon the financial mechanism? If these strains spring from useless speculative desires the answer is plain. Instead of trying the hopeless task of constructing a mechanism that will absorb the huge pressures of that type, effort must be directed towards closing the investment machinery to the play of irresponsible forces of such a character."

Dean Landis further declared:

"Investment rarely seeks the board room. It rarely follows the hunches of talkative customers' men or the advice of ignorant investment counsel, whose recent rise presents a problem of national consequence. Investment, though it does not despise close market spreads, regards them as of minor consequence in relation to significant trends. How far our trading mechanism is adjusted to emphasize these qualities, rather than to the minutes and seconds essential for the purposes of speculation, may well represent the difference between the hoped for sobriety of the new recovery and the mania of the old.

"One of the fundamental hopes of the [Securities] Exchange Act was that through some consciousness of the nature of corporate enterprise we, as a nation, should develop into investors—rather than speculators. Pure speculation we can tolerate at the race track or elsewhere, where it cannot stalk under the enticing garb of investment. But on the exchanges we sought a

[4] Address, December 4, 1936.

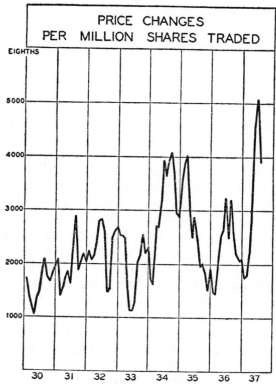

PRICE CHANGES
PER MILLION SHARES TRADED

"The diagram has been prepared to test whether or not there has been in recent years a real tendency for greater price changes to result from a given volume of share trading. The line shows for each month during the eight years beginning with 1930 the total volume of price changes measured in eighths that have been recorded for each million of shares traded on the Exchange. These eighths are the totals of the plus and minus changes recorded each day in the stock pages of the newspapers after all the net changes have been reduced to terms of eighths of a dollar."—The Cleveland Trust Company *Business Bulletin*, Vol. 18, No. 9, September 15, 1937.

reflection of values that have a relationship to something more permanent than mere liquidity. Yet today one wonders where the growing emphasis lies. One wonders just how the battle between the dull registration statements of listed securities and the fascination of the Trans-Lux will eventuate. And the responsibility for that outcome will not be ours alone, nor will its glory, if such there be, be the monopoly of political party or economic creed."

CONSEQUENCES

No measure of the inconvenience or loss resulting to owners or would-be purchasers as a result of thinness of the market or wide spreads between the bid and ask is possible. In the writer's opinion the net loss to the community probably has been exaggerated. Complete liquidity is unrealizable. Modification of some of the regulations could be made without a return to the evils of the twenties and present the maximum liquidity at not too great a price. Uncertain economic conditions and the widespread and deep-flowing differences of opinion between the administration and the financial world undoubtedly contributed materially to the lack of activity and the thinness of the market in the early part of 1938.

The *post hoc* argument is the only one that can be offered to prove that the regulations have curtailed activity and have made for a certain degree of illiquidity. Its weaknesses are obvious, for we can never be sure in the social sciences that one or more of the many other possible causal factors have not been partly responsible for the result. On the whole, the validity of the theory as it affects stock market activity under present regulations has been admitted. By the same token a plausible case can be made out for the opinion that these regulations have held within narrower bounds the extreme swings of the market. Reference to important data on economic conditions and the price of industrial stocks is presented below. Expressed in multiples of earnings or in relation to business activity, the highest prices in 1936 and 1937 were lower than in former years and higher in the early part of 1938 than at the low point of 1932 and 1933. Perhaps, then, when measured by the range of prices over a period of time the regulations have tended to level off the peaks and valleys.

This conclusion must be a tentative one, for it excludes the influence of differences in interest rates on stock prices, the shift to the industrial stocks because of inflation fears, and other possible explanations.

The tremendous increase in stock prices in 1928 and 1929 cannot be explained in terms of industrial production or corporate profits. Production increased only 2.8 per cent between 1926 and 1928; the rise in profits was 13.2 per cent. The average of stock prices advanced from 100 to practically 150, or 50 per cent. The further gain in 1929 was even less related to these fundamentals. In the accompanying tabulation the prices for the years since the Securities Exchange Act has been in effect follow a more logical and less extravagant line in relation to the basic forces that are supposed to determine stock prices. In the spring of 1938, when the production level fell to 76 or to about the same point as in January, 1934, or October, 1933, stock prices remained considerably higher than on these dates. The evidence is not altogether conclusive, but if the result of legislation has been to modify the extremes of price swings and bring them more closely in harmony with underlying factors, the investing public will be the gainer as well as the financial world, which has always suffered from wide, rapid, and unpredictable swings.

Trading Activity and New Financing

The second argument is a step removed. In barest outline it is: reduced volume produces illiquidity; illiquidity, in turn, hampers the sale of new issues and consequently clogs the flow of capital into industry. For many years there has existed a general relationship between the activity of the stock market and the marketing of new securities, especially stocks. New financing has generally risen and fallen in harmony with the phases of the business cycle. Market activity is usually greater in the expansion and boom phases of the business cycle, except for the brief periods of panic or semipanic. New issues are not, however, necessarily synonymous with the flow of new capital into business. Refunding operations and investment trust offerings have made up an astonishingly large part of the new security issues, both in recent years and also in 1928 and 1929. No differently than public works the invest-

STATISTICAL SUMMARY

	(1) Industrial Produc- tion 1923–1925 Aver- age—100	(2) Prices of Common Stocks 1926–100	(3) Corporate Profits (000 omitted)	(4) Volume of Trading Number of Shares	(5) Productive Financing (in millions)
1926......	108	100	$4,008,071	451,868,353	$1,801
1927.....	106	118.3	3,762,334	581,702,343	1,781
1928.....	111	149.9	4,538,027	930,893,276	1,495
1929.....	119	190	5,294,531	1,124,608,910	1,787
1930......	96	149.8	3,226,067	810,632,546	1,939
1931......	81	94.7	1,489,484	576,765,412	796
1932......	64	48.6	277,687	425,234,294	203
1933......	76	63	1,190,002	654,816,452	106
1934......	79	72.4	1,592,149	323,845,634	63
1935......	90	78.3	2,189,124	381,635,752	94
1936......	105	111	3,293,930	496,046,869	379
1937.....	110	112	3,511,200	409,464,570	630

SOURCES

(1) Index of the Board of Governors of the Federal Reserve System.
(2) Index of Standard Statistics Co., Inc.
(3) Compiled by Moody's Investors Service; 1,171 railroad, utility and industrial companies.
(4) New York Stock Exchange Yearbook.
(5) "Productive" issues are those adding to capital goods by raising funds for new construction, additions, improvements and purchase of new equipment (compiled by Moody's Investors Service).

ment of new capital would be most beneficial when industrial activity is declining or at a low ebb and when the nation's capital plant is not fully utilized. The attainment of this ideal is open to question.

The tabulation of productive financing and the volume of stock trading yields interesting results. The enormous increase in the turnover of stocks between 1926 and 1929 was unaccompanied by any increase in *productive* financing. In reality this type of financing was larger in 1924 than later. The larger totals in the succeeding years resulted purely from the sale of investment trust securities and other financial activities. For a time—between 1931 and 1935—the movement of these two series was in the same direction, although it is quite evident that the changes are not even roughly similar. The link breaks again in the subsequent years. With practically no increase in stock trading between 1935 and 1937, productive financing increased almost sevenfold. The increase, it is true, was from an extremely low level. The volume of new issues of this character was three times as large in 1937 as in 1932 when stock trading was somewhat larger. On the other hand, stock trading in 1926 was less than 10 per cent larger than in 1937, but the amount of new securities sold for productive purposes was almost three times as heavy. It seems unnecessary to labor the point. The causal connection between the two series is slight. The volume of stock trading and new capital investment through the sale of securities as distinguished from the reinvestment of corporate profits have not risen and fallen together, as is generally assumed.

INDEX OF TRADING VOLUME AND NEW ISSUES FOR PRODUCTIVE
PURPOSES

1926 = 100

Year	Trading Volume	New Issues	Year	Trading Volume	New Issues
1926............	100	100	1932............	94	11
1927............	129	99	1933............	145	6
1928............	206	83	1934............	72	4
1929............	249	100	1935............	85	5
1930............	180	106	1936............	110	21
1931............	128	44	1937............	90.5	35

Accordingly, whatever else may be the result of modification of present regulations on security trading, no evidence exists to support the thesis that the way to heavy corporate financing for productive purposes is through the encouragement of more active trading.

As the securities market becomes less attractive for the employment of funds for a possible quick profit, genuine investment should be encouraged. Investment in this sense means either lending funds (purchase of obligations in the form of bonds or debentures), the purchase of a limited equity interest (preferred stock), or purchase of a full proprietary interest (common stocks). The object is income and security, or appreciation of capital through the building up of a business enterprise, not the profit obtained through the vagaries of the market.

CHAPTER VIII

THE OVER-THE-COUNTER MARKET

CHARACTERISTICS

UNTIL recently, little information was available concerning the over-the-counter market. Despite its great importance, it was in a sense unorganized. Its very form and far-flung activities make generalization difficult.

What is the over-the-counter market, and what are its chief characteristics? The Securities and Exchange Commission has attempted the following definition or description: "The over-the-counter markets, in general, are the unorganized markets in which there are meetings of individual supply and demand as contrasted with the organized markets on exchanges where there are meetings of collective supply and demand. Over-the-counter market transactions take place in the offices of brokers and dealers and do not involve the facilities of an exchange." Under the Securities Exchange Act of 1934 the over-the-counter markets are deemed to include all transactions in securities which take place otherwise than upon a national securities exchange. Before further examining this phase of the financial world, the chief difference between an exchange market and an over-the-counter market should be mentioned. In the former, buyers and sellers concentrate, and transactions are effected as a result of the meeting of the highest bid and lowest offer under auction rules on the "floor" of an exchange. Over-the-counter transactions are not made in a particular place. Each purchase and sale involves negotiation, whether personally, by telephone (as in the greatest number of instances), by teletype, telegram, or correspondence. Buyers and sellers seek each other out. Transactions are not published and ordinarily are known only to the parties involved.

Early in 1938 there were 6,766 firms of brokers and dealers registered with the Commission, who transacted over-the-counter business, of whom only 1,371 were members of an

exchange. The over-the-counter market has been characterized as a nation-wide web of telephone and telegraph wires.
The volume of business transacted is huge. Over-the-counter
quotations are published for at least 60,000 stocks and bonds,
whereas only about 6,000 separate security issues are admitted
to trading on all the stock exchanges of the United States.
The securities dealt in include United States Treasury bonds,
Home Owners' Loan bonds, foreign stocks and bonds, public
utility stocks and bonds, guaranteed railroad stocks, railroad
equipment bonds, bank and insurance company stocks, investment trust shares, real estate bonds; miscellaneous industrial and railroad bonds and many others. Commissioner
Douglas cited an example of the significance of this vast
market. An estimate made in the summer of 1937 indicated
that insurance company securities with an approximate market
value of about $343,000,000 were admitted to trading privi-
leges on exchanges, as compared with some $1,209,000,000
of insurance company securities which were not admitted to
trading on any exchange. Nor is this all. Large blocks of
stocks listed on the New York Stock Exchange and other
exchanges are frequently dealt in "off the board," as such
transactions may be consummated more quickly and without
disturbing price movements. At one time this was confined
mainly to preferred stocks and inactive issues, but since the
markets have become less liquid, the extent of such transactions has increased and has become a problem to the exchanges.
For many years it has been common knowledge that the volume of listed bonds traded in over-the-counter is many times
heavier than on the stock exchanges. The Securities and Exchange Commission has stated that recent estimates indicate
a volume eight to twenty times greater than on the New York
Stock Exchange. To preserve for itself the largest volume of
business possible, the New York Exchange has adopted a rule
requiring its members first to present on the exchange bids or
offerings for fourteen bonds or less before turning to the over-
the-counter market.

A brief description of the mechanics of a transaction, sim-
plified for purposes of illustration, follows:

Let us assume that the holder of 100 shares of common

stock of Blank Chemical Co. of New Brunswick, New Jersey, who resides in Spokane, Washington, wishes to sell his stock. It is not listed on any exchange; the stockholder is not in a position to communicate with any of the 500 or 600 scattered stockholders; he does not have the stockholders' list and his interest in the situation is not sufficient to attempt to get in touch with the stockholders. He asks his broker or dealer, "What is the quotation on Blank Chemical Stock?" The broker or dealer probably will turn to his quotation sheets and find alongside the name of the security a list of firms with their telephone numbers, who currently appear in the sheets as making a market in the stock. The dealer will then inform the customer that the stock is quoted 18½ bid—offered at 19½; if the customer will advise him as to the number of shares he wishes to sell and at what price, he will endeavor to execute the order for which he will receive the usual commission; or the dealer may act as a principal, taking the stock for his own account at the bid price or at a fair price between bid and offer. The customer is advised as to whether the dealer acts as a principal or as a broker. Many dealers buy or sell for their own account certain securities in which they maintain active trading markets.

As a result of maintaining an active interest in particular securities over a period of time, firms become known as maintaining the best markets in these issues. The experienced dealer or trader, without reference to the sheets or to any other source, will at once communicate with such firms when he has an order in the stocks in which they specialize. Dealers often keep their own records showing who has been interested in particular stocks or bonds. These records have been accumulated over a period of many years at considerable cost and are of great value in obtaining for a customer the best bid or offer.[1]

Because of the structure of the over-the-counter market there is really a wholesale and a retail market. The over-the-counter quotations in the newspapers are usually a little wider

[1] Digested from pamphlet "The Over-the-Counter Market—What It Is and How It Works," issued by Robinson, Miller & Co., Inc., and prepared by the author.

than those of the "inside" market. In other words, if a stock is quoted 40-42 in the newspaper columns, it is often possible for the dealer to buy it at a price somewhat lower than 42, which is considered the retail market. On the other hand, it is not ordinarily possible to sell at a price higher than the bid side of the market; in this case, 40.

The associations formed pursuant to the Maloney Act should make this fact known to the public. Failure to understand it often leads to controversy or embarrassment. The difference made by the dealer is often no larger than the commission on the execution of a stock at the same price on an exchange. The intelligent investor does not object to a reasonable profit if the workings of the market are explained to him.

In addition to the function of the over-the-counter markets in providing a mechanism where investors may purchase and sell outstanding securities through brokers and dealers, this market has another equally important function. Few new securities representing current financing are immediately listed. The public sale and distribution of securities for the national government, the states and their political subdivisions, and of all types of private enterprise takes place over the counter. The primary operations of our greatest financial underwriters are as truly over-the-counter as those of the smallest dealer.

One of the reasons why the over-the-counter market has been an enigma is the absence of a record of transactions effected in over-the-counter markets. No ticker service exists, nor is there a central agency where the investing public can check the prices at which securities are sold. The disadvantages to the investing public have been in possible fictitious quotations and the ease of "rigging" markets under former conditions. The investing public derives some information from the newspapers as to over-the-counter quotations. The number of quotations published is small. Furthermore, the quotations, furnished by organizations of brokers and dealers in the important and financial centers, and by brokers and dealers elsewhere, do not purport to represent actual bids and offers at which purchases and sales may be made, but merely bids and offers between which it is believed that business may be transacted.

Commissioner Douglas, in picturesque language, has declared that the absence of a constantly spinning ticker and many of the casino aspects of exchanges deprives this market of much of the impact on the economic thinking of investors, industrialists, and the general public which is associated with price fluctuations on the exchange. He rightly stated: "It also renders over-the-counter markets very much less attractive as a medium for pure gambling since the score of the game is usually more difficult to ascertain and a rapid change of position more difficult to achieve." The speculator for a turn, on reading of an advance in steel operations or on being told of an impending rise in the price of steel scrap, will buy the leading steel stocks or general market leaders representing businesses in another field. Rarely will he turn to the over-the-counter market. The largest corporations in the great industries may not be represented in the over-the-counter market and, second, unlisted securities are less responsive to changes of monetary significance or of general importance and not directly affecting specific corporations. Furthermore, the investor who owns six stocks and does not "like the market" is more likely to sell the stocks whose fluctuations he may be aware of daily or even hourly than those over-the-counter. To this extent the over-the-counter transactions represent more nearly the results of investment transactions or, more accurately, of purchases made with the intention of longer retention. On the other hand, a greater part of the transactions in the over-the-counter markets is the result of trading among dealers. This was especially true before the advent of the Commission.

The trading department of unlisted firms, or of stock exchange firms with an unlisted department, executes orders for customers in over-the-counter securities and also for the firm in the event that it takes a position in securities. The trader in over-the-counter securities has no exact counterpart. It is his function to execute orders in over-the-counter securities. To this extent the trader combines the duties of the order clerk in a brokerage office and those of the broker on the floor of a stock exchange. He may also "make a market" in securities underwritten by his firm, or in which he specializes. This activity is somewhat similar to that of the specialist.

"Trading," or really the execution of orders in over-the-counter securities, involves a knowledge of the usual sources of supply and demand and familiarity with the activities of other dealers. It is not similar to the transmission of orders in listed securities. In the execution of orders for customers the trader who receives inquiries from dealers tries to anticipate whether the inquirer is a buyer or a seller, and the extent of his interest. In trading for his own or the firm's account a successful trader must have a keen market sense. Restrictions on manipulative practices or rigging of prices, and the reluctance of firms to take a large position, have reduced the trader's activities.

One of the difficulties of the over-the-counter market is that bid and ask quotations are not necessarily good for one hundred shares. On the New York Stock Exchange and other large exchanges a bid and ask, except for stocks in which the unit of trading is less than one hundred shares, is good for at least this amount. In the over-the-counter market, without previously ascertaining the size of the market, one hundred shares cannot be demanded or sold after the market in a stock has been quoted.

Toward Regulation

The need of regulating the over-the-counter market resulted from the possibility of defeating the purposes of the Securities Exchange Act if only the stock exchanges were to be regulated and independently from the practices that flourished unchecked to a large degree—practices that were responsible for the avoidance of over-the-counter stocks by many investors.

The report of the Senate Committee on Banking and Currency to accompany the bill which became the Securities Exchange Act of 1934 stated: "It has been deemed advisable to authorize the Commission to subject such activities [i.e., trading in the over-the-counter markets] to regulations similar to that prescribed for transactions on organized exchanges. This power is vitally necessary to forestall the widespread evasion of stock exchange regulation by the withdrawal of securities from listing on exchanges, and by transferring trading therein to over-the-counter members where manipulative evils could continue to flourish, unchecked by any regulatory authority."

Originally, Section 15 of the Securities Exchange Act of 1934, because of the lack of data or experience to enable Congress to determine upon a plan or regulation in detail, briefly set forth the objectives of and standards for such regulation. It expressly contemplated the adoption of rules and regulations concerning the over-the-counter markets "necessary or appropriate in the public interest . . . to insure to investors protection comparable to that provided by and under authority of this title in the case of national securities exchanges." To that end the Commission was authorized to adopt rules and regulations providing "for the regulation of all transactions by brokers and dealers on any such market, for the registration with the Commission of dealers and brokers making or creating such a market, and for the registration of the securities for which they make or create a market." In May, 1936, the section was amended as the result of the experience accumulated and it was made more specific. The need of regulation was confirmed by specific examples of the extent of the problems connected with the submarginal element among the over-the-counter dealers and brokers. In 1937 the Commission made field investigations in areas outside the main financial centers in Cleveland, Detroit, and the Pacific Northwest. In the space of a few months, as the consequence of inquiry into certain complaints and the making of a brief survey, 13 individuals were convicted in criminal proceedings, 16 more were placed under indictment, 17 corporations and 41 additional individuals were enjoined, and 2 firms were expelled or obliged to withdraw from national securities exchanges. The Commission, it is stated, has reason to believe that the same problem exists in other regions.[2]

Senator Maloney, in submitting the report on the bill that carries his name, summarized the principal aspects of the nature of regulation of the over-the-counter markets: "First,

[2] *Regulation of Over-the-Counter Markets,* Senate Report No. 1455, 75th Congress, 3d Session, p. 3.

to protect the investor and the honest dealer alike from dishonest and unfair practices by the submarginal element in the industry; second, to cope with those methods of doing business, which, while technically outside the area of definite illegality, are nevertheless unfair both to customer and to decent competitors, and are seriously damaging to the mechanism of the free and open market; and thus to afford to the investor an economic service the efficiency of which will be commensurate with its economic importance, so that the machinery of the nation's markets will operate to avoid the misdirection of the nation's savings which contributes powerfully toward economic depressions and breeds distrust of all financial processes."

Important steps were taken by the adoption of a series of rules relating to the requirement that on and after January 1, 1936, brokers or dealers using the mails had to register with the Commission. The Commission for proper cause could deny or revoke registration, which was equivalent to a license to do business. Disclosure and consent were made necessary in the event that a broker acted for both buyer and seller in any security transaction. Disclosure in writing was also made necessary in every transaction with customers as to whether the dealer or broker was acting as a dealer for his own account or as a broker for the customer, and in the latter event, the amount of commission had to be stated. It was also made necessary to state the name of the person from whom such security was purchased or to whom it was sold and the day and time when the transaction took place, or that such information be obtained upon the customer's request.

In August, 1937, the Commission complemented its regulation by the adoption of a comprehensive set of rules effective October 1, 1937, defining practices which it believed manipulative, deceptive, or fraudulent in the over-the-counter market. These rules, in substance, prohibit a broker or dealer from inducing the purchase or sale of any security by any act, practice, or course of business which would defraud or deceive. As fraud is always actionable, the reason for this rule, other than the desire to reiterate and emphasize the Commission's purpose to stamp it out, is to establish a basis for criminal liability. A broker or dealer was also prohibited from inducing a purchase or sale by any untrue statement of a material fact or any omission to state a material fact, if the statement or omission is made with knowledge or reasonable grounds to believe that it is untrue or misleading.

A broker-dealer in a relationship of control with an issuer is required to disclose to the customer the existence of such relationship before he effects a transaction in any security of that issuer. This disclosure may be oral if it is followed by written disclosure before the completion of the transaction, which ordinarily is the time of payment or delivery of the security. This rule was adopted to make manipulation more difficult. Such control gives the broker-dealer a dominant position in "making the market" of the security. For the same reason, restrictions are placed on the offering of an unlisted security at the market or at a price related to the market price, unless the dealer or broker has reasonable grounds to believe that a market for the security exists other than that made, created, or controlled by him or his associates. It is one thing to sell a security "at the market" where a genuine market exists and something else to control the market and pretend that a free and open market exists. Where, for example, an underwriter has disposed of only a small part of an offering, he must of necessity really be the market and, while it is neither illegal nor unethical to continue to sell the security, the customer should be put on notice of the fact. It may be difficult in practice to define "control," which does not necessarily imply ownership of a majority of outstanding stock. Control may be a matter of intent. An underwriter usually buys as a merchandiser and has control only because of the inability to dispose of a security.

A broker who is financially interested in the primary or secondary distribution of a security, or a dealer having such an interest and at the same time receiving a fee from the customer for giving investment advice, is required to give written notice to the customer of his interest before the completion of the transaction. An important prohibition is designed to eliminate the practice of stimulating exchange activity in securities which are being distributed. Anyone engaged in distributing security is prohibited from paying any other person for soliciting or inducing a third person to buy any security of the same issuer on an exchange.

Special rules affecting discretionary accounts were adopted owing to the possibilities of abuse of authority and the temptation of profiting thereby. Transactions which are excessive in size or frequency in view of the financial resources and character of such accounts are specifically made to come within the term of the sanction on "manipulative, deceptive, or other fraudulent device or contrivance." Records of transactions must be made immediately after effecting transactions in such accounts.

Suggestions have been made that, in view of the absence of information as to the actual market in over-the-counter securities, dealers should report to customers the profit on each transaction. The reasons for urging this innovation are clear and deserve sympathetic recognition, but the difficulties seem to be insuperable. The remedy for sharp practices lies in other directions. Let us assume that a dealer has purchased $5,000 principal amount of public utility bonds at 90. The bonds are outstanding in a small amount and transactions are not large. On the day of purchase, January 5, the bond market was weak owing to rumors of inflationary legislation. The dealer had no immediate buyer and has carried the bonds for a week. He has attempted to sell them at retail but without success. Over the week end a ruling interpreted favorably has been announced by the state Public Service Commission on a question pertaining to valuation. The bond market for similar issues turns strong and other dealers bid 94 for X utility bonds, with no offering under 96. One of the dealer's salesmen succeeds in interesting a customer and a memorandum is prepared containing a summary of the facts concerning these bonds. The customer, on reading the memorandum, is informed of the current market and decides to buy the bonds at 95. The dealer has made a gross profit of five points. If he had to report this profit, the customer might be incensed at what seemed an unreasonable profit. Yet the dealer accepted the risk in buying the bonds and partly through a fortuitous circumstance can dispose of them to other dealers at a substantial profit.

Part of the profit has been realized through an actual change in the market, and there is no reason why the dealer should sell the bonds materially below the best offering in the market. The market might have gone against him.

The situation is different where a dealer is really in control of the market. Here he alone, or with one or two other dealers, may arbitrarily raise his bid several points when he learns of the interest of a customer. In this instance he is creating an artificial situation to make a profit. It is this practice that one of the rules of the Commission is intended to prohibit. From time to time gross abuses come to light. These are not border-line cases and are the subject of criminal action. The Commission and the United States district attorney for the Eastern District of Tennessee obtained indictments against a group who sold the stock of Television Electric Corporation as underwriters; most of the funds derived from the sale were consumed by promotional fees. The stock was purchased at prices ranging from $1.25 to $1.50 per share, and these dealers sold the stock at prices ranging from $7.50 to $15 per share.

The rule requiring the dealer or broker to indicate in what capacity he is acting and the amount of his commission has been of great advantage. Many in the securities business had adopted this practice before it was incorporated in the Commission's rules. Unprincipled dealers and brokers sometimes make unjustifiably large profits or commissions on the execution of orders. In executing an order no commitment is required. Accordingly, no risk is involved, and the best practice is for the broker-dealer to act as a broker. For instance, Mr. Smith gives Mr. Jones an order to buy 100 shares of X insurance stock, quoted 19½-21. Mr. Jones may be able to buy 100 shares at 20¼ from a dealer who specializes in the stock. Ordinarily, if there is no difficulty in executing the order, Mr. Jones should be willing to accept a brokerage fee of one-quarter of a point, or $25 on 100 shares. If he has had to induce Mr. Smith to buy a stock, possibly preparing statistical material in the course of the effort, he should be allowed to act as a principal and earn a fair profit. At one time many unlisted firms did not hesitate to make four or five points in a transaction in a moderate priced stock on the execution of an order. The trader knew where he could obtain 44 for a stock, yet in quoting the market on being informed of a customer's intention to sell, would make the quotation 40 bid, offered at 42. Almost simultaneously with the purchase of the stock he would resell at 44.

In transacting unlisted security business the investor must rely on the integrity and high business principles of the broker or dealer to a greater extent than in trading listed securities. Unless he has confidence in the firm with which he is dealing, and reason for such confidence, he would do well to check carefully. Often the honest over-the-counter firm is harried by the investor who does not understand that markets change rapidly. At times situations similar to the following arise: An investor obtains a market in X stock from a firm. The stock is quoted 9½-10¼ in the afternoon, but the investor decides to do nothing until the next morning. He calls to sell the stock at 9½ and becomes irate when he is told that the best bid is now 9¼. Immediately he berates the unlisted market and the firm from whom he obtained the quotation. This is entirely unjust. Markets change, and change frequently and suddenly. If the investor will check the average listed security every fifteen minutes he will observe how often the bid and ask prices vary. Change is the great characteristic of all markets.

THE MALONEY ACT

The Maloney Act, sponsored by the Commission, embodied a plan of cooperative regulation resting upon three years of gradual and orderly growth. As outlined by the Senate Committee on Banking and Currency and by Commissioner Douglas, two alternative programs could be utilized. The first would have involved a pronounced expansion of the organization of the Commission; the multiplication of branch offices, a large increase in the expenditure of public funds; an increase in the problem of avoiding the evils of bureaucracy; and the rigid regulation of business conduct by law. It would involve the expanding of the registration of brokers and dealers with the Commission to include the proscription of not only the dishonest but of those unwilling or unable to conform to rigid tests of financial responsibility, professional conduct, and technical proficiency. In the words of Commissioner Douglas: "This would, of course, entail a regulation by the Federal Government of this business too detailed and pervasive for the brokers and dealers of the country to view with complacency. To select but one example alone of the many further possibilities which will occur to you, it might well be necessary to organize under Federal supervision a system for insuring public dissemination of only such quotations of bid and offering prices for securities as were demonstrably reflective of actual markets and perhaps for the recording of transactions to the end that the fiduciary obligation of a member could be enforced in courts of law. Such a solution of the problem of quotations, while entirely within the realm of possibility, would undoubtedly be burdensome to business and Government alike. Multiplied many times in terms of discretionary accounts, primary distributions, manipulation, advertising, fees, commissions, and spreads and the like, it would entail constant scrutiny of the business conduct of the entire industry. The prospect of such an undertaking is no more agreeable to our Commission than to the brokers and dealers of the country. It, however, is one from which we will not shrink should the logic of events demonstrate its necessity."

Instead, the principle of self-regulation or effective self-government was adopted. What did the proponents of the legislation mean by these phrases? The address of Commissioner Douglas on January 7, 1938, before the Bond Club of Hartford, Connecticut, one of the most important made by any member of the Commission, sets forth the implicit meaning of these phrases. The high standards enunciated are of more significance than a mere expression of hope. It was generally recognized that if the securities business did not prove its ability to maintain "effective self-government" more drastic regulation would be resorted to without hesitation. The Committee report on the Maloney Bill used almost identical language, giving added weight to the views of Commissioner Douglas:

"By self-regulation I do not mean private law making. By self-regulation I do not imply a private club whereby the few can control the many. By self-regulation I do not mean monopoly nor a monopolistic franchise. By self-regulation I do not mean a guild system operating above the law. I do mean, first, self-discipline in conformity to law—voluntary law obedience so complete that there is nothing left for government representative to do; second, I mean obedience to ethical standards beyond those any law can establish. I mean a form of organization of the general kind (but with 1938 improvements) which exchanges have evolved over a long period of time. I mean groups organized under federal auspices and operated under federal supervision with ample contractual powers over members to enable them to take a hand in enforcing the law. These groups would be voluntarily organized and have only such powers as the federal government deemed it wise to give them. The government would retain such power as was necessary or appropriate to make certain that their jurisdiction was adequately delimited, their activities properly circumscribed, their powers appropriately curtailed. The pattern is simply that provided by the Congress for the exchanges in the Securities Exchange Act of 1934. That is the type of self-regulation envisaged here, nothing more and nothing less, except as the differences between exchanges and over-the-counter markets call for an adaptation in details. This type of organization must be so restricted in view of constitutional limitations. It must be remembered in the first place that this is a government of laws, not of men. In the second place, the Supreme Court has often told us that the Congress cannot delegate its law making power. Hence, such organization must clearly conform to that pattern which constitutional law has prescribed."

Mr. Douglas continued: "This type of self-regulation has unquestioned advantages. From the viewpoint of the [securities] business, they are obvious. Self-discipline is always more welcome than discipline imposed from above. From the broad public viewpoint, such regulation can be far more effective, here, than it can be in case of the exchanges. Self-regulation of this kind can be pervasive and subtle in its conditioning influence over business practices and business morality. By and large, government can operate satisfactorily only by proscription. That leaves untouched large areas of conduct and activity; some of it susceptible of government regulation but in fact too minute for satisfactory control; some of it lying beyond the periphery of the law in the realm of ethics and morality. Into these large areas self-government, and self-government alone, can effectively reach. For these reasons such self-regulation is by far the preferable course from all viewpoints."

The method decided upon to provide the framework for regulation, while simple and in harmony with the avowed purpose to preserve the largest degree of autonomy to the over-the-counter business, set up provisions for a form of association. Brokers and dealers may register with the Commission as national securities associations under conditions similar to those covering securities exchanges under the Securities Exchange Act of 1934. However, the formation of associations and the application for registration by them are matters of voluntary choice. Membership in such a registered securities association does not supersede the obligation of the individual brokers or dealers to register. Eligibility to register is limited to such associations as are a proper subject of national concern. It is contemplated that associations, to qualify, should represent a substantial and economically cohesive region. The report of the Senate Committee suggested that the Federal Reserve System's districts might be regarded as an illustration of the type of region that would be appropriate. While particular associations may restrict their activities to a specified region or to members conducting their type of business, it is provided that all brokers and dealers who conduct an honest and responsible business shall be eligible for membership in some association. Improper conduct disqualifies a broker or dealer.

To ensure each member reasonable representation in the affairs of a registered securities association its rules must be fair. They must be designed, moreover, to prevent fraudulent and manipulative acts and practices and to provide safeguards against unreasonable profits or rates of commission. In general the rules must promote just and equitable principles of trade and protect the investor and the public interest, and remove impediments to and perfect the mechanism of free and open market. On the other hand, the rules must not be designed to permit unfair discrimination between customers, or issuers, or brokers or dealers, to fix minimum profits, or to impose any schedule of prices. The existing organizations were fearful that the Commission or the new associations would be directed to fix minimum commission rates or impose schedules of commissions, allowances, discounts, or other charges. All these are prohibited. To safeguard investors against unreasonable profits it is contemplated that associations may adopt rules designed to prevent each member from exacting in any particular transaction a profit which reasonable men would agree was unconscionable in the light of the facts and circumstances of that transaction.

The associations must have rules which provide that the members shall be appropriately disciplined for violations of the rules. Discipline may take the form of expulsion, suspension, fines, censure, or any other fitting penalty. Affiliated associations may be organized, the purpose being to enable soundly organized associations of brokers and dealers which are local in character to retain their identity as registered associations if by affiliation with a national securities association they bring themselves within a sphere that is a proper subject of national concern and make possible coordinated administration.

Any disciplinary action taken by a registered securities association against any member and any action denying admission to membership are subject to the Commission's review. To make the decision of an association final would be contrary to the spirit of the act, and place in the hands of the governing body tremendous power. The legislation differs in this respect from the long-standing New York Stock Exchange rule making disciplinary action final.

If the regulation by association is to be successful, brokers and dealers must be members. It is not made unlawful for brokers and dealers to conduct business if they are not registered. However, a registered securities association may provide that a nonmember broker or dealer may deal with a member only at the same prices, for the same commission or fees, and on the same terms and conditions as are accorded to the general public by members. Exclusion or nonmembership, therefore, will be attended by and implemented with economic sanctions which will make possible effective discipline within the association. The individual member is left free to determine his own business policy, but in so far as he differentiates between other bankers and dealers and the public generally, the rules of the association may compel him to classify nonmember brokers or dealers with members of the public.

The Commission is authorized to abrogate by order any rule of a registered securities association, after appropriate notice and opportunity for hearing, if this appears to the Commission to be necessary to assure fair dealing, a fair representation of the members of an association in the administration of its affairs, or otherwise to protect investors. Subject to notice and opportunity for hearing and only after written request that rules be supplemented or altered is the Commission empowered to order such action with regard to the following subjects: the basis for a procedure in connection with the disciplining of members or denial of membership; the method of choosing officers and directors; the method of adopting changes of additions to the rules and affiliation between registered associations.

Similar authority is granted the Commission with reference to suspension or expulsion and removal of officers and directors of registered associations and for the suspension or revocation of the associations as well. In addition, the Commission may prescribe rules and regulations to prevent fraudulent, deceptive, or manipulative acts or practices; prevent fictitious quotations; provide safeguards with respect to the financial responsibility of brokers and dealers; regulate the manner, method, and place of soliciting business; and regulate the time and method of making settlements, payments, or deliveries. An important provision authorizing the Commission to prescribe rules for the collection, recording, and dissemination of information relating to the over-the-counter markets was struck out. On the other hand, the suggestion of the Investment Bankers Conference, that the statute be changed to accord with the act of 1934 which refers principally to stock exchange activities so that only "willful" violation and not violation alone be penalized, was rejected. The Investment Bankers Association also requested that the Commission define the word "manipulative" fearing the effects on underwriters and dealers in "making a market" for new securities in the event that the precise practices held to be manipulative are unknown. Manipulation, like fraud, is a difficult term to define, and the Commission probably felt that to define the term at this time would restrict it before all the acts and practices that might come within the prohibition had been clearly disclosed. Manipulation on the stock exchanges is regarded as the employment of artificial stimuli for the purpose of controlling the prices or volume of trading of securities and inducing others to buy. Pegging and stabilizing operations during the distribution period of new offerings to prevent abnormal deviations from real values have been the subject of study by the Commission for some years, but it is believed that further study is necessary before definite rules are adopted.

Strong representations were made against the inclusion in the Maloney Bill to regulate the over-the-counter markets of dealers in state and municipal bonds. Dealers in these securities declared that the conditions affecting the sale of municipal bonds were entirely different from corporate securities. The present mechanism has been successful in that even the smallest municipality was able to raise funds without difficulty throughout the depression. The low rates of interest and the high degree of safety and liquidity were also brought forward as evidence of the satisfactory current methods of financing through competitive bidding after public advertising. There was no evidence of the demand from the investing public for regulation, and the law as enacted did not include state and municipal bond dealers.

The over-the-counter market must function well if it is successfully to resist the exertions of the exchanges to have Congress enact legislation to compel corporations whose securities are publicly owned and dealt in over-the-counter to file registration statements and annual reports similar to those filed by corporations whose securities are listed. The challenge is serious. The exchanges are irked by the existing inequality.[3] Naturally, they wish to add to the number of listed securities and are aware that one of the reasons why corporations refrain from attempting to list their securities is the absence of the registration requirements under the Securities Exchange Act and freedom from the need of furnishing fully detailed financial reports.

The increase in the work involved would be so tremendous as to require the Commission to multiply its personnel many times. The Commission, by adopting a neutral "wait and see" attitude at this time, occupies a strategic position, and will be able to move with greater authority after the new order in the over-the-counter market has obtained over a reasonable period of time. Reluctance to take on the burdens of a task of appalling size, except as a last resort, seems to favor the over-the-counter market in this struggle. In the long run, public opinion probably will cast the determining vote. There is also the constitutional question to be considered, since compulsory registration relates to small corporations of entirely local character.

A small minority, still wistfully glancing backward at the "good old days," scoffs at the new order and seemingly intends to cooperate only to the degree necessary to avoid difficulties with the authorities. The frank, admonitory advice offered by a former investment banker who temporarily left the business to work out the principles of self-regulation for the Commission, is none too blunt. The remarks go to the essence of the problem. "It is to the interest of the trade to do a real job. . . . To stall along and merely go through the motions of conforming to the Maloney Act will result in a weak meaningless organization which will have little standing before the public, a poor position in Washington and will be pushed further and further into the background by the exchanges."[4]

[3] See address of Mr. William McC. Martin, Jr., president of the New York Stock Exchange, December 20, 1938.

[4] Address of H. H. Egly, chief of the Over-the-Counter Section, Securities and Exchange Commission, December 7, 1938.

UNLISTED SECURITIES TRADED UPON STOCK EXCHANGES

A fairly important group of securities known as "unlisted securities" are traded upon stock exchanges. A listed security may be described as a security admitted to full trading privileges on an exchange upon application of the issuing corporation. As a condition to listing the issue is required by the exchange rules to file certain significant information concerning the corporation's history and financial condition. A security admitted to unlisted trading privileges, on the other hand, ordinarily has been admitted to trading upon application of a member of that exchange, and without regard to the preferences of the issuer. Consequently, the application is not supplemented by information furnished by the issuer, although the member of the exchange must usually file certain limited information concerning the security, such as capitalization and dividend record.

Although a security admitted to unlisted trading privileges for many purposes is deemed a security registered on a national securities exchange, it is exempted from certain sections of the Securities Exchange Act of 1934 and thus occupies a somewhat anomalous and favored position. The issuer need not file a detailed registration statement, and therefore escapes both the duty of disclosure and the risk of prosecution and criminal liability for false and misleading statements. The officers, directors, and principal stockholders could trade in the securities of the corporation without regard to the provisions concerning disclosure of ownership and accountability for trading profits which govern trading by them in equity securities registered under the Exchange Act, but this was altered by amendment.

In its report on "Trading in Unlisted Securities upon Exchanges," the Commission found that 1,370 issues of stock involving 1,875,291,931 shares and 564 issues of bonds with a face value of $6,882,396,343 were admitted to unlisted trading privileges on sixteen registered national securities exchanges. The New York Stock Exchange discontinued its unlisted trading department in 1911. The New York Curb Exchange is the primary market for unlisted trading: 691 issues of stock involving 400,204,695 shares and 499 issues of bonds with a face amount aggregating $5,976,488,335 are admitted to unlisted trading exclusively on this exchange.

The objections to unlisted trading privileges as assembled by the Commission are as follows:

1. Full and accurate information concerning the issuer is vital to the proper function of a free and open market. A properly functioning exchange market is therefore impossible for unlisted securities.

2. The exchange should not have power to determine the market in which the security is to be bought and sold without the consent of the issuer.

3. Exchanges frequently admit securities to unlisted trading when no real market for the securities exists on the exchange. In such cases it is frequently contended that the exchange quotation reflects only a kind of arbitrage against the over-the-counter market.

4. Manipulative practices have been rife in connection with unlisted trading upon exchanges.

5. The continuance of unlisted trading will involve an unfair discrimination against the issuers of listed securities and will, because of such discrimination, tend to discourage listing and encourage delisting.

6. As a practical matter, it is extremely difficult to bring home to the investing public, the distinction between a fully listed security and one admitted to unlisted trading privileges.[5]

The Commission in examining these objections found that to drive securities from an organized mechanism of control, such as exists on the exchanges, to the comparatively unorganized over-the-counter market, where manipulative or deceptive practices are more difficult to detect and prevent, would be profitless. It required that ticker quotations differentiate between listed and unlisted securities, removing the sixth objection. The exchanges adopted rules to forbid securities without adequate distribution to obtain unlisted trading privileges. The Commission made the point that neither the management nor an exchange was the best authority to determine whether under particular circumstances the public interest is

[5] *Report on Trading in Unlisted Securities upon Stock Exchanges*, Securities and Exchange Commission, January 3, 1936, p. 7.

served by permitting a security to be admitted to trading privileges upon an exchange. Complete termination, it was feared, would draw trading activity away from the local exchanges and promote "concentration in New York of control over the movement of capital in the Nation, a tendency which there is reason to believe the New York Stock Exchange recognizes as being fraught with serious implications."

The Commission recommended that unlisted trading privileges to which any security had been admitted prior to March 1, 1934, may be continued beyond June 1, 1936 (a two-year period of continuance had been originally granted), on such terms and conditions as the Commission might prescribe. The proposed amendments were adopted. No application for unlisted trading privileges shall be approved unless the applicant exchange shall establish that there exists in its vicinity sufficiently widespread distribution of the security and sufficient public trading activity therein to make the extension of unlisted trading privileges necessary or appropriate in the public interest or for the protection of investors.

The competition for business between the over-the-counter market and the exchanges on which unlisted trading privileges were granted was apparent to the Commission in its report. The characteristic of the securities of both types is nonregistration. Clashes between over-the-counter dealers and the exchanges have occurred as the result of the filing of an application for the termination of unlisted trading privileges. A case in point is the Piedmont & Northern Railway Company. A New York firm made the application for the termination of trading in the road's capital stock on the New York Curb Exchange. It appeared that this firm made or created a market in the stock. The railroad company advised the Commission that it did not desire to be represented and had no objection to the granting of the application. The facts were briefly as follows: There were outstanding 85,845 shares at $100 par value. Unlisted trading privileges were granted in June, 1926. The stock was not listed on any exchange. The ground for the application was that there had been inadequate public trading activity in the stock.

The volume of tradings between June 23, 1926, and September 1, 1936, follows:

Year	Shares	Year	Shares
1926	100	1931	None
1927	975	1932	None
1928	2,100	1933	100
1929	7,075	1934	25
1930	750	1935	None
	1936	50	

On this record the Commission found that there had not been adequate public trading. In considering the consequences of this fact the Commission found that during 1936 there had been offerings on only three days. Bids were highly irregular, moving as much as 10 points in one day. The applicant contrasted this record with its own purchases and sales:

	Bought		Sold	
Date	Number Shares	Price	Number Shares	Price
February 4, 1936	100	53	100	53½
March 11, 1936	100	54	100	54½
March 11, 1936	10	53	10	53½
March 17, 1936	25	53¾	25	54¼
April 7, 1936	25	54	25	55
April 16, 1936	50	54	50	55
July 10, 1936	20	54	20	54¾
July 20, 1936	10	54	10	54¾

The Commission found, that customers might have been deterred from buying the stock around 53 on the over-the-counter market because of the publicly printed bid of 35 or 40. Further, an order to sell might have been executed on the New York Curb Exchange at a price that would disturb the orderly over-the-counter market. The customer might recover upon complaint to the Exchange the difference between the best over-the-counter bid and the price at which the sale was effected, but the disturbance would have been created. The Commission held: "The excuse for the continuance of unlisted trading privileges rests primarily upon the ground that the exchange furnishes a valuable focal point for the trading in these securities. The contrary has been proved to be true in this case."[6]

[6] 1 S.E.C., pp. 916 ff.

A different set of facts was presented by the application of the New York Curb Exchange for permission to extend unlisted trading privileges on Utah-Idaho Sugar Company $5 par value common stock. It appeared that on October 15, 1936, 2,242 stockholders in the State of Utah owned 1,297,588 shares, or over half of the 2,370,000 shares outstanding. In the calendar year 1936, 220,728 shares were traded on the Salt Lake Stock Exchange. Of the 1,075,412 shares owned outside of Utah, 582 persons in the State of New York held 332,105 shares and 118 persons in the State of New Jersey held 270,543 shares. The New York Curb Exchange also emphasized the sizable holdings in several other states. The president testified that in the year ended February 28, 1937, 144 of its member firms alone bought or sold a total of 384,478 shares. The Commission held that sufficient public distribution and sufficient public trading activity existed in the vicinity of the Curb Exchange to render the extension of public trading privileges appropriate in the public interest and for the protection of investors.

Unlisted trading privileges have been obtained by a number of the smaller stock exchanges in securities already registered on the primary markets. The attitude of the Commission has been sympathetic to the endeavor of the smaller exchanges to build up their business. To obtain approval, the applicant exchange must provide evidence of sufficient distribution and active trading in the security in the vicinity of that exchange. The underlying policy is that if these exchanges are placed in a position to serve more effectively as a market for local securities, a regional consciousness will be developed and a barrier will be raised against further concentration of the capital markets. The privilege has been granted where the basic requirements are met and the investors' interests are safeguarded in the execution of orders.

The Boston Stock Exchange has taken the leadership in the movement, having obtained unlisted trading privileges for odd lots in fifteen security issues, thirteen of which are listed on the New York Stock Exchange and two on the New York Curb Exchange. Other beneficiaries have been the markets in Los Angeles, San Francisco, Philadelphia, Pittsburgh, Detroit, and Cincinnati.

CHAPTER IX

NEW FINANCING

PURPOSE OF SECURITIES ACT OF 1933

THE choice of securities most suitable for various types of financing is a proper subject for treatises on corporation finance. The larger subject of capital investment and its economic consequences is also outside the scope of this book. The present method of financing and the changes wrought by the Securities Act of 1933 concern the businessman, on the one hand, and the investor, on the other. The act grew out of the revolt against financial practices with which the decade leading to the collapse of 1929 has become identified. In reality, this period only underlined defects that were prevalent since the rise of the modern corporation. Not all public financing, however, was tainted with the abuses which inevitably hastened the demand for change and resulted in the losses that spurred the nation into action. To eliminate losses resulting from economic change or poor judgment is not the purpose of the act. But too large a part of the new financing was conducted so that the losses of the investing public were inherent in the new issue. Failure to disclose the facts, misstatements, lighthearted disregard of the responsibility of investment banking and the duties of directors, all amidst a background of dazzling speed, were the main evils to be corrected. These evils cluttered the main avenues of new financing; the bystreets and alleys with their flimsy promotions and sucker lists needed other correctives.[1] The Act of 1933 has been referred to aptly as the "Truth in Securities Act," which describes its primary purpose and is the broad underlying principle. To achieve this aim the act does not set up,

[1] If anyone wishes to refresh his recollection as to the desirability of national legislation, he is referred to the convenient summary of Investment Banking Practices published by the Senate Committee on Banking and Currency, Report No. 1455, 73d Congress, 2d Session Stock Exchange Practices—1934.

as it might have if it had been the legislative embodiment of a totalitarian philosophy, positive standards, or pass upon the desirability of permitting an industry to ask for a part of the capital available for investment, or dictate the channels into which capital may flow.

The method adopted was to proscribe fraud, but not to seek to thrust any responsibility upon government to earmark the good, bad, and indifferent:[2] "Instead, it placed upon government the duty to secure a measure of disclosure in the hope that an informed public would have both the ability and independence to guide the direction of its national savings. It does not strike at the inalienable right of the private investor to make a fool of himself. He was still free to choose if he wanted them, speculative mining shares, participation in race tracks, and other speculative enterprises. The hope is, that in the light of knowledge, investment can most profitably be still a matter of private choice."

The main objective—to require a full and fair disclosure of the material facts regarding securities offered for sale or sold in interstate commerce or by use of the mails, and to prevent fraud in the sale of securities—is accomplished by the means of registration statements required to be filed with the Commission in respect to all but exempted securities.

REGISTRATION

The registration statement must contain information set forth in great detail in the act. In a general way the information concerning corporations may be grouped under the following headings:

Pertaining to corporations (issuer)
    State of Incorporation
    Location of principal business office
    General character of business
    Statement of capitalization and description of securities
    Statement of securities, if any, covered by options
    Purposes of financing

[2] Address of former chairman of the Securities and Exchange Commission, James M. Landis, at the National Alumni Association Meeting of Princeton University, February 22, 1936.

Estimated net proceeds to be derived from the security to be offered

Price at which proposed security is to be offered

Commissions or discounts to be paid

Expenses of financing, including legal, engineering, etc.

Net proceeds of previous financing within two years preceding filing of registration, and details as to price, underwriters, etc.

Names and addresses of vendors and purchase price, etc., of any property acquired or to be acquired (not in the ordinary course of business) to be defrayed out of proceeds of financing, and details regarding commissions or other expenses relating thereto

Name and address of counsel who have passed on legality of issue

Details of every material contract (not in the ordinary course of business) to be executed at or after filing of registration statement; any management contract or contract providing for special bonuses or profit sharing arrangements; patent contracts, and certain contracts with public utility companies

Balance sheet as of a date not more than 90 days prior to date of filing registration statement; if not certified by an independent public or certified accountant, a similar balance sheet so certified as of a date not more than 1 year prior to filing of registration statement

Profit and loss statement for latest fiscal year and two preceding fiscal years, certified by an independent or certified public accountant

Balance sheet and profit and loss statement for three preceding fiscal years of acquired business, if any part of proceeds is to be applied to purchase of any business

A copy of the opinion of counsel in respect to the legality of the issue

A copy of all material contracts referred to, but disclosure is not required if Commission determines that disclosure would impair value of contract and is unnecessary for protection of investors

A copy of articles of incorporation; trust agreement of issuer if a trust, articles of copartnership if a partnership, etc.

A copy of underlying agreements or indentures affecting any security to be offered

Any amount paid within two years preceding filing of registration statement or intended to be paid to any promoter

Pertaining to Underwriting

Names and addresses of underwriters

A copy of underwriting agreement

Commissions or discounts paid to underwriters, including cash, securities, contracts or anything else of value (such as options)

Pertaining to Officials, Directors and Large Stockholders

Names and addresses of directors, chief executive, financial and accounting officers, and of promoters if business has been formed within two years prior to filing of registration statement

Names and addresses of all persons owning more than 10 per cent of any class of stock of issuer; or more than 10 per cent of aggregate stock within 20 days prior to filing of registration statement

Amount of securities held by officers and directors, underwriters within 20 days prior to filing of registration statement and if possible as of 1 year thereto; and amount to which such persons intend to subscribe

Full particulars of interest of directors, executive officer and stockholders owning more than 10 per cent of stock of any class or aggregate in any property acquired or to be acquired (not in ordinary course of business) within two years preceding filing of registration statement

The financial statements must be more than the perfunctory skeleton forms required by some state laws. The balance sheet must show all the assets of the issuer, the nature and cost thereof, whenever determinable, with intangibles segregated. Loans in excess of $20,000 to directors, officers, or controlling stockholders must be stated in detail. The surplus account must show how and from what sources such surplus was created. The profit and loss statement must show what the practice of the issuer has been as to the character of the charges, dividends, or other distributions made against its various surplus accounts. Depreciation, depletion, and maintenance changes shall be set forth in proper detail, and the statement will differentiate between any recurring and non-recurring income, and between any investment and operating income.

The registration statement must be signed by the issuer, its principal executive officer or officers, its principal financial officer, its controller or principal accounting officer, and the majority of its board of directors. The fee paid to the Commission at the time of filing the registration statement is 1/100 of 1 per cent of the maximum aggregate price at which such securities are proposed to be offered, but in no case shall the fee be less than $25. If any accountant, engineer, or appraiser, or any person whose profession gives authority to a statement made by him, is named as having prepared or certified a report or valuation for use in connection with a registration statement, the written consent of such person shall be filed with the registration statement.

The registration statement is intended to be examined by the experts of the Commission, although it is made available to the public and copies are furnished at a reasonable charge per page. The arrangement of the data and the length of the contents make it unserviceable as a document to submit to the investor. The prospectus, in the language of the statute, means "any prospectus, notice, circular, advertisement, letter or communication, written or by radio, which offers any security for sale." Securities are offered through the prospectus, which is based on the registration statement, but it need not contain the documents specified in the Act.

Before examining a representative prospectus, it is to be observed that in the case of corporate issues the information falls into two major classes: that having a direct bearing upon the financial worth of the securities and that tending to show whether there has been an abuse of trust on the part of persons holding fiduciary or quasi-fiduciary relationships with the issuer.[3]

THE PROSPECTUS

While new security offerings must be made by means of a prospectus, the prospectus need not be used by the underwriter to the exclusion of other selling documents. Annual reports, supplementary information of a descriptive character, comparison with other securities, opinions of investment advisory services, and other material may be, and as a matter of practice are, in common use. Investment bankers and other critics of the Securities Act of 1933 have complained that the

[3] Harold H. Neff, "Forms for Registration of Securities under the Acts of 1933 and 1934," *Harvard Law Review*, Vol. LI, No. 8, June, 1938.

prospectus is excessively cumbersome. The director of the Division of Forms and Regulations of the Commission, Harold H. Neff, in two statements concerning the method of condensing the description of securities in prospectuses, admitted that in many instances they have been so long and cumbersome as to destroy their usefulness. He stated that the prospectus is intended to be read by people making business judgments, and that the meticulousness of lawyers in drawing such documents as corporate indentures is out of place in a prospectus.[4] By its rules and instruction books the Commission indicated that it understood the problem of underwriters. In one of its instructions books, the Commission states: "The information set forth in the prospectus, except as to financial statements required to be furnished, may be expressed in condensed or summarized form." And, "where the incorporation by reference in the registration statement proper of matter contained in exhibits is permitted a similar incorporation by reference may be made in the prospectus." The Securities Act specifically provides that no liability imposed shall apply to any act done or omitted in good faith in conformity with any regulation of the Commission. Lawyers have been slow to avail themselves of the chance to make the prospectus more readable and less cumbersome. In the statements referred to, the spokesman for the Commission illustrated how five pages of material concerning the issuance of further securities under an indenture securing an issue of first mortgage bonds of an operating public utility could be summarized in less than a page. The condensation was stripped of as much technical verbiage as possible and to the average investor would be clear, whereas in the original the important statements were obscured in a mass of detail. Some progress has been made in this direction. A number of draftsmen now use the one-page newspaper prospectus as a convenient summary.[5]

[4] Securities and Exchange Commission, Securities Act of 1933 Release No. 1503, July 12, 1937, and Release No. 1580, October 19, 1937.

[5] The prospectus of the $100,000,000 10-year 3¼ per cent debentures of the United States Steel Corporation, dated June 2, 1938, contained 58 pages. The great mass of material in the registration statement was skillfully summarized, and the description of the corporation's properties and activities make interesting reading.

A more serious objection to the Securities Act was the outcry that the liabilities imposed must stifle the offer of new securities. The stringency of the civil penalties in the original act was modified by the amendments of 1934. Briefly, false registration statements that become effective create a liability on the part of every person who signed the registration statement; every person who was a director of or performed similar functions at the time of filing; every person who, with his consent, is named as about to become a director or person performing similar functions; every accountant, engineer, or appraiser, or any person whose profession gives authority to a statement made by him, and every underwriter. The amendment makes the right of recovery conditional on proof that the plaintiff, if he acquired the security after the issuer has published a statement of earnings covering a period of at least twelve months after the effective date of the registration statement, acquired the security relying on the registration statement. However, reliance may be established without proof of the reading of the registration statement. The amendment reduced the liability to purchasers who have made their investment more than a year after the original public offering. All other investors may recover whether or not they relied on the false statement or were aware of the omission.

All persons except the issuer may be relieved of liability in any event by showing that they acted in good faith and exercised due care. The standard of reasonableness prior to the amendment, in determining what constitutes reasonable investigation and reasonable ground for belief, was that required of a person occupying a fiduciary relationship. Furthermore, the amount of recovery has been limited in the present law by providing specific rules for measuring the damages. These rules provide that the recovery shall represent difference between the amount paid for the security (not exceeding the offering price to the public) and

(a) the value thereof at the time the suit was bought, or
(b) the price at which the security was sold before suit, or
(c) the price at which the security was sold after suit but before judgment if such damages shall be less than the damages representing the difference between the amount paid (not exceeding

the original offered price) and the value at the time the suit was brought.

The last is intended to avoid the temptation of investors to hold a security in the hope that a rise will reduce the actual loss with the thought that they will be protected against further depreciation. In all cases, if the defendant proves that any part of the damages represents other than the depreciation in price resulting from the part of the registration statement with respect to which liability is asserted, this portion of the damages shall not be recoverable. Under the present law the liability of underwriters is restricted to the offering price of the portion of the issue underwritten by him, whereas the original act made each underwriter responsible up to the entire amount of the issue. No action may be maintained under the civil liability provisions arising in connecton with false registration statements or in connection with prospectuses unless brought within one year after the discovery of the untrue statement or omission; or after such discovery should have been reasonably made; or if it has been brought within one year after the violation upon which it is based if it relates to the prospectus. In no event shall any action be brought more than three years after the security was offered to the public or three years after the sale. The limitations period has been drastically reduced—originally, suits could be initiated within ten years after the security was offered for sale.

To afford a measure of protection against "strike" suits, the court may in its discretion require an undertaking for the judgment of costs, including reasonable attorney's fees. If judgment is rendered against a litigant, costs may be assessed against such party if the court believes the suit or defense was without merit, these costs being assessable in an amount sufficient to reimbuse him for the reasonable expenses incurred in connection with the suit—this provision was added by amendment.

If one were assumed to know nothing of the evils which the statute was intended to eradicate, or the provisions of the law, would not the standards required in the registration provisions be regarded as reasonable? The information required to be disclosed is not dissimilar to what a prudent commercial banker requires in making an important loan (bank loans are usually for short periods, whereas corporate obligations in the form of marketable securities are mainly long-term) or the information without which a businessman would not enter a business enterprise as a partner. As a matter of fact, when a large financial institution purchases an entire bond issue and the transaction is exempt from the registration provisions of the act, because both the issuer and the purchaser are incorporated within the same state, the information required by the investor (in this case a financial institution which is an expert investor) is not less searching or extensive than required by the act. An outline of the questions to be asked of and the data to be furnished by corporations seeking funds from the "new business" department of an important investment banking firm prior to the Securities Act is strikingly similar to the questions in the registration forms.

The development of proper forms and the standardization of practices naturally required time and involved changes. Delays and uncertainties proved irksome to issuers and underwriters. The Commission wisely pursued a trial-and-error course instead of rigid policies. Forms have been adopted for various types of business, such as that for seasoned corporations with the purpose of eliminating "from the old registration form requests for information not specifically required by the act and which was not essential to adequate protection of the investor, and to phrase questions and explain the nature of the information to be filed so clearly that all uncertainty would be removed from the minds of the officials of the issuing company." There are special forms for mining securities, investment trusts, certificates of deposits, and securities in reorganization. It is encouraging to note that the Commission is constantly endeavoring to improve the administration of the act. A different basis for the registration forms to fill certain gaps and reduce the total amount of formal regulation has been suggested.[6] Rules of the Commission provide that persons wishing to object to public disclosure of any application, re-

[6] Harold H. Neff, "Forms for Registration of Securities under the Acts of 1933 and 1934," *Harvard Law Review*, p. 1370. Vol. LI, No. 8, June, 1938.

port, or document filed by them may file the confidential portion of such material with the chairman of the Commission, together with a statement of the grounds on which the objection is based. Aside from applications concerning annual reports, etc., during the year ended June 30, 1937, 68 applications were made for confidential treatment of material contracts or portions thereof in registration statements. Of these 65 were granted in their entirety, 1 was granted in part, 1 was denied, and 1 was withdrawn.[7] On the whole, registration imposes no onerous burden. For the first time the investing public has access to information enabling it to appraise intelligently the securities it is asked to buy. For the first time, too, the investor has adequate protection against abuses by those in a position to misuse their knowledge or office.

LIABILITIES IMPOSED BY THE ACT

Have the liabilities imposed opened the gates to a multitude of suits against underwriters or corporate officials? Are the standards set so high as to frighten business and finance into avoiding registration, at the expense of industrial progress and the expansion of business? The original act, we have observed, has been drastically amended. These modifications, already noted, corrected its stringent standards and practices and met the bona fide contention that they rendered the law unworkable. Yet the widespread impression has remained that the law invites lawsuits and leaves issuers and underwriters wide open to great losses without enabling them to interpose adequate defenses. A perusal of the law provides its own answer to these allegations.

The acid test of a depression and bear market in which new offerings suffered large depreciation in value has been met. As noted in a judicious survey of the Securities Act of 1933: "It is a significant fact that the principal criticism of the Act has been directed against the civil liability provisions, which have been virtually unused by the public."[8] Companies

[7] Third Annual Report of the Securities and Exchange Commission. See also the interesting comment in "The Administrative Process" by James M. Landis, (1938) p. 42, etc.

[8] Jay W. Blum, "The Federal Securities Act, 1933-1936," *Journal of Political Economy*, Vol. XLVI, No. 1, February, 1938, p. 92.

EXPENSES OF FLOTATION OF 217 COMMON STOCK, PREFERRED
COMPARABLE DATA WERE AVAILABLE). REGISTERED UNDER
SIZE OF
EXPRESSED IN PERCENTAGES OF GROSS AMOUNT OF SECURITIES PRO

Size of Issue (000)	COMMON STOCK						PRE			
	Under $250	$250 to $499	$500 to $749	$750 to $999	$1,000 to $4,999	Total	Under $250	$250 to $499	$500 to $749	$750 to $999
TOTAL										
Number of Cases	33	19	21	10	22	105	9	11	8	3
Commission and discount	19.9	17.8	17.2	15.8	14.3	15.8	14.3	17.5	10.0	14.1
Other expenses	2.5	2.0	1.9	2.4	1.4	1.8	3.0	2.0	1.8	1.6
Total	22.4	19.8	19.1	18.2	15.7	17.6	17.3	19.5	11.8	15.7

BREAKDOWN OF "OTHER EXPENSES" OF ISSUANCE AS INDICATED IN THE REGISTRA
BOND, NOTE AND DEBENTURE ISSUES EXPRESSED IN PER

Number of Cases	33	19	21	10	22	105	9	11	8	3
Listing fees	.085	.083	.035	.130	.053	.065	.079	—	.128	.089
Registration fees	.013	.010	.010	.014	.011	.011	.011	.013	.012	.023
Revenue stamps	.097	.025	.058	.034	.020	.035	.085	.064	.075	.093
State qualification fees	.140	.092	.036	.108	.039	.061	.206	.150	.042	.075
T. A. & reg.: Trustee fees	.035	.042	.056	.114	.032	.048	.028	.012	—	—
Printing and engraving	.220	.228	.213	.323	.197	.221	.407	.269	.329	.222
Legal fees and expenses	1.046	.764	.694	.923	.659	.739	1.566	.745	.763	.680
Accounting fees and expenses	.550	.225	.442	.537	.239	.335	.482	.400	.271	.275
Engineering fees and expenses	.038	—	.070	.021	.032	.034	—	.017	—	—
Other & miscellaneous expenses	.265	.505	.316	.220	.111	.216	.147	.284	.167	.173
Total other expenses	2.489	1.974	1.930	2.424	1.393	1.765	3.013	1.954	1.787	1.630

that have registered new issues have not been harassed by suits
for damages. There is no record of any suit to enforce the
civil liability provisions during the first two years it was in
effect. Two actions were reported in the third annual report
of the Commission as cases under the Securities Act of which
the Commission was informed. Other suits may have been
commenced, but the fears, still encouraged by careless statements in the press, that the investor would rely on suits to
recover losses caused by material misrepresentation in registration statements are unfounded. The care with which statements are examined and the cooperation of reputable issuers
and investment bankers have removed the likelihood of the
civil liability provisions ever becoming the bogey which they
were made out to be. There is no evidence whatsoever that

STOCK AND BOND, NOTE AND DEBENTURE ISSUES (FOR WHICH THE SECURITIES ACT OF 1933 DURING 1937, CLASSIFIED BY ISSUE POSED TO BE OFFERED FOR CASH SALE FOR ACCOUNT OF REGISTRANTS

FERRED STOCK					BONDS, NOTES AND DEBENTURES								
$1,000 to $4,999	$5,000 to $9,999	$10,000 to $24,999	$25,000 or More	Total	Under $250	$250 to $499	$500 to $749	$750 to $999	$1,000 to $4,999	$5,000 to $9,999	$10,000 to $24,999	$25,000 or More	Total
17	2	2	2	54	5	7	5	2	15	3	13	8	58
8.1	3.2	2.8	2.7	4.4	5.9	6.4	5.6	2.8	3.3	3.6	2.1	1.8	2.1
1.2	0.5	0.5	0.3	0.6	3.3	2.9	4.2	1.4	1.5	1.2	1.0	0.5	0.7
9.3	3.7	3.3	3.0	5.0	9.2	9.3	9.8	4.2	4.8	4.8	3.1	2.3	2.8

TION STATEMENTS ANALYZED ABOVE, OF COMMON STOCK, PREFERRED STOCK AND CENTAGES OF AMOUNT OF CASH OFFERING IN EACH SIZE GROUP

17	2	2	2	54	5	7	5	6	15	3	13	8	58
.028	.016	.014	.018	.022	—	—	—	—	.007	—	.020	.014	.015
.011	.010	.011	.010	.011	.016	.016	.010	.011	.011	.044	.011	.010	.011
.073	.103	.115	.100	.097	.049	.011	.214	.053	.100	.110	.149	.123	.128
.057	.020	.008	.003	.020	.081	.042	.031	.012	.089	.011	.005	.009	.013
.046	.020	.022	.018	.023	.421	.110	.198	.148	.081	.065	.128	.057	.078
.269	.086	.077	.046	.109	.226	.111	.512	.169	.304	.187	.201	.080	.129
.388	.158	.102	.058	.171	1.606	1.200	1.676	.486	.617	.426	.223	.067	.160
.161	.012	.064	.037	.081	.503	.368	.468	.210	.180	.105	.076	.026	.053
.016	—	—	—	.003	.054	—	.245	—	.024	—	.030	.008	.016
.224	.065	.109	.018	.087	.348	1.033	.805	.324	.134	.216	.108	.110	.120
1.223	0.490	0.522	0.308	0.624	3.304	2.891	4.159	1.412	1.547	1.164	0.951	0.504	0.723

legitimate public financing has been held back by these provisions.

A third objection remains. It is contended that the cost of registration weighs heavily on new financing, or that the necessary costs are actually prohibitive. In the year ended June 30, 1937, registered securities with estimated gross proceeds of $3,633,086,000 were offered for cash for the accounts of registrants. In connection with the sale of these securities the registrants estimated that they would incur $140,963,000 of expense, of which $26,013,000, or .7 per cent of the estimated gross proceeds, represented expenses of registration, such as fees of experts, printing, legal expenses, etc. In other words, on the sale of securities for which the issuer received $1,000,-000 the expenses of flotation and issuance, other than commissions and discounts, would be $7,000. Part of this expense would be necessary in any event.

The tabulation on pages 208-9, prepared from data compiled by the Securities and Exchange Commission, is a complete answer to the "too expensive" theory. The breakdown of expenses other than underwriting commissions and discounts shows that even for common stock offerings of less than $250,000 the other expenses are only 2.5 per cent. Commissions and discounts in this group were approximately 20 per cent.

The expense entailed by the Securities Act must be discarded as a possible explanation of the failure of the market for new issues (other than refunding or investment trust issues) to expand more rapidly. It is true that the expense is a more important factor for the relatively small enterprise, but the very small corporation has been relieved of the registration requirements. Under the terms of the Securities Act the Commission is authorized to add to the statutory exemptions any class of securities where the aggregate amount at which the issue is offered is $100,000 or less, "if it finds that the enforcement of this title with respect to such security is not necessary in the public interest and for the protection of investors by reason of the small amount involved or the limited character of the public offering." Pursuant to this section of the act, the Commission has adopted reasonable rules.[9] In compliance with the request of President Roosevelt to consider "such simplification of regulations as will assist and expedite the financing, particularly of small business enterprises," it reduced the financial information required in registration statements for issues of established enterprises and broadened the exemption for issues under $100,000.[10]

COMPARISON OF PROSPECTUS AND OFFERING CIRCULAR

Generally, attention has been centered on the abuses in large underwritings and the outright frauds practiced by swindlers. A large number of secondary issues of the class that authorities

[9] Rules 201 and 202.

[10] Securities and Exchange Commission, Securities Act of 1933, Release No. 1722. See also "Security Financing under SEC Exemptions," pamphlet published by the Twentieth Century Press, Inc.

have been anxious to promote show in striking manner the changes wrought by the Securities Act of 1933.

To illustrate concretely the difference in the information because of the disclosures now required and the responsibilities fixed by law, comparison has been made of two stock underwritings of small corporations of similar size and engaged in a kindred business. These were offered by the prospectus of Philip A. Singer & Bros., Inc., dated September 8, 1937, and an offering circular of Federal Fur Dyeing Corporation, whose stock was offered in 1928. In choosing these as illustrations, no reflection on the corporations is intended. More informative prospectuses and less informative circulars could have been used for purposes of illustration. The issues represent a fair example of the financing of the small corporation at present and before the Securities Act of 1933. It is a coincidence that the pro forma balance sheet of one showed total assets of $769,911 and of the other $786,465. The earlier offering was made by a circular containing four pages, of which the first was solely a title page and the fourth contained the pro forma balance sheet. The 1937 offering was made by a 22-page prospectus. Although information is not to be measured by the number of words used, the reader will be able to judge for himself the value of the prospectus in making an intelligent appraisal of the value of a security as either a speculation or an investment.

I am aware of the allegation that the average investor does not read the prospectus. Agreed. I am ready to go further. The average investor is not competent to interpret or evaluate the data made available by the prospectus and registration statement. The persuasion of salesmanship and the confidence reposed in investment banking firms and dealers, more than voluminous reading matter, are responsible for the distribution of securities. That the underwriter and issuer have had to compile the required information is of itself some advantage to the investor. The benefit is enhanced by the liabilities imposed for violating the full disclosure principle.

The careful, intelligent investor has been given more information than ever before, and those who are not able to use the data may at all times refer to qualified individuals for an

Present: Securities Act of 1933 and Rules of Securities and Exchange Commission	Before Securities Act of 1933

Business and History

General statement of origin and development	General statement of origin and development
Peak production and lowest activity stated	No statement
Average number of employees	No statement
Details of terms, option as to price, etc., details of business, connection if any, of owners of business optioned and officers and directors of issuer, or leading stockholders; financial statements of optioned business	Option to purchase stock of two corporations, business of which is peculiarly adapted to and will fit in with business of issuer

Plants

Details of leases, rentals, renewals, contracts, etc.	Premises are occupied under long-term leases, with provisions of renewal
Construction of plants	No statement
Statement of pending suits for infringement of trademarks, royalties, etc.	No statement
Statement that issuer knows of no proceedings contemplated by governmental authorities	No statement

Capitalization

Present capitalization and previous changes, especially changes leading to capitalization after new financing	Present capitalization

Underwriting and Offering

Statement as to: Net Proceeds to company	No statement except offering of 20,000 shares of common stock
Provisions of underwriting agreement as to price paid corporation, underwriting discounts or commissions; proceeds to issues, proceeds to stockholders; options to underwriters and officials and terms of options	
Agreement to make application to list within 12 months, and statement as to payment of expenses, etc.	Agreement to list—no time limit
Concessions to be allowed selling group	No statement
Statement that underwriter may buy and sell for long or short account and description of limitations	

Purpose of Financing

Details: Payment of bank indebtedness	
Payment to other creditors	Only statement: "and the proceeds of the issuance thereof will be used for general corporate purposes"
Payment of mortgages	
Payment for redemption of preferred stock or bonds	

| Present: Securities Act of 1933 and Rules of Securities and Exchange Commission | Before Securities Act of 1933 |

Present: Securities Act of 1933 and Rules of Securities and Exchange Commission

Payment for improvements or additions to plant or for purchase of machinery (in detail)

Balance for working capital

Earnings

Complete year to year statement of income, profit and loss statements,
Details as follows:
Gross income or sales
Less discounts and allowances
Cost of production
Selling and shipping expenses
Administrative expenses
other income
other deductions

Balance Sheet

Over 60 separate items
Balance sheet as of May 31, 1937
Pro forma balance sheet as of May 31, 1937, after giving effect to proposed financing and acquisition of the assets and liabilities of corporation and the liquidation of certain liabilities
Inventories (as taken and valued by the company)
Chemicals
Work in progress
Finished work
Note to balance sheet:
"The inventories were certified by the officers of .... No check was made of this item"
Fixed Assets:
Land and building
Machinery and equipment
Furniture and fixtures
Automobile trucks

Total
Less reserves for depreciation
an appraisal dated July 1, 1937 made by the American Appraisal Company shows:

Before Securities Act of 1933

Net profits only for nine months;
Estimated net profits for year—
Net profit after eliminating certain nonrecurring changes and other income items, and after giving effect to service contracts now to be in effect

Approximately 25 separate items
Only pro forma balance sheet after recapitalization and new financing

Inventories of merchandise, supplies, and work in process
No breakdown or basis of valuation

Fixed Assets:
Machinery and equipment, less reserve for depreciation

Delivery equipment, less reserve for depreciation

| Assets | Reproduction Cost New | Sound Value |

Present: Securities Act of 1933 and Rules of Securities and Exchange Commission	Before Securities Act of 1933
Land	Not broken down
Improvement to leased buildings	
Building construction and fixtures	
Machinery and equipment	
Office furniture and fixtures	
Automobiles	
Notes payable	Notes payable
Banks	
Creditors	Not broken down

Notes to balance sheet:

"We have made an examination of the Balance Sheet of Philip A. Singer & Bros. Inc., as at May 31, 1937, and the Statement of Operations and the Surplus Account for the five months ended May 31, 1937. In connection therewith we have examined or tested accounting records of the Company and other supporting evidence and obtained information and explanations from the officers and employees of the Company; we also made a general review of the accounting methods and of the Operating Statements for the years 1934, 1935, 1936, but we did not make a detailed audit of the transactions. We did not verify the quantities and conditions of the inventories, which quantities and conditions were certified to us by responsible officials of the company.

"In our opinion, based upon such examination, the accompanying financial statements fairly present, in accordance with accepted principles of accounting consistently maintained by the Company during the period under review, the financial position of the Company as at May 31, 1937, and the results of operations for the five months ended May 31, 1937."

"We have examined the books of account and records of the Federal Fur Dyeing Corporation, a New York Corporation, as at September 30, 1928. We have also examined the agreement dated October 23, 1928, providing among other things for: (a) amendment of charter of Federal Fur Dyeing Corporation, changing the authorized capital stock to 150,000 shares without par value and the issuance of 80,000 shares in exchange for presently outstanding capital stocks of said company: (b) the sale of 20,000 additional shares for cash: and (c) the reduction of value of processes and formula to $1.00.

"We hereby certify that the above pro forma balance sheet correctly sets forth the consolidated financial condition at the date stated as it would have appeared had the above mentioned transaction been consummated at that date and after giving effect to the retirement of bank loans to cash received in a part liquidation of a certain account receivable and the subsequent acquisition by the Federal Fur Dyeing Corporation of the entire capital stock of David Goldberg, Inc."

Management

Names and Addresses	Names
Salaries—agreement to limit for 3-year period	No statement

Present: Securities Act of 1933 and Rules of Securities and Exchange Commission	Before Securities Act of 1933
Persons owning 10 per cent or more of stock	No statement
Names	
Amounts	
Per cent of class of stock	
Reference to further information in registration statement	
(18 items), including:	
Remuneration paid to officers, directors, employees, and others	No statement
Revaluation of investments	
Consents of experts	
Names of certified public accountants who have certified financial statements since February 1, 1932	

informed opinion. Without the information, intelligent appraisal is impossible. In the relation of trustee and cestui que trust, and in other relationships growing out of confidence and good faith, extreme care is used in drawing the legal documents. They alone are no assurance of wise and honest administration, yet none would advocate the omission of carefully drawn legal documents.

Extended comment is hardly necessary on the major differences between the facts contained in the foregoing documents. Above all, the detailed financial statements stand out in one instance. Without them the beginning of an analysis cannot be undertaken. In the case of Federal Fur Dyeing Corporation a single item, "net profit" is published. This item is adjusted "after eliminating certain nonrecurring charges and income items, and after giving effect to service contracts now to be in effect." The investor is left to guess at the amount of the "nonrecurring charges" and the nature of the "service contracts." Since the gross business handled and the various classifications of operating expenses are not furnished, neither the margin of profit nor the relative importance of various groups of costs is available. Not one economic characteristic of the industry is made known. The single pro forma balance sheet is worthless. Every business executive, credit manager, banker, or security analyst knows that comparative statements over a period of years are necessary to determine the progress of a business. Even the single balance sheet is seriously deficient. Inventories are lumped into one item, and the basis of the valuation of fixed assets is not made known. Important items are not broken down into their component parts.

The price at which the underwriters bought the stock is lacking. Furthermore, no one can determine if they have a commitment or simply a contract under which they act as selling agents.

To secure firsthand knowledge of the inclusiveness of a typical prospectus the reader is urged to obtain a prospectus from an underwriter of an industrial or public utility security. To illustrate further the effect of the Securities Act of 1933 by direct comparison, there is shown at the end of this chapter an outline comparison of two offerings of the same issuer, Commonwealth Edison Corporation.

By taking at random a number of prospectuses, the type of information previously unavailable and now placed before the investor is illustrated.

The Montana Power Company in offering its first and refunding mortgage bonds set forth the fact that the Anaconda Copper Mining Company is its largest customer. It went further and in a footnote to the statistical data gave the percentage of electric energy sold to the Anaconda Copper Mining Company in relation to the total output. The gross revenues from sales of industrial electric revenues were broken down into divisions, such as smelting and reduction and metal mining. The balance sheet item "plant, property account and equipment" contained in parentheses the amount of intangibles and referred to a comprehensive note on the subject. As the intangibles made up $57,000,000 out of a gross amount of $117,154,253, the importance to bondholders and stockholders is obvious.

The offering of Cleveland Electric Illuminating Company general mortgage bonds has over a page of data on municipal and other competition. Public utility offerings in territory probably affected by government projects are careful to refer to this probability.

The prospectus of the Bath Iron Works Corporation showed that, of 194,000 shares offered at $12 a share, 50,000 shares were bought from the company at $10 a share and 144,000 shares from a group of large stockholders at $6 a share. The prospectus of Rochester Button Company disclosed that when the corporation had been formed in April, 1926, as a consolidation, the land, buildings, and equipment forming part of the assets acquired were $780,755, the net values shown on the books of the vendor companies. The accounts were immediately written up on the same date to appraised values of $2,217,767. Many of the uneconomic consolidations of the twenties would not have been so successful in offering their securities had such information been published.

To help the reader visualize the difference between the information made available in a typical prospectus and an offering circular prior to the enactment of the Securities Act of 1933, a comparison of the items has been made between two bond issues of the Commonwealth Edison Company. The offering circular of August 2, 1932, incidentally, was an unusually complete document for that period and followed the change of management consequent upon the Insull collapse. Other offering circulars might have been used which would have made the difference even more striking.

It may be that only the trained specialist will read the 69-page prospectus, whereas the four-page document is more likely to be read. By using a one-page summary (as in the prospectus of $58,830,000 Consumers Power Company first mortgage bonds, dated March 19, 1936) a convenient outline may be presented suitable to the average investor. This answers the objections offered against the length of the present prospectuses. We have become so accustomed to reading of vast sums that we forget the importance of a $25,000,000 to $100,000,000 bond issue. It is difficult to point to a large measure of superfluous material in the prospectus as it is issued under the Securities Act. The requirements regarding disclosure of material facts or omission seem to be reasonable, if it be conceded that the investor should be informed. Information may reach the purchaser directly, or indirectly through the services of experts. At present the essential material is generally available. Before the Securities Act of 1933 it was too often available to only a few.

Supplement

COMMONWEALTH EDISON COMPANY

FIRST MORTGAGE 3¾S, SER. H DUE 1965   First Mortgage
5½% ser. G'
due 1962

		Page		Page
Dated	April 1, 1935	3	June 1, 1932	1
Due	April 1, 1965	1	June 1, 1962	1
Date of Prospectus	June 6, 1935	1	Aug. 3, 1932	1
Amount	$29,500,000	1	$18,000,000	1
Underwriters	Names	1	Names	1
Price to Public	98 and interest	1	93 and interest	
Underwriting Discounts	2%	1	_____	
Concession to Selling Group	1½%	3–4	_____	
Purpose	Summary	4	Summary	1
Business	Area served			
	Electric energy produced, purchased and sold	4–6	_____	
	No. of customers and revenues by divisions:		_____	
	Residential		_____	
	Small commercial light and power		_____	
	Large light and power		_____	
	Municipal			
	Railways			
	Other electrical supply companies			
Rates	Summary of schedules		_____	
Property	Description of each generating station	6–8		2
Investments and Advances	Description of Commonwealth Subsidiary Corporation	8	Summary	3
Consolidated Investments and Advances	Division into two groups:	9		
	1. Permanent		Lower than	3
	Book value and market value when available		book value	
	2. Temporary			
	Book value and market value when available		_____	
Earnings	Three-Year Consolidated Statement and Summary—18 items	10	Summary 1922–1932 6 items	3

Supplement

COMMONWEALTH EDISON COMPANY (*Continued*)

Supplement

COMMONWEALTH EDISON COMPANY (*Continued*)

FIRST MORTGAGE 3¾s SER. H, DUE 1965   First Mortgage 5½% ser. G due 1962

		Page		Page
Rate Case	Statement—Summary of Reports of Accountants and Engineers			
Other Pending Litigation	Summary	24–26		
Pending State and National Legislation	Summary	26		
Miscellaneous Factors Affecting Earnings	Tax increases, increases in freight rates, salary and wage restoration	27		
Management	Directors and officers and addresses	28	Brief statement of policies	3
Stockholders	Number—no holder owning 10% of stock	28		
Underwriters	Name and respective amounts underwritten	29		
Historical information, particularly as to revaluation of Assets	Summary	29–30		
Property, Plant and Equipment and Intangible Assets	Summary	30–31		
Combination of Balance Sheets not Consolidated		56–57		
Combination of Income Accounts not Consolidated		62–65		
Combination Earned and Capital Surplus Accounts		66–68		
Restatements of Capital Stock	Summary	31–2		
Auditor's Certificate	In full	32		
Principles of Consolidation Statement		33		
Balance Sheet	Assets—29 items	34–35	Pro Forma assets 20 items	4
	Liabilities—29 items		Liabilities 16 items	
	Notes—3 pages	36–39		

Supplement

COMMONWEALTH EDISON COMPANY (*Continued*)

FIRST MORTGAGE 3¾S, SER. H, DUE 1965   First Mortgage
5½% ser. G
due 1962

		Page	Page
Statement of Investments and Advances	Name of issuer, Amount owned, per cent of issue, book value, market value where available	40–43	
Consolidated Income Account	43 items—1932–1934	44–45	
Consolidated Earned Surplus		46–47	
Balance Sheet	Parent Company only	48–49	
Income Account	Parent Company only	50–54	
Notes Explaining Certain Accounts and Certain Accounting Principles, followed by Subsidiary Companies Not Consolidated	2½ pages	58–66	
Combination of Income Accounts of Subsidiary Companies not consolidated	Three-year statement	62–65	
Combination of Earned Surplus — same		66–67	
Additional information contained in Registration Statement	References to Selected Items Follow: Material Provisions of Underwriting Contract Business experience of principal executive officers Information as to securities of record or beneficially held by each director, officer and each underwriter Rumuneration of Directors and officers Financial Statements and schedules Combination of Balance Sheets of Subsidiary Companies not consolidated December 31, 1934	69–70	

Supplement

COMMONWEALTH EDISON COMPANY (*Concluded*)

FIRST MORTGAGE 3¾s, SER. H, DUE 1965   First Mortgage
5½% ser. G
due 1962

Page

Combination of Income
Accounts of Subsidiary
Companies not consoli-
dated years 1931–1934   ————————
Schedules
15 items   ————————

FULL DISCLOSURE

The registration statement and prospectus may be used in extraordinary ways. During the labor difficulties of the Remington Rand Corporation union leaders protested to the Securities and Exchange Commission, declaring that the description in the registration statement covering an offering of common stock was inaccurate.

The illustrations used above show that care is used in the preparation of the prospectus. Disclosures may be favorable as well as unfavorable to the company or its securities. The facts must be weighed. A doubtful accounting practice, no longer followed, may be offset by other factors. The wide spread between the price paid and the offering price may be due to the anticipated difficulty in overcoming the prejudice against the industry in which the corporation operates. Whatever the facts may be, it is obvious how the present law has helped to reduce the difference in the position of the prospective investor and the so-called insider.

Some indication of the nature of disclosures made as a result of the examination of the Commission is portrayed by the seven typical cases briefly summarized by it:[11]

1. A company engaged in the business of creating and selling to the public a class of securities known as investment contracts sought to register $10,000,000 face amount of certificates to be offered under a so-called investment trust accumulation plan. These contracts provided for either a lump sum payment or monthly installment payments on the part

[11] Securities and Exchange Commission, *Third Annual Report.*

of the purchaser, the net proceeds being used for the purchase of shares of an underlying investment trust which were to be deposited with a trustee, who was to hold them for the account of certificate holders. The plan of investment thus involved a trust upon a trust with two sets of loading or service charges, one on the underlying trust shares and the other on the investment certificates.

2. The certificates to be issued under the periodic or installment investment plans were stated on the face thereof and in the prospectus as having a "maturity value" of $2,000 for each $1,200 agreed to be paid by the investor. The prospectus did not disclose the fact that this figure of $2,000 was purely arbitrary, representing nothing more than the sum which the investor would obtain only when, as, and if the value of the underlying trust shares purchased with the funds paid in, less the charges and reductions, had reached $2,000. The investor had no assurance that the so-called "maturity value" would ever be reached. In fact, by reason of the substantial charges deducted from the $1,200 paid in by the investor, amounting to approximately $200, the attainment of the stated "maturity value" would require a total appreciation of almost 100 per cent of the market value of the underlying securities. This element of contingency was artfully concealed and the use of this term, appearing in the prospectus no less than twenty times, indicated an endeavor to impart to the concept of "maturity value" a specious reality for apparently no purpose other than to mislead prospective investors. The prospectus further, in connection with an elaborate recital of the routine duties of the trustee under the plan, gave unwarranted prominence to the name of the trustee, which was a well-known financial institution, in what appeared to be an unjustified attempt to trade on its reputation. In consequence of such misleading representations and the failure of the prospectus in certain other respects to set forth clearly the information required to be furnished, the Commission instituted stop-order proceedings. The registrant subsequently amended its registration statement and prospectus, eliminating all reference to "maturity value" and otherwise revising the prospectus in keeping with the re-

quirements of full and fair disclosure of the material facts relating to the investment plan.

3. A registration statement filed by a bottling company in connection with a proposed public offering of common stock contained a balance sheet of the issuer which included among its assets franchise rights at a stated valuation of $2,500,000. It appearing from information contained in the registration statement that the valuation ascribed to the franchise rights was excessive, the Commission proceeded to a hearing under Section 8(e) of the act. At this hearing evidence was adduced to indicate that no basis existed for the valuation placed upon this intangible asset, whereupon stop-order proceedings were instituted under Section 8(d) of the act. Upon notice of hearing, the registrant filed an amended balance sheet reducing the valuation of the franchise rights from $2,500,000 to $1.

4. In a similar case involving the matter of property valuation, the balance sheet of a newly organized manufacturing company set forth its fixed assets at a valuation of approximately $700,000. The properties in question had recently been acquired at a cost of $200,000 and were appraised, on the basis of reproduction cost new, less depreciation, at approximately $1,200,000. For balance sheet purposes the company placed an arbitrary valuation of $700,000 on the properties, thus creating a "surplus" of approximately $500,000. The Commission instituted stop-order proceedings on the grounds that the balance sheet representations were misleading and that, in this instance, reproduction cost less depreciation did not constitute a criterion of value since the issuer had not demonstrated successful use of the properties warranting such valuation. As a result of the proceedings the issuer amended its balance sheet to show the properties at cost, $200,000, thereby eliminating the "surplus" of a half million dollars which appeared on the balance sheet as originally filed.

5. A business trust filed a registration statement covering an issue of $800,000 of certificates of beneficial interest, proposing to use the proceeds from their public sale to acquire oil properties which it had previously contracted to purchase from an oil operator in the Mid-Continent Field. Shortly after the effective date of the registration statement a preliminary

investigation was undertaken, which disclosed that the income of the properties was insufficient to support the dividends paid during the promotional period and, in addition, that the sponsors of the trust were misappropriating the proceeds from the sale of securities offered to the public instead of applying these proceeds on the purchase price of the properties. Injunction proceedings were instituted in the Federal Court, as a result of which the promoters were forced to restore the funds that had been diverted and the company was required to make full disclosure to prospective investors regarding the current earnings of the properties. Further investigation established that the estimates contained in the registration statement regarding the value, productivity, and income of the properties had been grossly exaggerated, the estimate of recoverable oil being overstated almost 500 per cent. In addition it was revealed that a certain over-the-counter dealer was selling the trust certificates in a nation-wide campaign involving willful and reckless misrepresentation.[12] Stop-order proceedings were instituted under the Securities Act of 1933 to suspend the effectiveness of the registration statement and proceedings under the Securities Exchange Act of 1934 were also instituted with a view to revocation of the dealer's license.

6. An express trust, created in accordance with the laws of the State of Oklahoma with assets consisting of oil and gas interests in Oklahoma and Texas, filed a registration statement with the Commission on Form A-1 on December 12, 1935. The statement become effective, as amended, on February 19, 1936. Some $1,070,000 of certificates of interest in the trust were sold to the public. In January, 1937, stop-order proceedings were instituted under Section 8(d) of the Securities Act. After full and complete hearings before an examiner and argument before the Commission on exceptions to the examiner's findings, the Commission[13] issued its order stopping the effectiveness of the registration statement. The registration statement was found to be deficient in the following respects:

[12] On July 7, 1937, proceedings to revoke the registration of this dealer were instituted pursuant to Section 15 (b) of the Securities Exchange Act of 1934.
[13] The Commission's order issued after the close of the fiscal year, on September 23, 1937.

(a) The registration statement failed to disclose the identity of the one promoter and failed to disclose the amount of profit that he had made. A great majority of the assets of the trust had been purchased from him.

(b) The statement that quarterly reports would be furnished, when at the time of the hearing no reports at all had been issued.

(c) The failure to disclose certain pending litigation relative to certain of the properties in the trust.

(d) The engineer's reports attached as exhibits to the registration statement were found to include misstatements of material physical facts and to omit facts necessary to prevent the estimate arrived at from being misleading. The reports also, in some instances, failed to follow methods approved in the profession.

(e) The statement of the present monthly income in the registration statement was found to be erroneous. Motions to dismiss the proceedings and to withdraw the registration statement were made in the proceedings, but were denied by the Commission.

7. A manufacturing company filed a registration statement with the Commission for the purpose of registering a large block of its common stock of which approximately 80 per cent was outstanding and to be offered for the account of certain stockholders and 20 per cent represented unissued stock to be offered for the account of the issuer. The registration statement stated that approximately 60 per cent of the company's output was sold to one customer, a large automobile manufacturer. The registration statement contained also, as part of the required financial information, a profit and loss statement covering a six months' period subsequent to the close of the issuer's last fiscal year which apparently indicated, in comparison with profit and loss statements for the three years preceding, a pronounced upward trend in its profits. Investigation by the Commission revealed that the principal customer of the registrant intended in the immediate future to reduce substantially its purchases from the issuer in consequence of certain changes effected in the design of its own product, and, further, that this customer purchased most of its annual re-

quirements during that portion of the year covered by the aforementioned six months' profit and loss statement, a circumstance which would render such statement misleading unless the seasonal nature of the business were clearly indicated. Since full and fair disclosure respecting these matters had not been made in the registration statement, the Commission instituted stop-order proceedings whereupon the registrant, upon notice of hearing, withdrew its registration statement. The issuer later filed another registration statement. This statement properly set forth the limitations attached to the six months' profit and loss statement and indicated clearly the possibility that a large portion of the issuer's business which had accounted for its profits in recent years might be lost as a result of an adverse change which appeared imminent in the business relationship between the registrant and its principal customer.

Sometimes the questions raised are close ones. The ruling of the Commission's examiner may be contested and brought before the Commission for a hearing. The case of the American Kid Company is an illustration of the care exercised and the investigation made by the Commission in reaching a determination. The issue in this proceeding was whether the registrant's statement of "Estimated Returns" was misleading in that the volume and profit figures shown assume the ability to obtain letter of credit financing to the extent of $250,000 without making it clear that the availability of such financing was at least doubtful and perhaps impossible.[14] The principal facts concerning the financial program were these: The aggregate offering price of the stock issue was $500,000. Of the $450,000 net proceeds remaining after allowing for the underwriting costs the registrant proposed to spend $350,000 in securing a factory site, erecting a factory, and purchasing equipment and machinery for the manufacture of glazed kid. The remaining $100,000 was to be allocated to working capital. After the first year of operations the estimated average annual net profit would be $160,000. This figure was based on the assumption that the plant would be operated at its full tanning capacity

[14] Securities and Exchange Commission, *Decisions,* Vol. I, No. 3 (pamphlet), pp. 694 ff., and Release No. 1678, Securities Act of 1933, February 11, 1938.

of 6,000 dozen skins a day. The $100,000 of proposed working capital was to be used exclusively for operating expenses.

The crux of the situation was the statement that the purchase of raw skins would be financed entirely through bankers' letters of credit with trust receipt privileges. It was estimated that the credit accommodations recurrently required would not exceed $250,000 at any one time. The amended prospectus read: "Should Banking Conditions at any time be such that the Corporation could not get credit accommodations in the amount of $250,000, the Corporation would be obliged to curtail its production program of 6,000 dozen skins per day to a production program in keeping with its credit accommodations, and in this instance the estimated profit figures shown on Page 5 of this prospectus and the estimated returns above on this page could not be maintained."

The Commission held that three questions presented themselves. Was the availability of the proposed line of credit doubtful? If there be such a doubt, did the prospectus make this doubt clear? Third, must the doubtful character of the premise be affirmatively revealed? The Commission had three Boston bankers testify as experts. The opinions were strongly against the prospects of lending a company, even with a capable management and one year's successful operations, two and one-half times its working capital on letters of credit with trust receipt privileges. The registrants relied on abstracts of balance sheets on file with the Massachusetts Commission of Corporations, and practices current from 1915 to 1919 and from 1927 to 1929. It was testified that credit standards had been thrown to the winds during the earlier period. In rendering the decision continuing a stop order, the Commission emphasized the implications that might be drawn from the use of the phrase "at any time" and the stress laid upon "Banking Conditions." The Commission held: "The implication which arises from the use of the phrase 'at any time' in this statement and the stress laid upon 'Banking Conditions' is that under normal banking conditions the registrant could undoubtedly obtain credit accommodations of the type and to the extent set forth in the prospectus. In sharp contrast to the implications of the prospectus, favorable to the registrant, is the doubt, if not the impossibility, that it can in fact procure any such line of credit. In view of the grave doubt as to the availability of such extensive credit accommodations under current banking practice, and in view of the further fact that their availability is a prerequisite to the registrant's figure of estimated returns, we find that the prospectus still omits to state a material fact necessary to make the future earnings as estimated therein not misleading."

The few cases that are appealed and the smaller number in which the ruling of the Commission have been upset by the courts is at least prima-facie proof that its functions are being performed without hamstringing legitimate financing.

Every now and then a prospectus reminiscent of the pre-SEC period is issued, but even Homer nodded and the Commission must be careful not to overstep its authority. The 6 per cent cumulative convertible preferred stock of the Brooklyn Daily Eagle Properties Corporation was offered at $25 a share, the par value, plus accrued dividend, and the same underwriter simultaneously offered the Brooklyn Daily Eagle common stock at $1.75 a share. New interests have purchased the newspaper, and this discussion is not a criticism of the present management. For purposes of convenience, Brooklyn Daily Eagle Properties Corporation will be referred to hereafter as the Company and the Brooklyn Daily Eagle as the Eagle. The stock capitalization of these companies was as follows:

COMPANY

	Outstanding
6% cum. conv. pfd. stock (par value $25)...................	40,000 shares
Common stock* (no par)................................	100 shares

EAGLE

Common stock (par value $1)............................	2,689,700 shares

* Owned by the Brooklyn Daily Eagle.

The Company had acquired 400,000 shares of the Eagle's common stock for conversion purposes, since the preferred stock is convertible into Eagle common stock at the rate of ten shares for each share of preferred. The Company previously had acquired two parcels of real property from the Eagle, for which it issued the preferred and common stock. The property consisted of a building originally constructed in 1892, now used as an office building, and a modern building, separated from the older structure by an alley and used as a newspaper plant. The properties were subject to a $990,000 mortgage. From this point the complexities increase.

The next step is that the Eagle, after "selling" the properties, rents them from the Company. It agrees to pay taxes and interest, and a sum sufficient to enable the Company to declare and pay dividends on its preferred stock and, beginning in 1940, to retire a certain amount of preferred stock annually. Until now all that has happened is that the public will purchase $1,000,000 preferred stock; the net proceeds will go to the holder of the common stock of the Company, which is the Eagle, and are to be used principally to buy certain assets, including the circulation and good will of the Brooklyn *Times Union*, a newspaper published in Brooklyn. The Eagle will henceforth publish both papers in its plant and a considerable saving is anticipated. The money to be raised from the sale of 300,000 shares of common stock of Eagle will be used principally for the payment of the Eagle's promissory notes, amounting to over $500,000.

We may review the transaction in outline: The consolidated picture is that outside of the purchase of the Brooklyn *Times Union*, the earnings assets of both corporations remain the same. What were the earnings? And here we find the answer, in all likelihood, to the complex transactions and switching back and forth of assets and obligations. The Company, it will be remembered, owns only the buildings, which it has leased to the Eagle. The circulation and earnings of Eagle, on which rest the value of its rental agreement, were as follows:

	Average Circulation [1]		Earnings	
	Daily	Sunday	Gross	Net Loss
1932	100,407	85,974	Not published	
1933	95,591	75,666	$3,377,083	$239,927
1934	93,290	90,515	3,400,613	302,950
1935	91,839	87,873	3,182,318	232,119
1936 [2]..................	89,042	85,643	2,596,602	175,756

[1] Ten months ended October 31.
[2] Year ended March 31; for the 9 months following that date, 88,695 daily and 84,161 Sunday.

There is no information as to the earnings of the *Times Union*. It was common knowledge that the Company had not been successful. Only one statement in the prospectus refers to the financial experience of the *Times Union*. It read: "While the registrant has been unable to secure information from the Brooklyn Times Union, Inc., with respect to its losses or net earnings, it believes that for the past several years the company has not had any net earnings."

Should not the prospectus of the Company have pointed out the Eagle's losses? The prospectus was a joint one, and exceedingly involved. It appears that if the Eagle on its record had attempted to sell a preferred stock, the effort would have been futile. The lease and rental arrangement seemed to give the preferred stock of the Company added strength and security. It relieved the issuer from relying on a poor earnings statement. The control of the enterprises remained with the Eagle, which in turn was owned by the Brooklyn Publishing Corporation, which in its turn was controlled by the president. The Company's preferred stock had voting power only when six quarterly dividends were in default. It is not, we understand, the province of the Commission to formulate sound capital structures or to decide between more or less desirable plans. Nevertheless, the writer believes that it would not have been exceptional for the Commission to have required clarification of the prospectus and the fuller discussion of some phases of the transaction, especially the financial record of the *Times Union*.

In January, 1938, the 1936 annual report of the Eagle appeared. Summary and comparison with the previous year follows:

	1936	1935
Earnings, gross	$3,127,422	$3,182,318
Net loss	224,883	232,119

The smaller loss was attributable to a reduction in the charge-off for depreciation, $119,461, against $168,942 in 1935. Cash as of December 31, 1936, was $66,617, compared with $129,547 as of December 31, 1935. Net current assets were only $152,557. Earned surplus was down from $588,102 to

$217,163. Notes payable due 1938-1939 were outstanding in the amount of $505,500. Concern as to the ability to meet these obligations may have been the main reason for the new financing, through which they were largely liquidated. That the situation was a serious one is proved by the terms of the notes held by two banks. It was provided that if the excess of current assets over current liabilities fell below $150,000, the banks on their discretion could declare the notes immediately due and payable. As of October 31, 1936, current assets were $522,222 and current liabilities $338,179, making net current assets $184,083. Over 60 per cent of the current assets were in notes and accounts receivable, and while they were stated after a reserve for doubtful accounts, a small change in this or any other important item among the current assets or liabilities might have made the financial situation of the company a desperate one. Among the current assets were items due from officers and employees and "sundry accounts receivable" of $14,384.

At the beginning of 1938 the preferred stock of the Brooklyn Daily Eagle Properties Corporation was offered at 13; in April, 1938, the stock was offered at 5, with no bid. The common stock of the Eagle was offered at 50 cents a share, with no bid. An unsympathetic critic might call this deal "High Finance Under the SEC." Partisan commentators might contend that the reason for the passive attitude of the Commission was the fact that the Eagle has been a Democratic newspaper, albeit independent. At any rate, the needlessly complex capital structure, the brief, unsatisfactory statement of the prospectus with reference to the circulation and earnings of the *Times Union*, and the absence of an appraisal of the important real estate assets, should have been regarded as danger signals. What efforts were made to obtain the information from the *Times Union*? Is it conceivable that a large business enterprise has no records that would have enabled the registrant to make more than the laconic statement that the "company has not had any net earnings"? The sale of the preferred stock of the Company represented, in effect, the capitalizing of the losses of two losing enterprises in a joint venture that it was hoped might prove profitable, and incidentally, the parent Company through the sale of its common stock possibly staved off impending financial difficulties.[15]

PRESENT METHODS OF NEW FINANCING

The actual distribution of securities has not changed nearly as much as is generally assumed. The background is altogether different but the mechanism is generally similar. One important exception grows out of the Securities Act and is fundamental; others concern internal changes in investment banking.[16]

A registration statement becomes effective twenty days after it is filed, providing that its "effectiveness" has not been postponed or suspended through a stop order or deficiency letter. The security may not be offered or sold during this period. In this way the characteristic of speed in the offer and sale of a new security has been eliminated. The whole background of speed contributed to hectic excitement; issues were offered and sold before a prospectus had been made available. The twenty-day waiting period permits inspection by the Commission and by the public. The ordinary investor does not examine the registration statement, but it is analyzed by the investment services who publish digests of the main features. The metropolitan newspapers and the financial periodicals carry the announcements of the registration of important new issues, usually based on releases of the Commission. The price at which a security is to be offered and the price paid by the underwriter is usually left open to be inserted by amendment. Price is adjustable to changes in market conditions, and a measure of flexibility is thus introduced. The information concerning the underwriting agreement is ordinarily filed between the fifteenth and the nineteenth day after the original filing.

[15] The Eagle reported a net loss of $386,205 for 1937; this included reorganization and merger expenses of $61,936 and expense of the newspaper guild strike in the amount of $76,585.

[16] Some of the information in the following paragraphs is based on the authoritative article of Dr. Paul P. Gourrich, Technical Adviser to the Securities and Exchange Commission, in "Three years of the Securities Act—Part I," in *Law and Contemporary Publications*, School of Duke University, Vol. IV, No. 1, January, 1937.

At present, although one investment banking firm originates the issue and acts as the manager of the purchase group, the contract is generally made between the issuer and the entire underwriting syndicate. Formerly the agreement ordinarily was made by one banker. By permitting a number of bankers to enter into contract with the issuer, each making a several purchase, the liability of each firm is limited to the part of the total issue purchased by it. This practice also is of advantage under the civil liability provisions of the Securities Act. Dealers who are invited by the underwriters to enter the selling group usually are communicated with several days before the effective date and receive preliminary prospectuses (known as "red herring" prospectuses because of the legend in red ink appearing on the face thereof) and preliminary selling group letters. The preliminary prospectus often is identical with the final prospectus, but does not contain the facts relating to price, commission of the bankers, amount of participation, allowance to selling group members, etc.

Principal underwriters are not permitted to offer participations to subunderwriters through the use of the mails or interstate commerce during the twenty-day period. Subunderwriting formerly enabled the principal underwriters to reduce their risk by allotting subparticipations to these subunderwriters, but this has fallen into disuse. Amendment to the Securities Act to permit this practice has been advocated and seems to be a simple method of forestalling the consequences of a possible shortage of capital for underwriting purposes.[17]

The "selling group" refers to dealers who have facilities for retail distribution, but who because of their size or limited financial resources are not in a position to carry the liabilities of members of the underwriting syndicate. Members of the selling group merely agree to buy for resale a stated amount of the offered security in return for a stated selling commission. On bond offerings the spread averages slightly under 45 per cent of the gross spread, which is the difference between

[17] Arthur H. Dean on Practical Results of Corporation Financing under the Securities Act Today, p. 30 of "Operations under the Federal Securities Act," Financial Management Series F.M. 46, American Management Association (1935).

the offering price to the public and the purchase price to the underwriters.

"BEATING THE GUN"

This practice used to describe the custom of selling or agreeing to allot securities to a customer prior to the date of the actual public offering, existed prior to the Securities Act, but has probably increased in recent years. Large buyers like banks and insurance companies watch closely all possible new financing. In the nature of things, investment bankers and salesmen are anxious to inform them of forthcoming issues. Especially when so large a part of the new bond financing is for refunding purposes, these buyers, aware of the redemption of bonds in their portfolio, wish to assure themselves of obtaining the amount of new bonds that they have decided to take. Formerly they were able to purchase their requirements directly from the underwriters or members of the banking group.

Strict enforcement of or compliance with the law raises nice questions. The Commission, through its general counsel, in two opinions drew distinctions between furnishing information either through bulletins published by statistical services or through circulars prepared by underwriters and dealers during or prior to the twenty-day "cooling" period when it is unlawful to attempt to dispose of a security or to solicit offers to buy a security. Presumably purely descriptive matter is permissible; but if the bulletin contains favorable comment or "opinion material," the underwriter or dealer assumes a substantial risk in its distribution. A "fair summation" of the salient information distributed and prepared by an underwriter is unobjectionable, but it must not "stress or in any way emphasize the favorable as against the unfavorable aspects."[18] The law may be observed on the surface and so far as written matter is concerned. However, in speaking with a possible investor who has been furnished with the bulletin or summaries not out of academic interest, but because he wants to use the information to formulate an opinion, the

[18] Securities and Exchange Commission, Securities Act of 1933, Release No. 464 and 801, August, 1935, and May 23, 1936.

banker or dealer or their representatives can hardly refrain from some comment or observation that would probably be a violation of the law if strictly construed. One writer has suggested that the law be amended exempting institutions and professional buyers so as to allow free and open discussion with, and offerings of new securities to, institutions and professional buyers prior to the effective date.[19] Probably the significance of the practice has been overemphasized, but this suggestion is sound.

"Market Out" Clause

The "market out" clause is used in underwriting agreements to enable underwriters to withdraw without liability, and is a common clause in underwriting agreements. Two typical provisions are quoted below:

"The underwriters have the right in their uncontrolled discretion to terminate the underwriting agreement without liability of the several underwriters to the company if, prior to the closing date (which shall be within twenty days after the effective date of the registration statement), in their judgment any change in the company's condition or existing political, economic or market conditions or any substantial loss to the company on account of fire, flood, accident, or other calamity, or any transaction entered into by the company out of the usual course of business, without the written consent of the underwriters, renders it undesirable, impracticable, unprofitable, or otherwise unsatisfactory to offer the common stock at the price or in the manner contemplated by the underwriting agreement."

Another form, not quite so comprehensive in its terms, relates more exclusively to the company's affairs and is more suitable to offerings of bonds that are not so sensitive to general market changes as equity security offerings of secondary corporations. It reads:

"On the date of the public offering of the issue a firm commitment will have been made by the principal underwriters severally to purchase from the company the amounts

[19] "The Securities Act and Its Effect upon the Institutional Investor," C. John Kuhn, in *Three Years of the Securities Act*, Part 1.

of bonds set forth opposite their respective names above, subject to approval of counsel, to a stop order not being issued or threatened, to the company or its subsidiaries not having sustained since the end of the calendar year, any loss by reason of fire, flood, accident or other calamity which would materially affect the sale of the bonds, and to their not having occurred any substantial adverse change in the condition of the company or its subsidiaries, financial or otherwise, since the end of the year, except in the ordinary course of business, and the receipt of the company's certificate to that effect."

The first "market out" clause gives the underwriters the right to cancel the purchase if in their sole judgment certain conditions have arisen. These conditions are not limited to such major catastrophes as the outbreak of war, national calamity, act of God, or panic. It is not even necessary that any material change in the company's affairs have taken place. If the underwriters decide that it is "undesirable, impracticable, unprofitable, or otherwise unsatisfactory" to make the offering they need not proceed, because of existing "political, economic or market conditions." This makes the underwriting agreement, in effect, an option since the judgment of the underwriters is the sole standard. The language used has the merit of being so sweeping that it should certainly avoid giving rise to litigation. Markets are extremely sensitive and because of the time element some protection is necessary. A standard might be provided that would not give the underwriters the unqualified right to withdraw; a cancellation could be made contingent upon a decline in an accepted index of stock prices of perhaps 10 per cent to give the issuer some protection. The second type of "market out" clause is much more nearly a binding contract. Contingencies are restricted to changes in the affairs of the company. Instead of permitting the underwriters to be the sole judge of such adverse changes, the company determines whether this has taken place. Its certificate is made the standard. The ordinary market changes have no effect on an offering using this clause. As a rule, the right to cancel may be exercised to the date of public offering; in other cases, cancellation may be made even beyond and to the date on which payment for the securities is made. Recently the "market out" clause has been retained in the underwriting agreement in one form or other, but has been omitted from the prospectus.

The more extensive use of the "market out" clause than prior to the Securities Act may be ascribed to the greater uncertainties in the securities market. With reference to the marketing of secondary issues and stocks of the more speculative class it may denote a lesser willingness or ability of investment banking firms to "bank" an issue during the course of distribution. Stricter policies on loans may also account for the fear of having to carry a substantial part of an unsold issue.

TRADING ACCOUNTS

To prevent the market for a new security from showing price weakness during the period of distribution, syndicate managers generally were given the right to trade in the new securities. The demand for the syndicate trading account would thus act as a stabilizing influence. Overselling, on the other hand, minimized the possibility of runaway price movements, especially for stocks. Short sales are effected to offset sales by investors who often accept a quick profit on a new issue. According to Dr. Gourrich, out of fifty-nine bond issues offered in 1928, trading accounts were used in the distribution of forty, or about two-thirds. The rationale for the activities of a syndicate trading account were described in the investigation of the United States Senate Committee on Banking and Currency by a prominent investment banker in the following words: "In the case of a new issue, until it becomes thoroughly absorbed, the syndicate or the selling group, or whatever it may be, must be standing ready to purchase any bonds from customers who want to, so to speak, return their goods from a sale; and therefore, in order to be able to repurchase these bonds and give them a proper market till they find their ultimate investment status, you must stand ready to purchase them." This stabilizing or pegging process lent itself to abuse. The Securities Exchange Act of 1934 provides that the Commission may prescribe such rules as may be necessary or appropriate in the public trust to prevent the making of transactions for the purpose of "pegging, fixing or stabilizing of prices" on a national securities exchange. As a part of the registration statement, syndicate trading agreements are published and are summarized on the prospectus. Disclosure has removed one objection to these operations. Restrictions on "when issued" trading on the exchanges has also curtailed the possible harm of stabilizing activities. While syndicate trading accounts are still generally used, the average amount of trading actually done is probably considerably smaller than before the present investment banking era. A typical provision in a prospectus follows:

"By an Agreement between all of the principal underwriters, Morgan Stanley & Co. Incorporated has been authorized (1) during the term of said Agreement, to buy and sell Debentures in addition to the Debentures sold to the Selling Group, in the open market or otherwise, either for long or short account, on such terms and at such prices as Morgan Stanley & Co. Incorporated in its discretion may deem desirable, and (2) in arranging for sales to the Selling Group to over-allot, it being agreed that such purchases and sales and over-allotments shall be made for the account of each of the several principal underwriters in proportion to their respective purchases of Debentures from the Company; provided, however, that at no time shall the net commitment under said Agreement of any principal underwriter, either for long or short account, exceed 5 per cent of the aggregate principal amount of Debentures which such underwriter has agreed to purchase from the Company."

In the supplemental prospectus of the Pure Oil Corporation underwriting it was reported that between September 25, 1937, and February 2, 1938, there were purchased for the trading account 679 shares of the preferred stock and 1,442 shares were sold. The net short position, accordingly, was 763 shares.

PRIVATE PLACEMENT

The investment banking world has been troubled by the growing importance of private placement. Purchases by financial institutions without previous public offering of entire issues eliminates the investment banking function even though in some instances investment bankers have negotiated the transaction. During the fiscal year ended June 30, 1937, 28 unregistered private placings with total estimated gross proceeds of almost $296,000,000 came to the attention of the Commission compared with 37 issues with estimated gross proceeds of over $213,000,000 during the preceding fiscal year. In the 1937 calendar year the total of private bond transactions exceeded $500,000,000, and this amount was surpassed in 1938. The proceeds of these privately placed issues were equivalent to approximately 8 per cent of the securities effectively registered during the year, compared with about 5 per cent during the preceding fiscal year. In relation to corporate bond registrations the percentage was much higher. Industrial corporations sold slightly over one-half of the reported private placings, and public utilities accounted for about 80 per cent of the rest. Securities placed privately but registered either on issuance or later amounted to less than $12,000,000 in the year ended June 30, 1937, against $211,000,000 during the preceding fiscal year. The estimate of private sales of new issues and the percent of total new financing placed in this way compiled by the "New York Herald Tribune" follow:

Year Ended Dec. 31	Estimated Total Volume	App. Per Cent of Total New Issues Offered
1934	$115,000,000	25
1935	225,000,000	10
1936	335,000,000	9
1937	360,000,000	23
1938	600,000,000	31

If there is a substantial saving to the issuer and an equally good or better price is obtained, the practice is economical and the investment banking community will merely have to accept it as another change. Among the representative issues privately placed in the past several years are the following:

REPRESENTATIVE BONDS

Privately Sold

Socony Vacuum Oil Co., Inc. Deb. 3¼s, 1955	$75,000,000
United States Rubber 1st 4½s, 1958	45,000,000
Kansas City Light & Power 1st mtg. 3¾s, 1966	38,000,000
Rochester Gas & Electric Gen. mtg. "F" 4s, 1960	15,000,000
Consolidated Gas Electric Light & Power Co. of Baltimore mtg. 3¼s, 1968	10,440,000

The purchase of an entire issue by one or several financial institutions must be regarded as a step away from liquidity or marketability. Private placement has been limited mainly to high-grade bonds. If it continues to expand, conceptions of the liquidity of financial institutions will have to be modified. There has been some saving to institutional buyers. On the other hand, the practice may be condemned as a means of circumventing the law. It is essentially undemocratic. It deprives other institutions and private investors from participation in desirable investments. In periods of poor business insurance companies may become the dominant power in enterprises of which they are the largest creditors. The McKesson and Robbins case illustrates the dangers of having one or two institutions own an entire issue, since the loss involved may be serious. Moreover, the effect on the investment banking business is likely to be serious. It removes one of the few avenues of profit still left. If equity financing is to be fostered, the higher grade issues should not be withdrawn from the field which the investment banker regards as the backlog of his business. This is a subject for examination by the Commission. It would be strange to strengthen the position of the large buyer, who is not without influence in the pricing of an issue in any case, when the national government is endeavoring to equalize the position of large buyers of merchandise. Selling group members are generally permitted to allow to banks and other financial institutions a concession from the offering price to the public.

SPREADS, PAST AND PRESENT

Complete data are not available as to the former gross compensation for the underwriting and sale of securities. On high-grade corporate bonds the average of a sample of issues offered between 1927 and 1931 was about 3 per cent of the principal amount. The average gross compensation of all domestic railroad bonds from 1920 to 1931 was slightly less than 3 per cent of the principal amount. The gross spreads on a sample of preferred stocks of $2,000,000 or over sold in 1929 averaged about 5 per cent of the public offering price. As shown in the following tabulation, average spreads on bond issues are now lower, probably because of the larger proportion of high-grade issues representing refunding operations.

SELECTED ISSUES OFFERED IN 1937

Gross Underwriting Spreads	1st Quarter	2nd Quarter	3rd Quarter	4th Quarter
Bond issues of $5,000,000 or over				
No. of issues..........................	14	9	3	5
Weighted average spread (%) of Public offering price........................	2.22	2.05	2.01	2.21
Preferred stock issues of $1,000,000 or over				
No. of issues..........................	13	9	8	3
Weighted average spread..............	4.25	2.90	4.14	3.37
Common Stock Issues (of $1,000,000 or over)				
No. of issues..........................	14	22	4	1
Weighted average spread..............	15.11	12.50	12.65	20

Note: Weighted by the dollars of gross proceeds of each issue, thus giving the figure for each issue a significance equal to the proportion of the value of all issues. Abstracted from Securities and Exchange Commission, Statistical Series Release No. 94, April 22, 1938.[20]

The gross spread has always varied in an inverse ratio to the quality of the issue. Accordingly, common stock financing has the greatest average spread, exclusive of rights to subscribe to additional stock which are often underwritten. Between June, 1935, and June, 1936, seven additional stock offerings were underwritten each of over $1,000,000 on listed issues. In six of the seven cases underwriters took less than 5 per cent of the issue; in one case, 11.7 per cent. Chairman Douglas criticized the underwriting commission of about 3½ per cent of the whole issue because 90 per cent or more of the stock was taken up by shareholders. He suggested that the "double load" be reduced so that the corporation would pay either for the insurance feature of having the issue underwritten or only on the stock not taken by the stockholders. A single loss, however, may wipe out a large number of profits where the spread is narrow. An offer of preferred stock of Pure Oil Company in the amount of 442,443 shares was under-

[20] Data presented in article by Dr. Gourrich, p. 233.

written, although offered to shareholders. The market began to turn downward, the stock was probably priced too high in the first instance, and only a small part of the issue was purchased by the shareholders. The gross commission was $2.50 per share on the total issue. Eventually, the underwriters took a loss estimated at over $10 a share.

The cost of common stock financing seems to be excessively high. Underwriting is a highly competitive business—the acute competition stimulated the search for foreign issues to offer in the twenties. Hence, the spread is not the result of price fixing or of the absence of competition in a quasi-monopolistic industry. If over a period of time lower gross commissions were sufficient to attract underwriters, we may be certain that they would prevail. Several factors must be remembered in considering the spread. Out of the gross commission, dealers must be paid. The dealer ordinarily receives between 30 and 45 per cent of the gross spread, but if this were the only offset, the underwriting of common stocks would be immensely profitable. Public financing is spasmodic. There are periods in which the public will not buy. In a declining market it is difficult to sell the most meritorious offering. This means that the overhead of an organization must be met during many months when new financing is out of the question. Furthermore, the negotiation of new deals and investigation are time-consuming and expensive. Only a small percentage of the new deals proposed or investigated ever develop into a piece of new financing. The maintenance of an organization is expensive. Much time and energy must be devoted to the study of situations and conferences with executives of business seeking new funds which for some reason are rejected or do not materialize because of difference as to price or other considerations. Lower commissions probably are justified where the "market out" clause gives the underwriter the right to withdraw even after public offering is made. In such cases the underwriter does not assume the risk of having to carry an issue, having his capital tied up until the issue is disposed of, or of absorbing a heavy loss in the event it proves entirely unsuccessful.

DIFFICULTY OF EQUITY FINANCING

Unfortunately it has been difficult in recent years to obtain new capital by common stock offerings. Former Commissioner John W. Hanes, an investment banker before his association with the Commission, chided the investment bankers for side-stepping newer and smaller companies. Formerly bankers were willing to buy issues of relatively unknown companies, without immediate prospect for resale, and to nurse the corporation during its early stages. Financing along these lines requires considerable capital. Underwriting capital is unquestionably smaller than in the twenties. The business has been made less attractive. Without questioning the justification for the restrictions now prevailing, it is well to consider the new problems that have been created. The relatively small capital of investment banking firms engaged in underwriting equity issues may result in a fundamental change in the mechanism of investment banking. If the capital is not augmented so as to facilitate equity financing, it may become necessary to supplement the available means by modifying the severance of investment banking from commercial banking; another corrective might be the development of institutions to which the government has contributed capital, or intermediate capital credit banks.

A related problem is the stimulation of local interest in smaller enterprises and the decentralization of investment banking so that activities would be less concentrated in New York and a few other large cities. The encouragement given to local stock exchanges by admitting to trading securities listed on the larger securities exchanges is commendable as it may emphasize investment buying as against purely trading activities. To develop such agencies nothing would contribute as much as making it more profitable than in the past to place high-grade securities.

The mechanism of the origination and distribution of securities is not so greatly different under the Securities Act of 1933 as is generally supposed. Greater information and less haste have been introduced. Sound securities have been easy to market. The cost of registration is no barrier to financing.

The widespread notion that expenses of registration have thwarted new financing should disappear after consideration of the facts. The costs are relatively higher for smaller aggregates of financing, but in themselves are not obstacles to new financing. The smallest issues are exempt. The liabilities assumed under the statute by bankers and corporate officials are not excessive. The failure of the capital markets to open their doors for desirable equity financing of secondary corporations, one of the knottiest problems of the business world, is traceable in part to general influences as well as to gaps in the investment banking mechanism. Long-existing investment habits of security buyers are also responsible. The process of educating the investing public, at best a slow one, has been measurably aided. The removal of fly-by-night promotions and frauds from competition with honest corporations seeking capital from responsible and reputable investment bankers exercises a constructive influence on the entire national economy. Problems of administrative practice remain. With the cooperation of the Commission and the investment bankers, these should not be insuperable. Improvement in the law and its administration, and adjustment of the mechanics of security flotation, will continue so long as the financial world and the Commission recognize that neither is the final repository of wisdom.

We cannot deal fully with the broader aspects of the failure to use the available capital resources of this country or indeed throughout the world. The basic economic situation is different than in 1929-1931. The eighth annual report of the Bank for International Settlements contained some significant comments:[21]

"Government action, though creating work on the one hand, has on the other hand created, in many cases, an atmosphere of uncertainty hampering to private enterprise. Economic nationalism, though fostering certain branches of internal activity in all countries and the whole of economic life in the countries with a controlled economic system, has often unintentionally stood in the way of the development of foreign trade."

[21] The report appears in the Federal Reserve *Bulletin* for June, 1938.

The following quotation seems to go to the heart of the problem. It is from "The Movements of Interest Rates, Bond Yields and Stock Prices in the United States," by Frederick R. Macaulay: "If an economic society is to be a highly successful society it should function as a society. We must break away from the mysticism of 'Laissez-faire.' Times without number 'the invisible hand' has led mankind into the economic ditch. Positive social action is absolutely necessary. In spite of the inevitable difficulties, the hope of the world lies in truly social, as opposed to merely individualistic economic *planning*. To the extent that the future can be made, instead of awaited, the disturbing social errors of erroneous and inadequate individual forecasting may become a thing of the past. Of course, adequate public planning is extremely difficult. No system of 'trial and error' will take the place of brains. Without brains, public planning may be extremely dangerous. *We must always remember that the essential objective of public planning should be to make legitimate and desirable private plannings easier and not more difficult,* unless we are willing to 'go the whole hog' and lapse into a communist state."

REGISTRATION UNDER THE SECURITIES EXCHANGE ACT

Registration of securities listed on national securities exchanges has much the same purpose, but is made under Section 12 of the Securities Exchange Act of 1934. Provision was made for temporary registration, which was permitted to continue until July 1, 1935. It then became unlawful to trade in nonexempt securities unless permanent registration had become effective. To avoid confusion because of the pressure of time in which the Commission and registrants had to work, a fifteen day interval was allowed granting to all listed but unregistered securities an exemption from registration requirements to July 15, 1935.

The Securities Exchange Act of 1934 requires that a company seeking registration of its securities must file an application on the appropriate form prescribed by the Commission. This application must contain detailed financial data. In general, the same kind of information is required as for registration of new issues under the Securities Act of 1933. Some 2,485 companies having securities listed and registered have filed. These registrants include most of the leading nationally known companies in the United States as well as many with activities of a sectional or local character. Each of the companies must file within 120 days after the close of its fiscal year an annual report bringing up to date the financial and other important items of information contained in its application for registration. This information must be filed with the Commission and exchange on which the securities are listed. The market value of all sales on registered exchanges for the year ended June 30, 1938 was $14,759,498,000. The number of shares listed on these exchanges as of June 30, 1938 was 2,349,491,227 and the principal amount of the listed bonds was $24,710,308,905, which are indications of the importance of maintaining sound practices in dealings on the exchanges. It should be possible to combine the registration provisions of the two statutes into one form.

CHAPTER X

New Financing (*Continued*)

Credit and Capital Problems

THE difficulty of obtaining adequate credit through the banks, or capital through the ordinary investment banking channels has been canvassed and has given rise to the possible creation of new agencies or facilities.

In the Seventh Federal Reserve District, selected as a sample area because it embraces a wide variety of industrial and business conditions, containing a large industrial and a large commercial city, the situation was thoroughly examined as to availability of bank credit to small and moderate-sized business concerns.[1] The more important findings as to this district were:

1. That there existed a genuine unsatisfied demand for credit on the part of solvent borrowers, many of whom could have made economically sound use of working capital.

2. That the total amount of this unsatisfied demand for credit was considerably smaller than is popularly believed, but was large enough to be a significant factor in retarding business recovery.

3. That a large proportion of would-be borrowers were persons or corporations whose equity in the business operated was so small that any bank or individuals lending them substantial would be taking an unwarranted risk.

4. That there was a larger unsatisfied demand for long-term working capital loans than for one-turnover credit; that the pressure for liquidation of old working capital loans, even sound ones, was one of the most serious factors in this unsatisfied demand; and that the pressure was partly due to a

[1] Report on the Availability of Bank Credit in the Seventh Federal District, submitted to the Secretary of the Treasury by Dr. Charles O. Hardy and Dr. Jacob Viner (1935).

determination on the part of bankers to avoid a recurrence of the errors that led to the previous wave of bank failures.

5. That the pressure was also attributable in large part to the attitude of bank examiners.

6. That the efforts to relieve the difficulties through the direct lending by the Federal Reserve banks (in this case the Chicago bank) and the Chicago agency of the Reconstruction Finance Corporation had a negligible effect on the general state of credit. It appears that the publicity given to the lending operations of these agencies aroused hopes that their policy was more liberal than the law permitted.

7. That the then existing restrictions on the use of funds to clear up existing debt interfered to a marked extent with the attainment of the purposes of the legislation by which the direct lending system was set up.

The line of demarcation between bank credit and capital loans is often blurred. Unquestionably the merger of banks in the large cities, the limited authority of branch bank managers, and the greater importance assumed by financial statements as against character and business record have affected the smaller merchant and manufacturer. Some of the larger institutions are not geared for the making of this type of loan. The need for definitely long-term capital on the part of small industries was sympathetically considered by the Business Advisory Council, on the basis of material assembled by it from 6,158 replies to a questionnaire addressed to small manufacturing establishments and of data furnished by the Reconstruction Finance Corporation and Federal Reserve Board regarding their experience to February, 1935.

The conclusion was significant, and follows in part: "As a matter of fact, long term financing for small industry has always been difficult. It is not simply a depression problem. Through private investment bankers, it has been available only to concerns of sufficient size and standing to warrant the investment banker to bring out an issue as small as for instance, $1,000,000. So it may be said that this facility has been practically denied to smaller concerns. Such enterprises have been obliged to develop their capital structures gradually out of undistributed earnings or to attract the attention of individual capitalists. They have not received the benefit of recourse to the capital markets for their long-term requirements." The Council was impressed by the fact that the bulk of advances and commitments made by the Federal Reserve banks were for periods of more than one year.[2] The Council was not entirely correct in its statement that private underwritings for less than $1,000,000 are uncommon; otherwise the conclusion is supported by the facts.

The relapse of business late in 1937 brought about renewed efforts on the part of the Reconstruction Finance Corporation and the Federal Reserve banks. Pressure resulted in the liberalization of banking regulations and policies. The Reconstruction Finance Corporation's authority was liberalized by amendment which became a law April 13, 1938. The change made it possible for the Corporation to purchase the securities and obligations of, and to make loans to, any business enterprise when capital or credit is not otherwise available, subject only to the opinion of the board of directors that the investments would be of sound value, or so secured as reasonably to assure retirement or repayment. This was interpreted to mean that the Reconstruction Finance Corporation had the broadest discretion in the making of capital loans, but could not purchase an equity interest in private business. The loans were to be made either directly or in cooperation with banks or other lending institutions through agreements to participate or by the purchase of participations. In all instances the business had to be solvent. The Reconstruction Finance Corporation announced that since the amended act provides that loans thereunder shall be made for the purpose of maintaining and promoting the economic stability of the country or encouraging the employment of labor, it would make loans for the following purposes:

1. For labor and materials.
2. For the purchase of machinery.

[2] "Capital and Capital Requirements of Small Industry," Summary of Report to the Secretary of Commerce by the Business Advisory Council for the Department of Commerce, and "Survey of Report of Credit and Capital Difficulties submitted by Small Manufacturers," United States Department of Commerce, 1935.

3. For the establishment of new business enterprises and for the expansion of existing enterprises.
4. To finance industrial construction.
5. To pay existing debts and taxes.

Loans to carry inventories or for the financing of the development or purchase of new inventions were eschewed.

Previously, in January, 1935, the Reconstruction Finance Corporation announced a liberalization of its policies with respect to direct loans to industry. One change provided that consideration be given to applications where a "substantial" rather than an "incidental" portion of the proceeds was used to satisfy or compromise existing indebtedness. The second modification, designed to be of assistance in the stimulation of demand for capital goods, provided for consideration of applications when the funds were to be used principally for the replacement and modernization of plant and equipment. In the same month the Reconstruction Finance Corporation was relieved of requiring "adequate security" for loans to industry. The time period was extended five years to January 31, 1945, and loans were authorized which could be repaid only over a period of years, and in addition the securing of long-term credits by business concerns through the pledging of assets was facilitated.

Under Section 13b of the Federal Reserve Act, as amended, the Federal Reserve banks were authorized to make loans, purchases, and commitments and to extend discounts to provide working capital for established industrial or commercial businesses. These accommodations can be made through banks or other financing institutions. In exceptional cases, when it appears that established industrial or commercial businesses are unable to obtain requisite financial assistance on a reasonable basis from the usual sources, Federal Reserve banks are authorized to make these "working capital" loans with a maturity of not more than five years. Immediately following the legislation the Board, to facilitate as much as possible the performance of the new functions granted the reserve banks blanket authority to grant such accommodations directly on their own responsibility without reference to Washington, although the law permits the making of direct loans only when authorized by the Board. To assist the reserve banks, an Industrial Advisory Committee was organized in each Federal Reserve district consisting of five members actively engaged in some industrial pursuit within the district. As a step in the concentrated attempt to stimulate recovery early in 1938, each Federal Reserve bank as of February 16 addressed a letter to all banks, financing institutions, and others concerned in its district, observing that the power to make advances and commitments under Section 13b is a continuing one; the Federal Reserve Bank of New York reminded the banks of facilities in this field of credit and asked for "continued cooperation" in bringing these facilities to the attention of those who might be interested. It continued: "If you know of any established industrial or commercial businesses in this district, which are in need of working capital and which cannot obtain much capital from the usual sources but could, nevertheless, in your opinion, be given financial assistance on a reasonable and sound basis, we shall be glad to discuss with you or with them the possibility of their obtaining accommodation under Section 13b of the Federal Reserve Act."

The authorities went further. Not without some misgivings, restrictions as to investments in securities by national banks were removed so as to liberalize the test of marketability. Examiners were instructed to be less eager to criticize or call attention to loans if sound and properly secured but slow. A lively controversy ensued in which the chief participants were Jesse H. Jones, chairman of the Reconstruction Finance Corporation, Marriner S. Eccles, chairman of the Board of Governors of the Federal Reserve System, Henry Morgenthau, Jr., Secretary of the Treasury, the Comptroller of the Currency and the head of the Federal Deposit Insurance Corporation.

In every instance the early expectations as to the possible increase in loans or investments failed to materialize. Between March 31, 1938, and June 30, 1938, the Reconstruction Finance Corporation's loans to industrial and commercial businesses increased only $3,681,000 to $72,688,000 and the financial journals good-naturedly countered the chairman's remarks that the banks were "bulging" with loanable funds by referring to his own bank's experience. The letters of the Federal Reserve banks implied that the volume of working capital loans had not come up to expectations. The Federal Reserve Bank of New York later noted a considerable increase in the number of inquiries from business concerns regarding the possibility of obtaining loans. However, in a large percentage of cases discussions with prospective borrowers showed that the needs were for permanent additions to proprietary capital or for other types of loans that are ineligible under the law; or that the condition of the business did not provide a sound basis for bank credit. The total amount of advances made by the Federal Reserve Bank of New York during the four-year period to June, 1938, was approximately $24,500,000. In many cases the loans made, either directly or in conjunction with commercial banks, served a useful purpose. Yet, although great care was exercised in the original review of the applications and constant supervision was maintained, the Bank had to place a number of loans on the "trouble list," and in a few cases the borrowing firm failed despite the receipt of the loans. The Bank declared that its experience indicated that the income received, even at rates as high as 6 per cent, was not adequate to cover expenses and losses.[3] The experience of all the reserve banks to July 20, 1938, was that they had received 9,173 applications for loans of $387,039,000. Applications recommended for approval by the Industrial Advisory Committee numbered 2,853 for a total amount of $167,666,000. Of these, 2,583 loans were approved in the amount of $161,-920,000. As of July 20, 1938, the principal data were as follows:

Federal Reserve Bank advances outstanding......... $18,093,000
Federal Reserve Bank commitments outstanding.... 13,432,000
Financing institution participations outstanding..... 8,328,000

The largest amount of advances was at the end of 1935, $32,493,000, when the outstanding commitments were also the largest, $27,649,000; at that time the participations of financing institutions were $8,718,000.[4] It is still probably true that the member banks are reluctant to approach the Federal Re-

[3] Monthly Review of Credit and Business Conditions, Second Federal District, Federal Reserve Bank, New York, August 1, 1938.

[4] Monthly statistics for both the Reconstruction Finance Corporation and the Federal Reserve banks appear in the *Federal Reserve Bulletin.*

serve banks, and are slow in suggesting that borrowers apply directly to the regional institutions.

The Reconstruction Finance Corporation is barred from the purchase of stocks. The Federal Reserve banks may make only working capital loans. Underwriting of comparatively small issues is difficult, and the impression is growing that a supplement to the existing avenues now open to business is necessary. The opinion exists despite the results of a survey announced in April, 1938, by the Investment Bankers Conference, Inc., a nation-wide organization of brokers and dealers in securities. This survey was made through inquiries to investment bankers and was confined to industries that needed funds for capital improvements not exceeding $1,500,000, and through a direct communication with about four thousand manufacturing concerns by questionnaire. Over three-quarters of the replies were to the effect that there was no lack of new capital for the expansion of sound companies; but as less than eight hundred replies were tabulated, the evidence is hardly conclusive.

A bill for the establishment of a system of regional industrial banks was introduced in the 75th Congress, 3d Session, by Senator Claude Pepper "so as to furnish additional credit and capital facilities for business purposes."[5] The bill provided for the creation of a Board of Governors to be composed of one member from each region in which such bank shall be established. The Board, to be appointed by the President, shall divide the country into a minimum of five regions and a maximum of twelve and establish a regional bank in each region.

The banks shall begin business with a capital stock of $100,000,000 to be subscribed by the Secretary of the Treasury for the use and benefit of the national government. The amount of capital stock to be subscribed by the Treasury might be increased to as much as $1,000,000,000 for each bank, upon the recommendation of the Board of Governors with the concurrence of the President. The capital stock shall be subject to acquisition by the public in amounts and at prices

[5] S.3630, 75th Congress, 3d Session, which was read twice and referred to the Committee on Banking and Currency.

to be fixed by the Board of Governors. The operations of the banks are to be governed by a board of directors of seven, who are authorized to establish subregional banks or field agencies.

The regional banks shall have authority to make loans "upon such terms and conditions, with or without collateral, and at such rates of interest" as the board of directors shall determine. Further, "each of such regional banks shall also have authority to buy preferred stock, common stock or bonds of any business enterprise, or any public agency, or any government body, or to take such steps as the board of directors of each such regional bank shall determine to be proper, to furnish needed capital and credit facilities in the United States."

The regional banks shall also have authority to rediscount paper acquired from either national or state banks, and to sell any assets acquired in the due course of their business. They shall not, however, accept deposits. Each regional bank may issue debentures to be insured by the Secretary of the Treasury and these debentures would be lawful for investment by national banks. An insurance fund could be established to protect the Treasury against loss arising out of the defaults of the regional banks.

Structurally the bill seems to be modeled on the Federal Reserve Act, with a supervisory board, and regional banks directly managed by boards of directors. Four of the seven directors are to be appointed by the President and three in a manner to be prescribed by the Board of Governors, by those doing business with or through such regional banks or those owning the securities of the banks. It is questionable if this dual system of responsibility and management through the appointive power will be successful.

The authority vested in the proposed banks, both as to the possible capital to be utilized and the scope of the investments, is deliberately so broad as to challenge the commercial and investment banking world as well as the Federal Reserve System. The Reconstruction Finance Corporation even with its expanded powers is small in comparison with the potentialities of the proposed "regional industrial banks." The Pepper bill may not become a law, or it may be enacted only in modified form. But the bill is significant as an expression of opinion as to the need of supplementing the existing credit and investment machinery and facilities.

A minimum of five banks with capital stock of $500,000,000 is envisaged with a possibility of twelve banks with $12,-000,000,000 capital stock. In addition each bank may issue an unlimited amount of obligations in the form of debentures. There is practically no limitation on the loans or investments that the regional banks may make. Unless the directors restrict the loans or investments, the banks could finance new enterprises as well as existing businesses; buy entire issues of preferred or common stocks or bonds, of industrial, public utility, or railroad corporations; aid in effecting reorganization plans, and refunding operations; municipal obligations or bonds of public authorities such as port authorities might also be acquired. The securities of private corporations purchased could range from the smallest enterprise to those of the greatest businesses.

Rather than enact legislation that might jar the investment banking world during a period when it has had to absorb many changes and adapt itself to the far-reaching legislation of recent years, I suggest that use be made of the already existing organizations and agencies such as the Reconstruction Finance Corporation and the Federal Reserve banks. In the larger cities it is urged that the commercial banks themselves be authorized to use a small part of their resources to form industrial banks which could make loans and investments beyond the scope of ordinary commercial bank practice. The advantages of this method over that proposed in the Pepper bill are important. The existing mechanism will be free to develop without the impact of a step that might prove disturbing. The added agency, under private management, will begin to function in a friendly atmosphere and without the impediment of alleged political favoritism or influence in its lending policies. I have already admitted the necessity of abandoning a laissez-faire policy, and the achievements of a constructive governmental program have been, I believe, generously acknowledged in this book. Had the financial world formulated and placed in effect its own sufficiently inclusive reforms, the multiplication of governmental instrumentalities might have been avoided. The tendency toward active participation by the government to aid the smooth operation of business will continue and in itself is not alarming, always providing that administration is in capable hands and administrative procedure permits the curing of possible abuses. At the same time it seems to be wise to proceed slowly wherever there is a reasonable doubt as to the need of further infiltration of governmental processes, and first to attempt changes that may be initiated by industry and finance.

PROPOSAL FOR
REGIONAL CAPITAL
CREDIT BANKS

The writer proposes that there be created twelve regional "capital credit" banks,[6] one in each Federal Reserve district. These banks are to begin business with capital raised through subscriptions by the member banks in the two central reserve cities, New York and Chicago, and the sixty-one reserve cities. As of June 30, 1938 national banks which are located in these central reserve and reserve cities had capital stock, surplus and undivided profits of approximately $1,931,000,000; deposits (eliminating interbank deposits) of roughly $13,800,-000,000 and assets of about $20,900,000,000. Unfortunately, exact figures for state banks that are members of the Federal Reserve system are not available. However, by applying a 55 per cent increase, the approximate percentage of state member bank deposits to total member bank deposits, the following approximate figures are obtained:

Deposits (exclusive of interbank deposits).......	$21,390,000,000
Capital stock, surplus and undivided profits.....	3,103,000,000
Total assets................................	32,395,000,000

By investing an amount equal to 10 per cent of their capital stock, undivided profits and surplus, the member banks would contribute $310,000,000 to the new capital credit banks. This amount would be equivalent to about .7 per cent of the

[6] The term used by A. A. Berle, Jr., in his memorandum to the committee investigating monopolies, officially known as the Temporary National Economic Commission.

deposits of these banks. These banks would be empowered to make loans to and purchase the securities of industrial corporations. A condition precedent to the obtaining of aid would be the previous effort, in good faith, to obtain credit from a commercial bank. Except for the additional power to buy stocks, authority would be similar to that of the Reconstruction Finance Corporation to make loans to industry. The management of the banks would be in the hands of a board of directors, elected by each bank every two years, as follows:

Two by the member banks, classified by size so as to assure the small member banks proper representation, each of whom shall be an experienced commercial banker, and

Two by the member banks from industry or agriculture.

Three directors shall be appointed by the president of the reserve bank of the district, one of whom shall have had investment banking experience; appointments subject to approval of the Board of Governors.

The members of the Board of Governors of the Federal Reserve System would act in a supervisory capacity as governors of the capital credit banks. Their power would include the fixing of maximum and minimum rates of interest, the making of regulations as to the character of investments to be made, and the fixing of maximum amounts to be invested by the capital credit banks in any one industry. Additional capital could be obtained, if necessary, by the issuance of debentures in an amount not more than five times the capital and surplus of the capital credit banks. The capital would be furnished by banks that would not be disturbed by the reduction in their excess reserves. A net return of 4 per cent on the initial capital would amount to $12,400,000 annually; member banks do not receive a return on their reserves, and because of the increase in reserve requirements from the percentages that obtained for many years prior to 1936, the income would be welcomed by the banks. In June, 1938, all member banks in central reserve and reserve cities had excess reserves of $2,304,000,000. The capital to be provided will be drawn from the large existing reservoir and will put to work funds that are now redundant; that is, dead capital will be vitalized. The banks in central reserve and reserve cities are located in the larger cities in which the demand for a supplementary avenue for obtaining capital is greatest. The capital credit banks would be authorized to establish branches with the approval of the Board of Governors.

The capital credit banks could be established as part of the Federal Reserve System Act as amended, Section 13b of the Federal Reserve Act could be repealed; the Reconstruction Finance Corporation's authority under Sections 5d and 14 of the Reconstruction Finance Corporation Act could be revoked. The new capital credit banks, although managed in part by directors appointed by the member banks, would have directorates in which nonbanking interests would have a voice. The supervision of the Board of Governors of the Federal Reserve System and the directors appointed by the president of the Federal Reserve district in which the bank is located could be relied on to preserve and promote the public interest. Possible overlapping of authority, as at present, would be avoided, as well as reputed political management. The Board of Governors would be vested with important powers helpful in making its broader monetary policies more effective. At the same time further centralization, through the establishment of a body with the right to veto any capital issue like the War Finance Board, would be avoided.

It is significant that between June 19, 1934, and December 31, 1937, out of authorized commercial and industrial loans (including participations and agreements to purchase participations) the Reconstruction Finance Corporation reported the following division as to size was to loans not exceeding $500,-000:

	Amount	Per Cent of Total
$ 25,000 to $ 50,000	$18,233,356	10.4
50,000 to 100,000	28,370,976	16.3
100,000 to 200,000	29,370,976	16.8
200,000 to 500,000	42,645,234	24.3

Textiles and lumber and timber products were the largest industrial divisions, neither of which is popular with purchasers of securities.[7]

As a large part of the loans was made in amounts that would bar security offerings, opposition from investment

[7] Reconstruction Finance Corporation, report for the fourth quarter of 1937.

bankers is not considered likely. In fact, should loans or equity investment in small amounts help a business to expand or establish it on a profitable basis, it may well be that many of the businesses will be able to turn later to public financing. Member banks would not hesitate to suggest that depositors seek the assistance of the capital credit banks; as the latter would not be banks of deposit, the member bank would not lose an account if the loan were made. It could cooperate with the capital credit bank in making certain that the funds were properly used. The deficiencies mentioned in the report made for the Treasury Department and in other studies would be cured by the establishment of a system of capital credit banks without adding another political administrative agency. Whatever these banks are called—capital credit banks, or investment banks, or intermediate credit banks—the need for certain types of venture capital could be supplied in a large degree by the plan outlined. The plan presupposes that the new institutions will only supplement the present methods of obtaining capital, filling a gap for which the reasons ascribed may differ but which is generally conceded to exist. By placing the banks in the Federal Reserve System, the authority of the Board of Governors would be extended directly into an important segment of the financial world. This authority, or similar powers, is necessary if it is to meet the changed conditions in banking. Broad as its authority appears to be under the Banking Act of 1935, it is mainly of a negative character, directed to enable the Board to check the development of an inflation based on security loans. To promote investment of capital, it may bring into play the powerful lever of easy money rates. The last several years have proved decisively that a more direct, positive force is necessary since easy money does not seem to percolate far enough. Large corporations and businesses with excellent credit obtain the full advantage of easy money. Small enterprises requiring additional capital or credit benefit little, if at all.

CHAPTER XI

THE FUTURE OF WALL STREET

THE AGE OF THE CORPORATION

THE present has been described as the iron age; the age of chemistry and electricity; the credit era; the developed stage of the industrial revolution; the age of big business; the period of finance or securities capitalism. To a degree these descriptions are all true, yet none is completely descriptive. The typical business unit through which the economic processes are conducted is the corporation. To a greater and greater extent property is owned in the corporate form, and the corporation has become increasingly the owner of the nation's productive capital and the manufacturer and distributor of the commodities that are the basis of trade. It is also the recipient of, and the channel through which the component parts of the national income are made. This is the corporate age. The corporation and its activities and problems typify our modern American life, just as the New England village constituted the essence of colonial New England. As the manor was the focal point of medieval England, the corporation is the keynote of our day. The great characteristics of the corporation—continuous life, limited liability, and easy transferability of the units of ownership and indebtedness—have become so common as to be taken for granted.[1]

After all, the publicly owned corporation in its present magnitude is still a relatively new phenomenon. As with democracy, the ways in which it has been abused and its shortcomings sometimes blind one to its great essential service and still greater possibilities. The corporate system inherently has the qualities of economic democracy; and if this be true, Wall Street should be an instrumentality in its accomplishment.

---

[1] The implications are reviewed in *The Good Society*, by Walter Lippmann, pp. 277-281 (1937).

A reminder of the vast import of the corporation is contained in a statement of Dr. Nicholas Murray Butler, referred to approvingly by such different authors as Sereno S. Pratt and Walter Lippmann. He said: "I weigh my words, when I say that in my judgment the limited liability corporation is the greatest single discovery of modern times, whether you judge it by its social, by its ethical, by its industrial or, in the long run,—after we understand it and know how to use it,—by its political, effects. Even steam and electricity are far less important than the limited liability corporation, and they would be reduced to comparative impotence without it."

The formation of corporations without special act of the legislature is also taken for granted and has eliminated almost all trace of the early fear of the corporate form of doing business and skepticism as to its practicability. From a historical standpoint the corporation as we know it is only a recent institution. A little over a hundred years ago the London *Times* thought that joint-stock companies soon must go out of fashion. It expressed the widely held view that corporations could not compete with individuals and "can never successfully resist the vigilance and skill of their more active rivals." The *Monthly Review* wrote in 1825:

"The age of companies is passed. The application of capital in masses to some splendid object beyond the reach of *individual* enterprise will always distinguish Britain . . . But the proper occasions for such associations are comparatively rare and the principal degenerates into a pestilential abuse when it is applied to an ignorant and impertinent interference with the smaller details of trade, endeavoring to curse the humbler industry of individuals by the overwhelming power of capital *alone*."[2]

The advantage of the corporation quickly overcame the doubts of legislators and jurists both here and in England. The economic progress of the nineteenth century could not have taken place without the corporation. Paeans of praise gave way to renewed questioning with the rise of the trusts, but it was not until the twentieth century that the works of

[2] The foregoing quotations are from B. C. Hunt, *Development of the Business Corporation in England 1800-1867*, p. 55 (1936).

such writers as Justice Louis D. Brandeis (*Other People's Money*), Dr. William Z. Ripley (*Main Street and Wall Street*), and Messrs. Berle and Means (*The Modern Corporation and Private Property*) formed a basis for the institutional studies of corporations. All had one point in common—the recognition of finance or securities capitalism and its effects. This form of economic organization, essentially stock and bond capitalism, has three underlying characteristics: (1) the severance of capital and management; (2) the creation of corporate securities; and (3) the impersonalization of the financial relationship between the corporation and the investor.[3]

The constant increase of securities in relation to the national wealth creates a serious strain on the theory of marketability, one of the properties sought by investors, and lends to every phase of security issuance and security markets a national aspect. There can no longer be "rich men's" panics when securities are so widely held by individuals and financial institutions. The facts are summarized as follows: "The result of the figures is striking in the extreme. Liquid claims and the national wealth, strike a rough proportion of 16 per cent in 1880. This drops slightly in 1890; it increases to 18 per cent in 1900; and to 20 per cent in 1912. . . . The war decade, ending in 1922, shows a jump equal to that of the entire previous thirty years—from one-fifth to one-fourth. In ten years it had increased one-fourth. By 1930 it had increased to about 40 per cent. . . . The financial chaos of the depression of 1929 is possibly measured by the drop in ratio from 40 per cent (in 1930) to 33 per cent (in 1932), a fluctuation which in historical perspective is enormous; and the figure turns up, resuming the upward trend of proportion, in 1933."[4]

SECURITIES REGULATION

The issues of the World War deflected attention from the growing concern over the evils and defects brought to light in the prewar years. An unprecedented boom and collapse took place before the enactment of national legislation. In the

---

[3] Based on *The Evolution of Finance Capitalism*, by G. W. Edwards, pp. 5 ff. (1938), one of the most significant studies of the past decade.

[4] *Liquid Claims and National Wealth*, by Berle and Pederson, p. 77 (1934).

writer's opinion a new era was ushered in by the stinging rebuke to financial America contained in President Roosevelt's first inaugural address. The nature of the legislation might have been softened if the attitude of Wall Street's spokesmen had been different, or if consideration of the Securities Exchange Act had not been accompanied by rank manipulation and indefensible pool operations. The public might have forgiven the mistakes that were only a part of the excesses in almost every field of business during the "new era." It has always seemed to the writer that Wall Street, for a period after the reopening of the Stock Exchange in 1933, had the ball, but fumbled badly. Later the public and Congress were no longer in a mood to pay attention to pleas that finance could regulate itself. Details may be changed, but the imprint of the examples of bad faith and recklessness has been stamped on the public mind so thoroughly that national regulation seems certain to be permanent. The basis of this regulation, the nature of which has made up a large part of this book, is a rejection of both the theory of laissez-faire and complete governmental control. As Dr. Edwards states in the study above referred to: "The third, or liberal policy, is opposed to the abolition of security capitalism but at the same time is based on the conviction that the system cannot function without control. The liberal theory aims rather to develop a proper mechanism of control by private and public agencies which will overcome the evils of security capitalism and at the same time retain the benefits which the system yielded to society in leading capital-accumulating countries of the world throughout the nineteenth century."

One of the administrators of the new legislation, Commissioner J. D. Ross, now administrator of the great Bonneville Dam project, and a scientist without animus, described the Commission as the "policemen of America's securities." His judgment, however, extended to the constructive side of the Commission's influence: "So, it is coming about that while the Securities and Exchange Commission is instituted to protect the bondholder and the stockholder, it is also protecting the man who is willing to put out bonds and stocks that have a real value back of them. It helps such a man by exposing the man who has little or nothing back of the securities he offers for sale. The nation wants to see the man with proper principles succeed. . . . So it is that in many quarters those who originally opposed the SEC are now pleased with its results and realize that it is a help and not a hindrance to any legitimate business."[5]

Neither the legislation nor the Commission is perfect, and an open mind is as greatly needed in Washington as in Wall Street. It would be surprising if the statutes could not be improved upon or administration technique bettered with the passage of time. When the Transportation Act of 1920 was passed and the Interstate Commerce Commission given authority over the issuance of new railroad securities, enthusiasts believed that the investor was now assured against loss. Partly through errors of judgment, but more largely because of unpredictable economic changes, some railroad securities offerings in the ten years that followed lost as great a part of their value as did the much-maligned foreign securities. Too much must not be expected either by or from the Commission. As its sway over finance expands there will be a danger that it will fall into the inconsistency of advocating economic decentralization while it is effectuating political centralization. Despite the strong language of Chief Justice Hughes in the J. Edward Jones case, I am not fearful over the alleged assumption of arbitrary power by the Commission. As the late Justice Cardozo observed in his trenchant dissenting opinion in the same case, the act invests the Commission with only restricted authority. He said: "A commission which is without coercive powers, which cannot arrest or amerce or imprison though a crime has been uncovered or even punish for contempt, but can only inquire and report, the propriety of every question in the course of the inquiry being subject to the supervision of the ordinary courts of justice, is likened with denunciatory fervor to the Star Chamber of the Stuarts. Historians may find hyperbole in the sanguinary simile." Against abuse of the appointive power we must rely on the watchfulness of the Senate and the force of public opinion. The successive heads

[5] Address of J. D. Ross, before the symposium on the "New Wall Street," New School for Social Research, March 31, 1937.

of the Commission to this writing—Joseph P. Kennedy, James M. Landis, and the present incumbent, William O. Douglas —have established a standard of administrative justice, without weakening the execution of the statutes, from which it will be difficult to depart. There can be no guaranty of continued excellence any more than in other arms of the government.

WALL STREET'S ATTITUDE

Gradually the new Wall Street must remove the association of the financial world with opposition to all measures of reform. One cannot deny that the matchless description of a certain type of conservative by the distinguished English statesman and writer, John Morley, frequently suggests Wall Street. The typical conservative, "with his inexhaustible patience of abuses that only torment others; his apologetic words for beliefs that may not be so precisely true as one might wish, and institutions that are not altogether so useful as some might think possible; his cordiality towards progress and improvement in a general way, and his coldness or antipathy to each progressive proposal in particular; his pygmy hope that life will one day become somewhat better, punily shivering by the side of his gigantic conviction that it might well be infinitely worse."

In the past Wall Street too often arrayed itself on the side of the ruthless financier and industrialist, and in politics accepted the status quo indiscriminately. A moderate publicist like Alexander D. Noyes stood out as an exception because he supported President Theodore Roosevelt's attacks on evident abuses by big business and finance, although he had no great liking for the President. Wall Street opposed the Hepburn Act that strengthened the Interstate Commerce Commission; the Income Tax Amendment; the Federal Reserve Act; and the establishment of the Federal Trade Commission. It supported the Fordney-McCumber tariff and acclaimed the Harding administration. During the investigation of the Teapot Dome Scandal one would have concluded that Senators La Follette and Wheeler had been accused of a crime. It is difficult to name a reform or progressive measure which Wall Street supported, much less originated. On the brighter side was the general sentiment against the raising of the tariff during the Hoover administration, the work of the Committee on Stock List, and the earnestness of the new administration of the Stock Exchange in its own program of reform and protection of the investor. The work yet to be done does not minimize the progress that has been made. Three incidents illustrate that progress and epitomize the character of the Wall Street. About the time of the bizarre episodes described in *Chapters in Erie*, the New York Stock Exchange asked the officers of the Delaware, Lackawanna & Western Railroad Company for financial information. The officials replied bluntly that they "make no reports and publish no statements, and have not done anything of the kind for the last five years." It is not recorded that the stock was stricken from the list or why the Exchange waited five years. In 1912 the following colloquy took place between the United States Senate Committee and a respected member of the New York Stock Exchange:

"Is it legitimate for a member to give an order to sell a certain amount of stock to one broker and an order to buy the same amount of the same stock to another broker?"

"So long as there is no collusion and the commissions are paid, it is not illegitimate."

Pressed as to whether or not he approved such transactions, the witness replied: "You are asking me a moral question; I am answering you as to the Stock Exchange questions."

Recently the president of an important railroad was asked by the Stock Exchange to appear for questioning before a committee to explain how it was that a notice that interest would be paid on a bond in the regular way was permitted to be published, only to be followed later in the day by a notice that the company had decided to take advantage of the grace period. Wide fluctuations in the quotations for the bonds followed. The Exchange acted vigorously and promptly. Its action impressed the financial world and was brought to the attention of the investors throughout the nation by the financial press. One single episode of this nature is worth half a dozen steps taken only after the insistence of the Commission or an angry outburst of public opinion.

Beyond the quotations on the board and the sputter of the

stock ticker are the reasons why Wall Street fascinates the imaginative observer. The investor has had a great part in molding history. One might write a significant history of the United States in terms of investment. Whereas the business-man ordinarily is satisfied to tend to his own knitting, the world's affairs are the business of Wall Street. The operator of a sugar refinery is interested chiefly in the sugar market, crop developments, national legislation, and international plans concerning sugar. Wall Street knows that no industry stands alone or can be isolated from the general situation. It watches wage policies in the automobile industry, rate deci-sions of the Interstate Commerce Commission, the develop-ment of the textile industry in Japan, the Bank of England discount rate, gold mining in Russia, repressuring of oil wells, the formation of public corporations, the use of a semiplastic in the aviation industry, changes in depreciation policies, the growth of giant food markets, the change in the make-up of the population as to age, and a myriad of other factors. The Wall Street mind should be singularly broad. Wall Street must learn that the sun does not rise at 10 A.M. and set at 3 P.M. Time and time again it has come to the writer's attention that the judgment of intelligent Wall Street observers con-cerning an industry's tendencies or the price structure of a commodity is sounder than that of executives in the respective businesses, who inescapably perhaps are unable to get the proper perspective. The Wall Street man is often something of an economist, accountant, technician, constitutional lawyer, historian, and prophet. It is regrettable that much of the best work done in Wall Street cannot reach the public at large; in the nature of things, the reports and studies made for insti-tutions and others are confidential.

Occasionally a glimpse of the broadening influence of finance may be caught. A striking example is afforded by two ad-dresses made in 1934 by Russell Leffingwell, a partner of J. P. Morgan & Company. The speaker declared: "Gold is not an end to itself. It is a means to an end. That end is monetary stability. Gold is meant to give confidence in the currency at home and it serves to settle balances abroad. But when the nations and populations scramble for gold, and attempt to convert external and internal balances into gold, the value of gold rises, prices and wages fall and the horrible cycle of deflation, with its terrible consequences in human suffering, begins to revolve toward the abyss. Then the only hope for humanity was to stop gold payments, to go off gold. . . ."

"Government must intervene to relieve the sufferings of the people. It is intolerable that the monetary mechanism evolved for the sole purpose of achieving stability and human welfare should be permitted ever again to run amuck as it did from 1929 to 1933. . . . During the last three years government policy put an end to deflation, brought about some measure of recovery, achieved monetary stabilization and provided necessary relief. Let us not be unmindful of the depth of economic despair from which in three years we have emerged, nor the vital necessity of government action along these lines, however critical we may be of the extent and manner in which public expenditures have been made, or of this and that phase of monetary policy."

A comparison of these statesmanlike utterances with the vapid generalities that were current in financial circles and the repetition of the dirge of certain academic economists who imitated the loose talk of the "baloney" dollar will illustrate what the writer has in mind. As Mr. Leffingwell implied, recognition of the need of action by government and the imperious necessity of forging a more adaptable monetary policy need not indicate acceptance of or agreement with every step taken.

WALL STREET'S PROBLEMS

The internal problems of Wall Street are serious and deserve sympathetic consideration. Stock Exchange seats, once valued at over $600,000, have fallen to as little as a tenth of the highest price paid, with similar depreciation in the value of memberships on other stock exchanges. Not all members, of course, acquired their memberships at around the peak levels, but the shrinkage in the values is tremendous if the number of seats is multiplied by the depreciation per unit. No businessman can watch such shrinkage of part of his capital with equanimity and absence of ill feeling toward those allegedly responsible, directly or indirectly.

The Street, unfortunately, thought of the years immediately preceding 1929 as normal, and some have refused to admit that the easy profits and big incomes were mainly the result of purely adventitious circumstances, unlikely to repeat themselves. Accustomed to a high place in the nation's counsels, another blow has been the dwindling of Wall Street's importance. Perhaps the "most unkindest cut of all" has been the little-concealed indifference of businessmen toward the plight of the Street, a reminder of the feeling even among those who have used its services for their own ends that finance expected too much for its contribution. Retrenchment and adjustment have been difficult, for those accustomed to an income of $50,000 or of $5,000 a year. The process is still incomplete. The rise of the open-end investment trust has taken business from brokers and dealers. Low interest rates and a general belief in the advent of inflation have been partly responsible for the lack of interest in the purchase of corporate bonds by businessmen and small investors. A less continuous market on the Stock Exchange, shrinkage of activity, and larger margin requirements have discouraged active trading. Stories of the fortunes lost in the market and the revelations of the investigation of Congress into investment banking and stock exchange practices have hurt confidence in Wall Street. Lack of sympathy with the policies of the national administration have made capital timid—it is not our province to inquire here if this attitude has been wholly justified.

The many changes made necessary by the Securities Act of 1933 and the Securities Exchange Act of 1934; the regulations of the stock exchanges; the rules against practices long established and familiar have all tended to create uncertainty and a sense of instability. At this writing incorporation of Stock Exchange firms is being considered; policies regarding segregation have not been determined. Depletion of capital has raised questions concerning the sufficiency of the capital of underwriters to take care of the country's requirements were other conditions favorable to new financing. Financial institutions have made inroads on the business of underwriters and dealers by purchases of entire issues. Suggestions that the addition of associate memberships would shift business to the Stock Exchange are being considered. Changes so sweeping and rapid are bound to be painful. But change, ever resisted, is irresistible. The future of Wall Street is not so dismal as it seems. To suggestions for increasing the opportunities for service and profit of the new Wall Street, the remaining paragraphs of this closing chapter are devoted, in the belief that if they are followed we shall witness, to paraphrase the words of Benjamin Franklin at the Constitutional Convention, a rising and not a setting sun.

Around the information now made available to the general public by the Commission and the Stock Exchange is the material for rebuilding faith and confidence in the securities market. Throughout the provisions of the Securities Acts and the additional requirements by the Stock Exchange runs the dominant note of removal of the veil of mystery and secrecy from all matters pertaining to finance and securities, in so far as this is possible. In discussing the purposes of the legislation, Dean Landis, speaking then as the head of the Commission, classified the aims into three groups: first, control of credit for the purpose of buying or carrying securities, and third, the elimination of fraudulent and manipulative practices; the second aim, he declared, "and this is basic to the entire legislative scheme—is the work-a-day task of making the investment problem less a matter of mystery and more a matter of intelligence, by seeking and presenting adequate information about companies whose securities are traded upon the national markets or are offered for sale upon a national scale."

Before reviewing the information that has been opened to public scrutiny or made easily accessible, let us inquire what Wall Street has done with this priceless asset. The information has been used, but no campaign has been embarked upon to make the public understand the tremendous difference between the old and the new Wall Street. If half the effort had been expended in this direction that was originally directed toward defeating the pending legislation and decrying its provisions, the public would by this time have an adequate understanding of the progress achieved in this phase of the warfare in behalf of the investing public. It is a program on which Wall Street can unite, forgetting the differences over the division of the responsibility of the change, and the diverse groups in the financial district—underwriters, dealers, and brokers—should be one in this respect. The blunder in not utilizing this resource would drive the advertising managers of a large industry or its public relations counsel to commit hara-kiri; it is as if the meat packing industry, following the legislation for inspection and government certification, had devoted the following years to criticism of the law and mournful backward glances at the "good old days" before Upton Sinclair's *Jungle* and the crusade of President Theodore Roosevelt, instead of emphasizing the new protection to the consuming public. There is still time for an intelligent, comprehensive, dignified, but forceful program to acquaint the "consumers" of securities with the meaning of the new efforts in their behalf. It is a challenge to the vision of Wall Street, its ability to adapt itself to changing conditions, and its good business sense.

Around the information now made available to the investor by the Commission and the Stock Exchange, I repeat, is the material for rebuilding faith and confidence in the securities market. Let us review briefly the flow of information that would have astounded an investor, investment dealer, or broker ten years ago. The only complaint with reference to new financing is the difficulty in selecting from the wealth of data its essence. The sales and purchases of "insiders" are made public monthly. Reacquisition of securities by issuing corporations is published regularly; the extent of the short interest is now published monthly, and in addition, the number of shares of the individual stocks in which the largest short interest exists; the purchases and sales of odd lots appear daily, only a few days after the date on which the orders have been executed. The trading for the account of members is published weekly. The statistics are broken down further to show purchases and sales contracted on and off the floor; transactions of specialists in the stocks in which they are registered, and the percentage of all member transactions to the total. The latter consistently averages between 18.5 to 22 per cent. Fig-

SECURITIES AND EXCHANGE COMMISSION

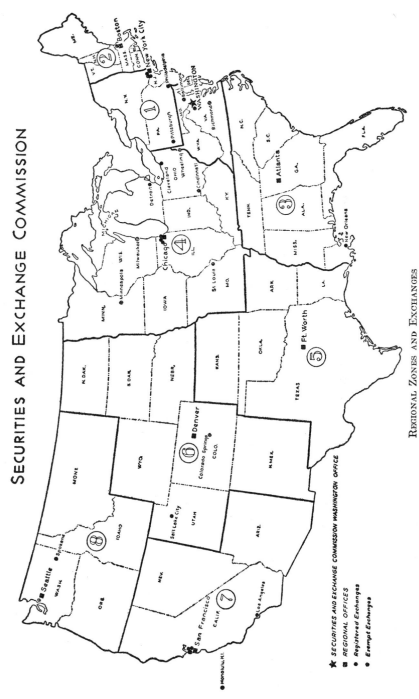

REGIONAL ZONES AND EXCHANGES

Note: Another regional office was established in Cleveland, Ohio, in November, 1938.

★ SECURITIES AND EXCHANGE COMMISSION WASHINGTON OFFICE
▣ REGIONAL OFFICES
● Registered Exchanges
● Exempt Exchanges

ures are regularly issued as to the "restricted" accounts of stock exchange firms, that is, the accounts that cannot make further purchases without the deposit of additional margin. The foregoing is exclusive of the brokers' loan data (first published in 1926) and the borrowings of New York Stock Exchange members on collateral from New York banks and trust companies, and from private bankers, brokers, foreign bank agencies, and others—the first weekly and the second monthly. For the first time in the history of Wall Street, the customer may examine the financial statement of his broker.

In relating what the Commission and the Stock Exchange do, let us not forget the wider services at which one can only guess. Manipulation that would take place but for fear of detection; withheld plans of reorganization prepared with an eye toward favoring one class of security; caution in purchases of raw materials because the facts must be made known; schemes that may or may not be actually fraudulent, but whose promoters shun the disclosure of the facts; more moderate fees in reorganization plans—these suggest the many ways in which the investor is protected in a quiet, unobtrusive manner that is especially effective, although not spectacular.

Slowly the financial map of the United States is being remade. The map itself has more detail than at any time in the past. There are fewer unsurveyed areas; in this respect the Commission's institutional studies have been explorations as notable as the famous Lewis and Clark expedition of the Northwest. The authorities and those engaged in the securities business have made travel safer and the roads have never been so free of highwaymen. When the treacherous roads of earlier days and the marauders are allowed to become historical curiosities, the map will be used by a greater number.

But if the police are forever recalling the days when travel was unsafe, and those who supply the travelers with their equipment constantly tell about the bad road conditions that once were prevalent, is it any wonder that would-be travelers are frightened? Perhaps it is expecting too much, but once the restoration of confidence in private enterprise revives, Wall Street may become a strong factor in the movement for economic democracy that underlies the great political issues of the times.

CREATING AN INVESTMENT MARKET

The origin of the commission rates on brokerage transactions and gross profits on the sale of securities has been given little attention and would make an interesting study. Commission rates have been changed from time to time. The present rates on the New York Stock Exchange became effective early in January, 1938. Commissions on bonds have remained the same for many years. According to calculations made by the Commission and used by Dr. P. P. Gourrich, in a study on investment banking methods, the average spread on high-grade railroad bonds sold between 1920 and 1931 and on high-grade corporate bonds of all descriptions sold between 1927 and 1931 was about 5 per cent. Recently the gross spread has averaged less than 2.5 per cent. On preferred stocks of investment character the spread has been about 4½ per cent of the public offering price. On speculative common stocks 15 to 20 per cent appears to have been a fair average. The spreads cited are the gross profit of the underwriters; selling group spreads are between two-thirds and three-fourths of the underwriters' margin.

Two assumptions about the securities business seem to be beyond controversy: (1) the tendency in the direction of an investment market and away from a speculative market is desirable; (2) the business is considered to be affected with a public interest. If these assumptions be correct, it is clear that commission rates and profit margins are too low. The method of compensation appears to require drastic change, or at any rate a thorough overhauling. Higher commission rates and profit margins, it is urged, will protect the public and at the same time place the securities business on a more satisfactory footing. The present conditions militate against the recommendation of investment securities and, in the opinion of the writer, stimulate the turnover of funds, often to no real purpose.

The customer of a Stock Exchange firm, for example, who wishes to invest in a high-grade bond is shown a list of five issues, with a brief description of each. He decides to purchase and places an order to buy $10,000 Consumers Power Corporation 1st mortgage 3¼s, 1966. The gross commission on this transaction is $25. If the bonds were bought at 103, the brokerage commission represents less than ¼ of 1 per cent of the amount invested. Let us change the facts somewhat. A customer of a dealer firm tells a salesman that he has $10,000 to invest. The salesman calls on this customer a number of times. A return of 7 percent is desired. The salesman can offer 100 shares of Ohio Edison Company 6 per cent preferred stock at around 99, or 800 shares of a speculative common stock at $12.50 a share; the gross profit on the Ohio Edison preferred stock, not a new issue, is $1 a share and on the common stock $1.50 a share. The gross profit in the first case is $100 and in the second $1,200. The scale of commission rates and spreads penalizes investment and encourages the recommendation of speculative securities.

The buyer of $10,000 principal amount of bonds pays $25 commissions, or ¼ of 1 per cent. The funds probably will remain "locked up" for a number of years. The broker would make a gross commission of $75 on the purchase of 500 shares of stock bought at $20 a share. Moreover, the chances of the customer selling, repurchasing, or exchanging his stock in three months or less is infinitely greater than if he purchased a high-grade bond. Naturally the broker will not be elated over the elimination of a potential source of future income; the meager commission from the original transaction is not sufficient compensation. A salesman receiving 40 per cent of the gross profit on business transacted is confronted with a chance to earn almost $500 if a customer buys a newly issued common stock as against $40 if he decides on a sound public utility preferred stock. Is he not being tempted unfairly? It would be expecting too much of human nature if the virtues of the more speculative stock were not emphasized. The purchaser of a public utility preferred stock of investment quality must seek continued income rather than possible capital gains. There is no reason to expect quick changes in market price.

In no other business would a broker be expected to consummate a $10,000 transaction for $25 or a salesman be expected to use his efforts for a commission of $40. One of the obstacles in the way of changing the market to an investment basis is the inability of the securities business to maintain itself on the earnings from the execution of brokerage orders in, or from the sale of, investment securities. This does not apply to the same extent to new securities, but these are only a small fraction of the total transactions or total available securities. The investing public does not gain from the low profit. Too large a part of the securities business proceeds on the theory of rapid turnover. To make income securities more attractive to those in the business would be a long step forward in eventually teaching the investing public to be income-minded. Acceptance of the principle of higher compensation would relieve the pressure on customers' men and salesmen to do business with a customer frequently. It might lead to many wholesome changes, one of which would be the greater care in the selection of securities owing to the knowledge that the cost of buying and selling, in itself, is of some moment. Secondly, the eagerness to sell new securities would be reduced, and customers would be more likely to purchase securities suitable to their needs. In all probability the profit in the sale of new securities will always exceed that of seasoned securities, but the difference can be cut down.

The real estate broker's commission rates are generally a fixed percentage of the purchase price, and vary according to the type of real estate involved. The schedule of commissions adopted by the Real Estate Board of New York, Inc. is 2½ per cent of the sales price, on real property in the Borough of Manhattan up to a price of $100,000. The brokerage fee is based not on the sum that changes hands, but on the total price. In the sale of a home for $10,000 subject to a $7,000 first mortgage, the buyer parts with $3,000, subject to minor adjustments. The broker's fee is $250; not 2½ per cent on $3,000, or $75. Few merchandisers work on so narrow a margin as the investment bankers and brokers. It has been suggested that few underwriters are willing to "nurse" a business along, carrying the securities until the condition of the business makes it possible to market the securities. To do this successfully the normal margin of profit would have to be larger, since the new issue business is highly irregular and the investment banking firm must maintain its organization during dull periods. The low basis of compensation also affects the segregation of brokerage and dealer activities. Many firms regard the former as a "bread-and-butter" business, which enables them to cover their overhead and expect their underwriting activities to furnish the biggest part of their profits. In smaller communities the difficulties of effecting segregation are especially difficult. Many brokerage houses depend on their own trading activities to supplement the income from the execution of customers' orders. It may be desirable to reduce the trading activities on firm capital, but if commission rates are to remain at present levels, and the volume of activity is reduced permanently, further restrictions on firm trading must result in radical changes in brokerage firms, since the present business arrangements will be unprofitable. In recent years consolidations, less elaborate offices, and general reduction of waste have reduced operating expenses. It is doubtful if much more can be accomplished through cuts in overhead. The aggregate number of undesirables has been reduced. As yet new securities are saleable only after genuine effort, except the issues of the largest and most successful corporations. In time decentralization tendencies may make it possible to sell the securities of secondary corporations in the regions in which they operate, with a lesser reliance on New York, Chicago, and other large financial centers. The need of creating an interest in securities will remain and the investment banking business particularly will have to receive encouragement if industry is to receive new capital through public financing.

At the present time no one in the securities business is engaged in selling high-grade securities already outstanding to small investors in the same way that hundreds of firms are actively engaged in the sale of speculative and semispeculative securities. By making it possible to earn a fair profit, sales of seasoned securities would be promoted. One of the reasons for the popularity of open-end investment trusts is the inducement offered to the dealer by the commission, which averages around 5 per cent. This is not pointed out in a critical sense, but the millions of dollars placed annually in these issues mainly through intensive sales efforts illustrates that the buying habits of the investing public may be changed. In the only previous recent period that bonds were sold to the small investor it was made possible because security salesmen were able to earn a commission of several points per bond. Unfortunately these were generally new securities of second- and third-grade quality, after the high interest rate bonds of the early twenties were redeemed. The same effort, if applied to seasoned securities, would have far-reaching effects on the securities business and on the experience of the investor. The business is geared to large turnover. The spirit of rapid in-and-out trading and the expectation of quick capital appreciation permeates the securities business. When it is remembered that the annual rate of appreciation of a fund invested on the industrial securities in the Dow-Jones averages during the extraordinary period from 1900 to 1938 was only 7.8 per cent, assuming that the dividends were spent, expectations of tremendous profits are shown to be groundless.[6] The whole economy would gain from an effort to make it worth while to interest the public in investing.

The story of the success of the open-end management trust illustrates what may be accomplished in the sale of securities. The open-end trust came into prominence after the glaring errors of the management trusts had been thoroughly aired and the obvious defects of the fixed trusts had led to the virtual abandonment of this type of investment trust. In the face of these handicaps the open-end trust has become of increasing importance. At times sizable distribution has continued when the general lack of interest was as striking as in the spring of 1938. From 1933 to 1936, 67.7 per cent of the effective registration statements for investment trusts and investment companies covered issues of open-end companies. The sales record of open-end management investment companies for the years 1932 to 1936, inclusive, and the percentage to total sales of investment trust and investment company securities follow:[7]

[6] Dwight C. Rose, address on "Common Stocks at the Current Price Level," 1928.

[7] Securities and Exchange Commission, *Investment Trusts and Investment Companies,* Part Two, Vol. 11, p. 11.

	Amount of Sales (in millions of dollars)	Percentage of Total Sales
1932	26	21.
1933	82	66.2
1934	69	45.4
1935	86	50.3
1936	₁23	61.1

The results from a management standpoint have been fair. Few have done better than the averages, or indices of common stock prices generally, but the period has been a trying one. In diverting the investor's purpose from trying to "trade" or "beat the market," the net result has been wholesome. The experience of the average investor in stocks undoubtedly has been poorer. From the Wall Street angle, the overcoming of sales resistance by effective merchandising has far-reaching significance. Investors do not buy investment trust issues on their own initiative; they must be sold. The successful distribution of these securities, although aided by the sentiment favorable to equities and the soundness of the investment trust principle, as well as by the repurchase contracts now general, points the way toward convincing the investor of the justice of a fair merchandising profit. Beginning with an appeal to the small, uninformed investor, who may not always have understood the "loading charge," the average sale of open-end trusts has shown an increase. Sales are being made to large institutional investors, estates, and sophisticated individual purchasers of securities. The gross profit in 1936, if an average 8 per cent load is assumed, was $9,840,000. Dealers, as distinguished from the originators, earned a gross profit of around $5,000,000 out of the total. The purchase of an equal amount of bonds on the stock exchange at par would result in gross commissions of $615,000 after doubling the $2.50 commission per $1,000 bond to include the commissions on both sides of the trade. At an average price of $100 per share for preferred stocks, the total commissions of the brokers would be $922,500.

The difference explains the aggressive, intelligent merchandising activities of open-end investment trust distributors and the general apathy of brokers and dealers toward high-grade income securities or seasoned equities, except when a block is available.

Until this problem is attacked, I am sure the organic defect of the financial world will not be corrected. Its correction is necessary to the soundness of the securities business. This is only the beginning of its importance. The transformation of the securities business, whose prosperity is now conditioned in great measure by turnover will have pervasive effects on the nation. Spurred on by the assurance of a fair profit through the sale or execution of orders for existing investment securities, efforts will be directed toward making security buyers investors in the sense that they purchase either for income or for long-term capital appreciation.

The principle of full disclosure has been established in the sale of new securities. Manipulation is effectively outlawed; the advantages of insiders have been reduced; brokerage practices have been improved; and the customer's funds are better protected. As additional changes are made and the new mechanism is adjusted, the machine will be as close to the optimum of perfection as we have the right to expect. Revision of the compensation of the operators is now required so that it will be more profitable for them to sell the finest quality of goods that the machine is capable of producing. Only in this way can the remaining vestiges of the "casino" aspects of Wall Street be removed and the securities business be lifted to the level of a profession.

APPENDIX I

New Securities Registration

Statistics, by Months, of New Securities,[1] Included in Registration Statements Fully Effective September 1, 1934–June 1, 1938

[Amounts in dollars]

Month	Total Securities Effectively Registered		
	Number of State-ments	Number of Issues	Total Amount Registered
1934			
September....................	18	22	$ 36,003,991
October.......................	13	16	29,567,475
November.....................	14	32	34,547,422
December.....................	18	26	40,240,879
1935			
January......................	13	18	11,044,405
February.....................	9	10	36,843,133
March........................	24	27	130,015,787
April.........................	27	30	154,596,548
May..........................	27	33	140,208,002
June..........................	30	39	192,630,681
Total, September 1934–June 1935	193	253	805,698,323
1935			
July..........................	47	52	530,474,751
August.......................	34	50	254,062,322
September....................	30	42	319,874,100
October......................	49	65	406,086,507
November....................	46	56	289,771,988
December....................	43	57	212,084,696
1936			
January......................	39	48	275,696,001
February.....................	42	56	212,088,937
March........................	53	83	583,391,363
April.........................	87	128	751,012,738
May..........................	59	83	319,318,654
June..........................	59	104	523,439,405
Total fiscal year..............	588	824	4,677,301,462

[1] New securities in this table include all securities registered with the Securities and Exchange Commission with the exception of reorganization and exchange securities, certificates of deposit, and voting trust certificates.

STATISTICS BY MONTHS, OF NEW SECURITIES,[1] INCLUDED IN REGISTRATION STATEMENTS FULLY EFFECTIVE SEPTEMBER 1, 1934–JUNE 1, 1938 (*Concluded*)

[Amounts in dollars]

Month	Total Securities Effectively Registered		
	Number of Statements	Number of Issues	Total Amount Registered
1936			
July..........................	67	110	$ 362,924,906
August........................	56	79	286,021,610
September.....................	52	79	260,079,511
October.......................	79	114	526,329,912
November.....................	49	67	266,025,753
December.....................	82	124	698,408,036
1937			
January.......................	47	69	429,989,754
February......................	56	93	491,399,718
March........................	79	113	469,907,443
April.........................	97	161	288,075,987
May..........................	62	88	238,067,626
June..........................	61	81	369,065,424
Total fiscal year 1937..........	787	1,178	4,686,295,680
1937			
July..........................	60	85	266,886,086
August........................	48	69	302,343,200
September.....................	38	52	156,394,527
October.......................	30	36	127,621,431
November.....................	37	52	38,158,526
December.....................	46	75	201,374,253
1938			
January.......................	17	36	79,909,170
February......................	22	29	206,697,937
March........................	18	29	69,211,924
April.........................	27	34	97,370,695
May..........................	24	36	93,634,322
June..........................	16	26	272,447,605
Total, July 1937–June 1938.....	406	598	$1,926,209,178

[1] New securities in this table include all securities registered with the Securities and Exchange Commission with the exception of reorganization and exchange securities, certificates of deposit, and voting trust certificates.

APPENDIX II

SUMMARY OF PART II OF THE REPORT OF THE SECURITIES AND EXCHANGE COMMISSION IN THE WHITNEY INVESTIGATION—RECOMMENDATIONS OF THE NEW YORK STOCK EXCHANGE AND THE COMMISSION

Part I of this report has related the chain of events which led up to and attended the eventual failure of Richard Whitney & Co., followed as it was by the losses which resulted from Richard Whitney's misuse of customers' funds and his embezzlement of their securities. There has been described the disciplinary action taken by the New York Stock Exchange when its responsible officials became aware of Richard Whitney's defalcation. There has also been set forth in detail the limited facilities provided by the former management of the Exchange for the supervision of the affairs of the members.

After the events described in Part I had occurred, the earlier plans for reorganization of the administrative machinery of the New York Stock Exchange and for the installation of a new management were speedily completed. That new management has been working cooperatively with this Commission in an endeavor to raise the standards of practices of the Exchange members and to improve the system which permitted Richard Whitney to operate to the detriment of the financial community for almost twelve years without let or hindrance.

PROGRAM OF THE NEW YORK STOCK EXCHANGE

The new management of the New York Stock Exchange has proposed to inaugurate various measures as an immediate step toward strengthening and improving methods of regulation by the Exchange of its own affairs and of the relations between the members and the public. The program includes the following:

1. FINANCIAL STATEMENT. QUESTIONNAIRES

Provisions for increased supervision of the conduct of members' business by the Exchange, through increase of financial statement

284

requirements and examinations. It is proposed to increase the number of periodic financial statements, or "questionnaires," required to be filed with the Exchange and to require annual independent audits of firms doing a public business. The Exchange will undertake supervisory audits and more frequent examination and inspection of member firms by Exchange auditors at irregular intervals and without prior warning.

2. MARGIN TRANSACTIONS

Prohibition of margin transactions and the maintenance of margin accounts by member firms and by partners of member firms doing a business with the public. This proposal is aimed at removing further risks to public customers growing out of speculative activity for the account of the house or its partners.

3. CAPITAL AND INDEBTEDNESS RELATIONSHIP

Establishment of a 15 to 1 ratio between a broker's indebtedness and his working capital.

4. SEPARATION OF BROKERAGE AND DEALER CAPITAL

Separation of capital employed in the brokerage business by firms doing business with the public from that used in incurring commitments by the broker as an underwriter or dealer. As a part of this measure, the Exchange proposes to encourage the formation of separate corporate affiliates of brokerage firms to handle the dealer and underwriting activities, thus attempting to insulate brokerage customers from the risks inherent in underwriter and dealer commitments. In this connection, the desirability of making such a program a requirement for all such firms is clearly set forth in a letter of the president of the New York Stock Exchange to the Commission, dated October 24, 1938.

5. SPECIAL LOANS

A requirement that members and member firms and partners thereof report to the Exchange all substantial loans made to or by such persons or firms except those fully secured by readily marketable collateral. It is also proposed in this connection to prohibit, so far as members are concerned, the making of any unsecured loan by or to any governor of the Exchange or any officer or employe thereof, unless the prior written approval of the appropriate committee is obtained.

6. CURRENT UNDERWRITING INFORMATION

A requirement that weekly information as to underwriting positions by members and any affiliated dealer corporations be filed with the Exchange.

7. CENTRAL SECURITIES DEPOSITORY

In addition, the New York Stock Exchange plans to establish for its membership a central securities depository, to receive, hold, and make deliveries of customers' securities whether margin, excess collateral, or safekeeping. This proposal is outlined in a letter received by the Commission from the president of the New York Stock Exchange under date of October 24, 1938, and published in adjoining column.

PROGRAM HELD CONSTRUCTIVE

The foregoing program is a constructive approach to many of the problems which are the products of the system so jealously protected by the old regime. It evidences the process which a progressive exchange should constantly undergo as it seeks through effective regulation to render greater service and to afford increased safety to its customers. Such steps are inevitable in a securities business in which we find combined in single firms and single individuals such disparate functions as those of broker and dealer and broker and banker.

The program of the New York Stock Exchange is suggestive of an appropriate commencement toward the solution of the many similar problems existing in other parts of our national securities markets. The Commission therefore recommends that the other national securities exchanges, as well as brokers and dealers contemplating the formation of national securities associations under the recently enacted Section 15A of the act, consider and appraise these proposals in the light of the situations peculiar to each. Certain of the measures which the New York Stock Exchange has proposed may not be applicable to members of all of the other securities exchanges or to all brokers and dealers. But a large measure of adaptation is possible.

PROGRAM OF THE COMMISSION

However, adoption of rules by this Commission is also desirable in order to assure uniform business practices by all brokers whether or not members of a national securities exchange. Rules of this

Commission are further necessary in order to supplement and to strengthen the programs of regulation which are undertaken by the exchanges themselves.

[Under Section 19 (B) of the Securities Exchange Act of 1934, the Commission is empowered to alter or supplement the rules of national securities exchanges relating to certain specified subjects, including, so far as is here relevant, "safeguards in respect of the financial responsibility of members." Section 8 (B) of the act requires members of national securities exchanges and other brokers doing business through members to establish and maintain their capital within such minimum relationship to their indebtedness as the Commission's rules may prescribe. Section 8 (C) prohibits members of national securities exchanges or brokers or dealers doing a business through members, from rehypothecating or commingling their customers' securities in certain circumstances if in contravention of rules and regulations which that section authorizes the Commission to adopt. Section 15 (C) prohibits all brokers and dealers from using the mails or instrumentalities of interstate commerce to effect transactions in the over-the-counter markets in contravention of rules and regulations of the Commission with respect to the financial responsibility of such brokers and dealers. By Section 17 (A) the Commission is empowered to require the making, keeping and preservation on the part of all members of exchanges and of brokers and dealers registered with the Commission, of such accounts, books and records, as the Commission may prescribe by regulation as necessary or appropriate.]

3. The Commission therefore proposes to issue rules and regulations establishing the same 15 to 1 ratio between a broker's indebtedness and his capital as is proposed by the New York Stock Exchange; and it will make appropriate definition of the terms "aggregate indebtedness" and "net capital" for the purposes of the regulation.

B. Regulations under section 8 (C) of the act will prohibit rehypothecation of customers' safekeeping securities, limit the extent to which customers' margin securities may be repledged and place restrictions on the commingling of customers' securities.

C. The Commission will also promulgate rules requiring the keeping and preservation of books and records essential to the proper conduct of a brokerage business.

D. The Commission is of the opinion that full realization of effective regulation of the industry in the public interest is to be found in the establishment of trust institutions to assume the banking and custodial functions of the brokerage business. Only such a system (hereafter described more fully) can be an adequate substitute for direct governmental supervision and control. Pending the establishment and full operation of trust institutions, no measure of protection can be overlooked. The machinery which the New York Stock Exchange will set up for the voluntary separation by its members of their brokerage and dealer businesses through the formation of separate corporate affiliates to handle their dealer and underwriting activities has constructive possibilities in this direction if properly encouraged by the Exchange. The Commission views the full development of this plan as an essential of interim regulation, and it is hopeful that such measures as these will prove to be an appropriate area for regulation by the industry rather than for further and additional regulation by government.

These combined proposals represent a program well balanced between regulation by the industry itself and regulation by the Commission, and the principles which underlie these various proposals rest upon a sound basis, since they undertake to deal with the problems arising from the broker-dealer and the broker-banker combinations.

THE BANKING ASPECTS OF BROKERAGE

The broker (both on an exchange and over-the-counter) who does a margin business performs a banking function at least equal in importance to his brokerage services. Yet, so well accepted is the practice of including banking accommodations along with brokerage service, that custom has obscured the full significance of the banking function performed.

Many activities regarded as incidental to the brokerage business are in reality banking activities. The broker loans money to margin purchasers from his own funds, retaining the purchased securities as collateral for the loan. He makes similar loans with funds obtained from banks. Just as banks receive cash deposits, so the broker receives and retains cash, or "free credit," balances for the account of customers, and, in the manner of a bank, makes loans from such funds. An increasing tendency on the part of customers to leave their fully paid-for securities with their brokers for safe-keeping, as well as securities which constitute excess collateral not needed to secure the customers' margin accounts, has resulted in the assumption by brokers of custodial functions traditionally performed by the banks or trust companies.

The banking business done by brokers involves hundreds of millions of dollars. As of August 31, 1938, member firms of the New

York Stock Exchange alone held deposits of customers' cash in the form of free credit balances aggregating approximately $272,-000,000. As of the same date, the total market value of securities held in margin accounts carried by New York Stock Exchange brokers has been estimated at more than $2,000,000,000. Loans to customers by New York Stock Exchange brokers have in the recent past regularly aggregated in the neighborhood of a billion dollars. The total market value of all customers' fully paid or excess collateral securities held by all brokers is not yet definitely known. Nevertheless, it has been conservatively estimated to be many times greater than the amount of customers' free credit balances.

[As of the end of August, 1938, bank borrowings by member firms of the New York Stock Exchange aggregated approximately $570,-000,000 while the total of their loans to customers was approximately $865,000,000. During the rising market in the spring of 1937 these figures reached a total of $1,215,000,000 for brokers' borrowings and $1,559,000,000 for the total of brokers' loans to customers.]

BANKING FUNCTION NOT REGULATED

This banking business, carried on not only by many members of exchanges, but also by those engaged in the business of buying and selling securities in other markets as well, is neither regulated nor supervised as a banking business by the government, state or federal. Its supervision has been left in the hands of the exchanges. The deficiencies in the system in vogue under the old regime of the New York Stock Exchange have been noted. In spite of such deficiencies, however, the record of stock exchange houses in terms of financial failures has been remarkably good. Yet the objective here is that of supplying further and more adequate safeguards so that inherent financial risks will be further minimized.

Furthermore, we have seen instances in which the handling of customers' securities has been both lax and in disregard of the ordinary standards of trusteeship. Customers' free or excess collateral securities have not always been kept segregated from the securities of the firm or its partners, or from securities held on margin for other customers. The use by brokers of these customers' securities to collateralize their own business loans in an effort to tide themselves over a crisis comes to light only in such cases as that of Richard Whitney, where failure of the effort resulted in its detection. Furthermore, despite exchange rules to the contrary, margin securities of customers have been rehypothecated with banks in excessive amounts which bear no relation to customers' indebtedness to the broker or have been so commingled with the securities of the firm or its partners or those of other customers as to subject their owners to unjustifiable hazards.

Customers' free credit balances have been regularly subjected to even greater hazards. Evidence adduced in the Whitney case indicates that it has been the usual practice among brokers to commingle customers' funds with those of the firm and to use them for whatever the daily demands of the business may require. The cash balances of member firms of the New York Stock Exchange have normally been far below the total amount of customers' free credit balances—the customers' cash held and used by the brokers.

Abstract from reports of New York Stock Exchange member firms to the Federal Reserve Board showing the relation between total cash on hand and in banks and customers' free credit balances:

Date	Number of Firms Reporting	Cash on Hand and in Banks (000 omitted)	Free Credit Balances (000 omitted)	Excess of Free Credit Balances Over Cash on Hand and in Banks (000 omitted)
August 31, 1938	388	$200,001	$272,100	$72,099
June 30, 1938	389	215,894	257,999	43,105
December 31, 1937	415	231,546	277,840	46,294
June 30, 1937	423	214,273	265,715	51,442
December 31, 1936	418	248,962	342,175	94,213
June 30, 1936	420	219,952	276,107	57,045

The risks to customers inherent in the merging of a banking business with the agency functions of a broker will always be accentuated where there is absent any real financial supervision. Yet in the conduct of those activities by brokers generally, there has been little supervision of a character comparable to that exercised over banks and the brokers are not subjected by public authority to banking standards or requirements.

THE BROKER'S BUSINESS AS DEALER

Some exchange houses do nothing but a brokerage business. More frequently, however, brokerage houses also trade for their own account and engage in the underwriting business. This combination of functions obviously entails certain risks. As we have earlier said:

"In addition to executing brokerage orders for customers, commission houses may perform a diversity of functions. They may act as principals in underwritings, in the primary and secondary distribution of securities, and in trading operations for firm account.

They may serve as fiduciaries in furnishing investment advice to customers, in conducting discretionary accounts and in managing investment trusts. These interrelationships may be further complicated when such firms extend credit to their customers, hold customers' securities in pledge or hold customers' free funds on deposit; or when partners of such firms trade for their own account or act as directors or officers of corporations whose securities are listed on exchanges.

"The financial interests of a commission house, the activities of which are thus diversified, may run counter to the best interests of those for whom it acts as agent. Such a commission house may solicit brokerage customers to purchase securities which it has underwritten or is distributing or in which it has a position or an option. In furnishing investment advice, its recommendations may be colored by its security commitments. It may sell its own securities to accounts over which it has discretion. Substantial participation in underwriting or distributing operations or excessive trading for its own account may impair the solvency of a firm, thereby jeopardizing the securities, equities, and credit balances of customers. A commission house managing an investment trust may use the trust as an outlet for issues which the firm has underwritten or is distributing; or it may employ the buying power of the trust to maintain the price of such issues.

"Undoubtedly, abuses incident to these multiple relationships are held in check by the standards of business conduct prevailing among reputable commission brokers. Practices on the part of a commission house which are detrimental to the interests of its brokerage customers would appear, in the final analysis, to be opposed to the dictates of enlightened self-interest. Nevertheless, such abuses have not been uncommon in the past."

But at this point we are concerned only with the manner in which the dealer functions increase the financial risks of an unregulated banking business. The problems of conflicting interests in the furnishings of investment advice, the handling of discretionary and investment trust accounts, and other like activities, which are raised by the presence of the combined broker-dealer function are not here dealt with. Nor do we deal with the conflict between a dealer's self interest and a broker's duty to his customers as it may exist in the case of specialists and others on the floors of exchanges.

Speculation by brokers or brokerage firms for their own account as well as their purchase of blocks of securities for primary or secondary distribution—a common cause of brokerage failures—

directly threaten the brokers' capital essential to the safe handling of their customers' affairs, funds, and securities. Theft and embezzlement of customers' funds or securities usually have been but the aftermath of a course of over-extension and over-commitment invited by permitting brokers to engage in trading or underwriting activities for their own account.

As we have said, however, in spite of the risks to customers inherent in the combination of brokerage, banking, and dealer functions, the record of Exchange houses in terms of financial failures has been an exceptionally good one. Yet the impact on the public, and on the Exchange members themselves, of those financial failures which have occurred has been serious.

REGULATION OF BANKING AND DEALER ASPECTS OF BROKERAGE BUSINESS

The program set forth above makes a significant advance on these problems of financial risks arising from a combination of banking and dealer functions with those of a broker. Further steps to the same end can and should be accomplished either by additional legislation, by administrative regulation, or by regulation and control by the industry itself. Regulation by the industry, if given adequate time to make the basic readjustments necessary, could effectively separate the banking and the brokerage functions so as to produce a more efficient and effective system.

One method of accomplishing this could be a self-imposed requirement that firms deposit customers' free credit balances in trust accounts separate from those of the firm and that customers' fully paid or excess collateral securities be deposited either in a central depository similar to the one proposed by the New York Stock Exchange, or held in trust account. If that system were followed, free credit balances would not be subject to any liens in favor of the depository bank to secure its own loans to the broker, or to the claims of general creditors of the firm. Nor would they be permitted to be commingled with the funds of the firm or its partners. Under that system, separate deposit of customers' fully paid or excess collateral securities would relieve a broker of responsibility for them, would regularize the methods of handling such accounts, and would afford the public greater protection than it has enjoyed in the past.

But it is our view that the ideally effective measure for dealing with customers' free credit balances and customers' fully paid or excess collateral securities would be the establishment of trust institutions in various financial centers. The establishment of a separate trust institution for these purposes was a suggestion originally advanced by various members of the New York Stock Exchange. Such an institution would assume all banking and custodial functions now performed by brokers as an incident to their brokerage business whether conducted on a cash or on a margin basis. It would be established under national or state banking laws. It would be subject to the same supervision and control as is now exercised over national and state banks and trust companies. Establishment of such trust institutions in the leading financial centers would be the most effective means of accomplishing a separation of banking functions from brokerage functions. Institutions of this character would have the advantage of placing centralized banking activities under appropriate supervision, reducing to a minimum financial risks to customers, and lessening the overhead expenses of individual brokers. Their use would also serve to remove customers' cash and securities from the risks of insolvency involved in the combination of the dealer with the brokerage function. Of equal importance would be the ability of trust institutions to protect customers from that confusion of conflicting and rival creditors' claims which follows the failure of a modern brokerage firm. Trust institutions could so operate that customers' rights might be realized without the difficulties and expenses which now result from the intricacy and costs of legal proceedings to wind up an insolvent brokerage house.

It is recognized that such a plan might not lend itself to immediate consummation. And exploration of the feasibility of the system proposed has, it is true, disclosed divergent points of view. Those who doubt its practicability point to the multitudinous accounts requiring banking service; the volume of cash balances and safekeeping items; the types of service demanded by customers in connection with the latter; the expense of the initial organization of such an institution and the resistance which might be met in both banking and brokerage circles. Nevertheless, it is our considered judgment that such a plan contains the desirable ingredients of self-determination on the part of the brokerage community as against direct governmental action requiring the separation of the banking and brokerage functions. Finally, trust institutions would, by their own safeguards, obviate the need for much of the program of present and future regulation on the part of the industry and government discussed in this report. This program of regulation will necessarily be complex since it is required by the very complexities which have resulted from the combination of banking and dealer activities with the brokerage business. It will also in some respects be unavoidably burdensome. Hence, it would be eminently desirable, from all points of view, if this multiplicity of regulation could be dispensed with as a result of the separation of functions by means of trust institutions to conduct the banking activities of brokers.

APPENDIX III

PROGRAM TO AFFORD ADDITIONAL PROTECTION TO THE PUBLIC IN ITS BROKERAGE DEALINGS WITH MEMBER FIRMS OF THE NEW YORK STOCK EXCHANGE

ADOPTED BY THE BOARD OF GOVERNORS
OF THE NEW YORK STOCK EXCHANGE,
OCTOBER 26, 1938

The following is a general summary of a program which has been worked out with a view to affording additional protection to the members of the public in their brokerage dealings with member firms of the New York Stock Exchange.

SEPARATION OF CAPITAL EMPLOYED IN FIRMS' AND PARTNERS' UNDERWRITING, SECURITY AND COMMODITY POSITIONS AND COMMITMENTS

A review of past failures of member firms indicates that the over-extension of security and commodity positions for firm and partners' account has been an important factor. With a view to affording additional protection to the members of the public in their brokerage dealings with member firms of the New York Stock Exchange, the Exchange proposes to permit member firms to organize separate corporations, to be known as affiliated companies, for the purpose of carrying underwriting, security and commodity positions for the company's own account and for the account of the member firm's general partners. When the details of the program for the formation and operation of such affiliated companies have been determined upon the Exchange proposes to increase the capital requirements applicable to member firms in such a way as to encourage member firms to conduct their underwriting and trading operations through the medium of such separate companies.

An outline of the remaining portions of the program is enumerated below:

I. REVISED CAPITAL REQUIREMENTS

Effective January 1, 1939, no member firm doing a general business with the public, except those subject to supervision by State or Federal Banking authorities, shall permit, in the ordinary course of business as a broker, its aggregate indebtedness to all other persons to exceed 1,500 percentum of the member firm's net capital. In computing the net capital and aggregate indebtedness of such a member firm the Exchange proposes to delimit further the type of assets and securities which may be included in net capital by requiring specific deductions in the computation of capital.

II. Prohibited Loans

Without the prior written approval of the Committee on Member Firms, no governor, member of a committee, officer or employee of the Exchange shall make any loan of money or securities to or obtain any such loan from any member, member firm or partner of a member firm, unless such loan be (a) fully secured by readily marketable collateral, or (b) made by a governor or committee member to or obtained by a governor or committee member from the member firm of which he is a partner, or a partner of such firm.

III. Disqualification of Governors and Committee Members

No governor or member of a committee shall participate in the investigation or consideration of any matter relating to any member or member firm with knowledge that such member or firm is indebted to such governor or committee member, or to any of his partners or to the firm of which he is a partner, or that he, his firm or any of his partners is indebted to such member or firm, excluding, however, any indebtedness arising in the ordinary course of business out of transactions on any exchange, out of transactions in the over-the-counter markets, or out of the lending and borrowing of securities.

IV. Financial Statements

The Committee on Member Firms will call for at least the following financial statements from all member firms:

(a) An answer to a "long form" questionnaire at least once in each year. This "long form" questionnaire will be in substantially the form heretofore used by member firms carrying margin accounts, which calls for a detailed financial statement.

(b) An answer to a special "short form" questionnaire at approximately quarterly intervals between the calls for answers to "long form" questionnaires.

V. Independent Audits

The Committee on Member Firms will require all member firms doing any securities business with others than members or member firms to have an audit of their books, records and accounts made by independent public accountants at least once in each year. The scope of the audit is now the subject of a study being made by the Exchange in conjunction with committees representing the American Institute of Accountants and the New York State Society of Certified Public Accountants.

The Committee on Member Firms will prescribe audit regulations when the scope of the audit has been decided upon.

VI. Exchange Auditing

The scope and frequency of the supervisory audits, examinations and inspections made of member firms' offices by the Exchange will be increased. The audits, examinations and inspections are being made at irregular intervals and without prior warning and include a test or spot check of safekeeping securities and segregated securities representing excess margin.

VII. Report of Member Borrowings

Every member, member firm and general partner of a member firm will be required to report forthwith to the Exchange the following:

(a) Each loan in the amount of $2,500 or more, whether of cash or securities, heretofore obtained (and now outstanding) or hereafter obtained;

(b) Each loan in the amount of $2,500 or more, whether of cash or securities, heretofore made (and now outstanding) or hereafter made to any member, member firm or general partner of a member firm;

provided, however, that no report shall be required with respect to:

(1) Any loan fully secured at all times by readily marketable collateral;

(2) Any loan of securities made by the borrower for the purpose of effecting delivery against a sale where money payment equivalent to the market value of the securities is made to the lender and such contract is marked approximately to the market;

(3) Any loan on a life insurance policy which is not in excess of the cash surrender value of such policy;

(4) Any loan obtained from a bank, trust company, monied corporation, or fiduciary on the security of real estate;

(5) Any loan transaction between general partners of the same firm.

VIII. Margin Accounts

After April 1, 1939, no member firm carrying margin accounts for others than members of a national securities exchange or registered brokers or dealers, as the terms "member" and registered "broker" and "dealer" are defined in the Securities Exchange Act of 1934, and no general partner of any such firm, shall trade in margin accounts with their own firm or with any other member firm. This prohibition will not prevent the obtaining of bank loans with which to purchase or carry securities nor embrace such activities as underwritings, etc. Appropriate exemptions to the rule will be considered for certain types of transactions by members on the floor.

IX. Partners' Accounts

No member firm shall carry an account for a general partner of another member firm without the prior written consent of another general partner of such other firm. Duplicate reports and monthly statements shall be sent to a general partner of the firm (other than the partner for whom the account is carried) designated in such consent.

All clearance transactions for a general partner of another member firm shall be reported by the clearing firm to a general partner of such other firm who has no interest in such transactions.

X. Individual Members Carrying Accounts

No member, doing business as an individual, shall carry securities accounts for customers.

XI. Qualifications of Personnel

Steps will be taken to provide for a more intensive control and supervision of persons now in or hereafter entering the business of Exchange members.

XII. Enforcement

The business practices of member firms are being more strictly supervised and the conduct rules are being rigidly enforced and, where necessary, severe penalties are being imposed for violations.

XIII. Report of Underwritings

Every member firm will be required to submit to the Exchange, weekly, a statement of its obligations in respect of underwritings and net positions resulting therefrom.

BIBLIOGRAPHY

GOVERNMENT PUBLICATIONS

SECURITIES AND EXCHANGE COMMISSION

Annual Reports

Compilation of Releases under the Securities Act of 1933, to and including December 31, 1936.

Compilation of Releases under Securities Exchange Act of 1934, to and including December 31, 1936.

Compilation of Releases under the Public Utility Holding Company Act of 1935, to and including December 31, 1936.

Decisions Vol. 1 (July 2, 1934, to December 31, 1936)

Report on the Government of Securities Exchanges.

Report on the Feasibility and Advisability of the Complete Segregation of Dealer and Broker Report on Trading in Unlisted Securities Upon Exchanges.

Report on the Study of Investment Trust and Investment Trust Companies.

General Rules and Regulations under the Securities Act of 1933.

Guide to Forms Adopted under the Securities Act of 1933, as amended.

Rules and Regulations under the Securities Act of 1934.

Guide to Forms Adopted under the Securities Exchange Act of 1934, as amended.

Rules, Regulations and Forms under the Public Utility Holding Company Act of 1935.

Report on the Study and Investigation of the Work Activities, Personnel, and Functions of Protective and Reorganization Committees

Part I: Strategy and Techniques of Protective and Reorganization Committees.

Part II: Committees and Conflicts of Interest.

Part III: Committees for the Holders of Real Estate Bonds.

Part IV: Committees for Holders of Municipal Obligations.

Part V: Protective Committees and Agencies for Holders of Defaulted Foreign Governmental Bonds.

Part VI: Trustees under Indentures.

Part VII: Management Plans Without Aid of Committees.

Regulation of Over-the-Counter Markets. Report of Committee on Banking and Currency, U. S. Senate, 75th Congress, 3d Session, Report No. 1455.

Releases Covering the Commission's Official Actions, Orders, Rulings, Opinions, etc.

Report on the Government of Securities Exchanges, 74th Congress, 1st Session, House of Representatives, Document No. 85.

Regulation of Over-the-Counter Markets, 75th Congress, 3d Session, Senate Report No. 1455.

BOARD OF GOVERNORS, FEDERAL RESERVE SYSTEM

Annual Reports 1934 to 1937.

Bulletin (monthly).

SECONDARY SOURCES

TWENTIETH CENTURY FUND, *The Security Markets.* Twentieth Century Fund, Inc., New York, 1935.

FLYNN, JOHN T., *Security Speculation.* Harcourt, Brace & Company, New York, 1934.

MEEKER, J. EDWARD, *The Work of the Stock Exchange.* Ronald Press, New York, 1930.

VAN ANTWERP, WILLIAM C., *The Stock Exchange from Within.* Doubleday, Page & Company, 1913.

BRANDEIS, LOUIS D., *Other People's Money.* National Home Library Foundation, Washington, D. C., 1933.

DUKE UNIVERSITY SCHOOL OF LAW, *Three Years of the Securities Act.* Vol. IV, Nos. 1 and 2, Duke Station, Durham, N. C., 1937.

TWENTIETH CENTURY PRESS, *Trading in 'When Issued' Securities,* 1938.

———— *Security Financing under SEC Exemption,* 1938.

———— *Stabilization of Security Prices during Distribution,* 1938.

FORD, BACON AND DAVIS, INC., *Recent Practice and Procedure in Securities Act Registration,* 1938.

———— *The Expert Clause of the Securities Act of 1933,* 1937.

———— *Economy, Convenience and Assurance in Securities Act Registration.*

Fortune, Volume VIII, Number 2, August, 1933: SECURITIES ACT— "Legal Opinion," by Arthur H. Dean; "Social Consequences," by Felix Frankfurter.

NEW YORK CURB EXCHANGE, *Annual Reports,* 1935 to 1938.

NEW YORK STOCK EXCHANGE, *Annual Reports* 1935 to 1938.

———— *Constitution* (Effective May 16, 1938).

—— *Rules of the Board of Governors of the New York Stock Exchange,* adopted May 16, 1938.

—— *Report of Sub-Committee on Size and Listing Requirements of Committee on Stock List,* 1938.

HOXSEY, J. B. M., *Accounting for Investors,* New York Stock Exchange, 1930.

—— *The Listing of Securities Upon the New York Stock Exchange,* New York Stock Exchange, 1937.

HASKELL, J., *The Growing Interdependence of the New York Stock Exchange and Listed Corporations,* New York Stock Exchange, 1937.

NOTE: No attempt has been made to duplicate the exhaustive bibliography in *The Security Markets,* Twentieth Century Fund, Inc.

INDEX

303

WALL STREET

AND THE

SECURITY MARKETS

An Arno Press Collection

Abbott, Charles Cortez. **The New York Bond Market, 1920-1930.**
1937

Adams, Henry C. **Public Debts:** An Essay in the Science of
Finance. 1898

Black, Hillel. **The Watchdogs of Wall Street.** 1962

Bond, Frederic Drew. **Stock Movements and Speculation.** 1930

The Boston Stock Exchange. 1975

Burr, Anna Robeson. **The Portrait of a Banker: James Stillman,
1850-1918.** 1927

Carret, Philip L. **The Art of Speculation.** 1930

Chamberlain, Lawrence. **The Work of the Bond House.** 1912

The Chicago Securities Market. 1975

Finance and Industry: The New York Stock Exchange. 1886

Flynn, John T. **Investment Trusts Gone Wrong!** 1930

Forgan, James B. **Recollections of a Busy Life.** 1924

Fowler, John Francis, Jr. **American Investment Trusts.** 1928

Galston, Arthur. **Security Syndicate Operations.** [1928]

Glass, Carter. **An Adventure in Constructive Finance.** 1927

Grayson, Theodore J[ulius]. **Investment Trusts:** Their Origin,
Development, and Operation. 1928

Greef, Albert O. **The Commercial Paper House in the United
States.** 1938

Haney, Lewis H., Lyman S. Logan and Henry S. Gavens.
Brokers' Loans. 1932

Hardy, Charles O[scar]. **Odd-Lot Trading on the New York Stock
Exchange.** 1939

Hillhouse, A|lbert| M. **Municipal Bonds:** A Century of Experience. 1936

Hodgson, James Goodwin, comp. **Wall Street:** Asset or Liability? 1934

King, Jos|eph| L. **History of the San Francisco Stock and Exchange Board.** 1910

Lamont, Thomas W. **Henry P. Davison:** The Record of a Useful Life. 1933

Lefèvre, Edwin. **The Making of a Stockbroker.** 1925

McElroy, Robert |McNutt|. **Levi Parsons Morton:** Banker, Diplomat and Statesman. 1930

Medina, Harold R. **Corrected Opinion of Harold R. Medina, United States Circuit Judge in United States of America, Plaintiff, V. Henry S. Morgan, Harold Stanley, et al., Doing Business as Morgan Stanley & Co., et al., Defendants.** 1954

Meeker, J|ames| Edward. **Short Selling.** 1932

Meeker, J|ames| Edward. **The Work of the Stock Exchange.** [1930]

Moody, John. **The Long Road Home:** An Autobiography. 1933

Moody, John. **Profitable Investing.** |1925|

Moulton, Harold G. **Financial Organization and the Economic System.** 1938

Moulton, Harold G. **The Financial Organization of Society.** [1930]

Moulton, Harold G. **The Formation of Capital.** 1935

Moulton, Harold G., George W. Edwards, James D. Magee and Cleona Lewis. **Capital Expansion, Employment, and Economic Stability.** 1940

The New York Stock Market. 1975

Nicolson, Harold. **Dwight Morrow.** |1935|

Palyi, Melchior. **The Chicago Credit Market:** Organization and Institutional Structure. |1937|

Peach, W|illiam| Nelson. **The Security Affiliates of National Banks.** 1941

Pratt, Sereno S. **The Work of Wall Street.** 1921

Regulation of the Security Markets. 1975

Reis, Bernard J. **False Security:** The Betrayal of the American Investor. 1937

Rice, Samuel O., ed. **Fundamentals of Investment.** 1925

Sakolski, A|aron| M. **Principles of Investment.** [1925]

Satterlee, Herbert L. **J. Pierpont Morgan:** An Intimate Portrait. 1939

Scott, James Brown. **Robert Bacon:** Life and Letters. 1923

Herbert D. Seibert & Co. **The Business and Financial Record of World War Years.** [1939]

Steiner, William Howard. **Investment Trusts: American Experience.** [1929]

Sturgis, Henry S. **Investment:** A New Profession. 1924

Townsend, William W. **Bond Salesmanship.** 1924

Twentieth Century Fund. **The Security Markets.** 1935

Two Private Banking Partnerships. 1975

U.S. Congressional House Committee on Banking and Currency. **Report of the Committee Appointed Pursuant to House Resolutions 429 and 504 to Investigate the Concentration of Control of Money and Credit.** 1913

U.S. Senate Committee on Banking and Currency. **Stock Exchange Practices.** 1934

Van Antwerp, W[illiam] C[larkson]. **The Stock Exchange From Within.** 1913

Warburg, Paul M. **The Federal Reserve System:** Its Origin and Growth. 2 Volumes. 1930

Weissman, Rudolph L. **The New Wall Street.** 1939

Willis, Henry Parker. **The Federal Reserve System:** Legislation, Organization and Operation. 1923

Willis, H[enry] Parker and Jules I. Bogen. **Investment Banking.** 1936

DATE DUE